XPRESS IT!

A STEP • BY • STEP GUIDE TO QUARK XPRESS 3.0

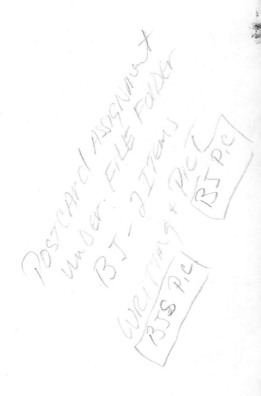

*X*PRESS IT!

A STEP • BY • STEP GUIDE TO QUARK XPRESS 3.0

Linda J. Peterson

Foothill Community College

WCB
Wm. C. Brown Publishers

Book Team

Editor *Kathy Shields*
Developmental Editor *Lisa Schonhoff / Doug DiNardo*
Production Coordinator *Audrey A. Reiter*

Wm. C. Brown Publishers
A Division of Wm. C. Brown Communications, Inc.

Vice President and General Manager *George Bergquist*
National Sales Manager *Vincent R. Di Blasi*
Assistant Vice President, Editor-in-Chief *Edward G. Jaffe*
Marketing Manager *Elizabeth Robbins*
Advertising Manager *Amy Schmitz*
Managing Editor, Production *Colleen A. Yonda*
Manager of Visuals and Design *Faye M. Schilling*
Production Editorial Manager *Vickie Putman Caughron*
Publishing Services Manager *Karen J. Slaght*
Permissions / Records Manager *Connie Allendorf*

Wm. C. Brown Communications, Inc.

Chairman Emeritus *Wm. C. Brown*
Chairman and Chief Executive Officer *Mark C. Falb*
President and Chief Operating Officer *G. Franklin Lewis*
Corporate Vice President, Operations *Beverly Kolz*
Corporate Vice President, President of WCB Manufacturing *Roger Meyer*

Cover design by Kay D. Fulton

LIST OF TRADEMARKS

QuarkXPress is a registered trademark of Quark, Inc.
Adobe Illustrator and Adobe Fonts are registered trademarks of
Adobe Systems, Inc.
Bitstream is a registered trademark of Bitstream, Inc.
MacWrite, MacDraw, MacDraft, Laser FX and Mac3D are registered
trademarks of Apple Computer, Inc.
Microsoft Word and Microsoft Works are registered trademarks of
Microsoft Corporation.
WriteNow is licensed by T/Maker Company.
FullPaint is a trademark of Ann Arbor Softworks, Inc.
SuperPaint is a trademark of Silicon Beach Software, Inc.
Pantone is a registered trademark of Pantone, Inc.

Library of Congress Catalog Card Number: 91-75859

ISBN 0-697-14003-2

Printed in the United States of America by Wm. C. Brown Communications, Inc.,
2460 Kerper Boulevard, Dubuque, IA 52001

10   9   8   7   6

Contents

Acknowledgements

It is probably impossible to adequately thank all of the people who inspired, encouraged, and facilitated this book, but I would like to try anyway. Thanks to Kathy Shields and Lisa Schonhoff at William C. Brown Publishers for their patience and flexibility as this book was developed and written.

To my students who have used the many fledgling versions of these exercises, who helped me find errors and refine the Learning Guide, thank you.

To my mother, Jacquelyn Carr, teacher and author, I owe thanks for inspiring and encouraging me in all my academic endeavors.

Thanks also to Verley O'Neal, Dean of the Computer, Technology, and Information Systems Department at Foothill Community College for forward-looking vision that enabled this course to begin and to grow.

Special thanks to my friends, Patrick Mahoney and Peggy Randall, who encouraged me and who sometimes worked by my side during the final "crunch."

Introduction

1

Introduction

ABOUT THIS BOOK

I was *forced* to write this book. Having "discovered" QuarkXPress in 1989, I quickly became its convert because of the precise layout and typographical controls that the program offered.

I persuaded the dean of Foothill Community College's Computer Information Systems Department that QuarkXPress would make headway in the marketplace and offered to teach the program during the winter of 1990. My first class was full, but I had no textbook. (During the winter of 1990, there were no college texts or trade manuals on the market for QuarkXPress.) Hence, the birth of XPress It!

This book evolved in two parts. The first six chapters comprise the Learning Guide, a step-by-step tutorial that takes the student from the beginning — launching QuarkXPress — to the completion of complex projects — brochures and newsletters. In the process, the student receives a thorough overview and gains familiarity with the program's features. The second six chapters and appendices comprise the Reference Guide.

WHAT THIS BOOK DOES

This book is a solid introductory guide to learning QuarkXPress. It not only follows a hands-on, step-by-step approach to improve the student's retention, but also contains a thorough reference section to answer any questions or problems the student may encounter. The reference section will continue to be a valuable resource to the student, long after the time when the tutorial is completed.

WHAT THIS BOOK DOES NOT DO

This text does not attempt to teach the student all there is to know about desktop publishing, design principles, or electronic publishing technology. There are many other texts on the market that do a fine job in those areas. Also, because most college computer labs are not equipped with color workstations, the Learning Guide does not address color definition and separation, but they are described in the reference section.

FORMAT OF THE LEARNING GUIDE

As the author and as an instructor it is important to me that a student can pick up a textbook and, without a lot of extra equipment, discover what he or she needs in order to produce effective publications with QuarkXPress. No special data disks or other programs are required in order to complete the exercises, only a full version of the QuarkXPress program.

I have assumed that the student is already familiar with the basic operations of the Macintosh system and is also familiar with a word processing and a paint or graphics program. While not *absolutely necessary* to learning QuarkXPress, this prerequisite knowledge will greatly reduce the mistakes and resulting frustration that accompany the learning of any new program. Because page layout programs have become increasingly complex, I recommend that the student complete an introductory Macintosh course before attempting to learn an electronic page layout program. Appendix A is included for those students who would like a review of Macintosh basics.

Except for the first chapter, which contains more general information than the other chapters, each two-page spread in the first six chapters is laid out as follows:

- The top of each page displays the current exercise emphasis in bold, reverse type (white type on a black rectangle).

- The left-most column of each spread displays major topics and subheadings. The right-most column is reserved for student notes and comments.

- The left page contains the step-by-step instructions and information for each exercise, while the right-hand page displays the actual computer screen pictures for each step. Each instruction is numbered and is preceded by a checkbox to help the students track their progress.

- Menu choices and options are in ALL CAPS for ease of reading.

- Text or commands to be entered directly from the keyboard are shown in the `10 pt. Courier font`.

- The bottom of each left page displays the keyboard equivalent for the FILE/SAVE command (⌘S) to remind the student to save his or her work.

An introductory tutorial, however, cannot contain *all* of the information a student needs to know to be productive with a page layout program: it would be far too complicated and lengthy. Therefore, the second six chapters (the Reference Guide) were included.

The Reference Guide is organized according to functional topic:

- Document Construction and Management

- Creating and Managing Page Elements

- Managing Text

- Managing Pictures

THE REFERENCE GUIDE

Introduction

THE APPENDICES

◆ Managing Color

◆ Using the Libraries Feature

Each chapter contains a description of all relevant menu commands and QuarkXPress features. In addition, the chapters discuss alternative methods of achieving a desired effect or goal.

Four appendices are included for additional reference:

◆ Macintosh Basics

◆ Keyboard Commands (quick keys)

◆ Glossary of Terms

◆ QuarkXPress Version 3.1 Update

Macintosh Basics is for the student who would like a quick review of Macintosh system components (hardware), the "desktop," mouse operations, working with windows, and menus, and disk and file management.

The Keyboard Commands appendix provides a handy desk reference for QuarkXPress keyboard commands. Students are encouraged to use keyboard commands instead of pull-down menus in order to increase speed and efficiency.

The Glossary of Terms gives definitions for often-used words associated with QuarkXPress, desktop publishing, and computer graphics.

As this book is going to press, QuarkXPress Version 3.1 is being released. The QuarkXPress Version 3.1 Update lists the new features offered by the program and gives a brief description of how to use these features. If your computer lab has upgraded to QuarkXPress Version 3.1, the instructor may wish to incorporate the new features into the Learning Guide exercises.

Chapter One

A First Look at QuarkXPress

CHAPTER OBJECTIVES

OPENING A NEW DOCUMENT

To start QuarkXPress, locate the application on the hard drive and double-click on the center of its icon. Or select the icon, pull down the FILE menu and select OPEN. You will see the QuarkXPress opening screen. Click on the XPress opening screen to go to the Quark desktop which consists of a blank (grey or colored) screen, XPress menus, and palettes.

Through the next few exercises, you will learn to

✔ Create a new XPress document.

✔ Become familiar the uses for XPress tools, menus, and palettes.

✔ Use Page Setup.

✔ Save your new document.

☐ 1. Pull down the FILE Menu (figure 1.1) and select NEW...or press Command-N (⌘N).

A New dialog box will appear that allows you to specify criteria for page size, margins and column guides. These specifications define the layout of the document's master page and also its first page.

Examine the default settings in the New dialog box as shown in figure 1.2. The *Page Size* is set to U.S. Letter (8.5" x 11") with .5" margins on all sides. The *Column Guides* section defines the default text box (one-column) which will automatically be placed on the page. All of these default settings can be customized by the user.

If you click the CANCEL button, Quark will return you to the same window as before you pulled down the FILE Menu and selected NEW.

☐ 2. Click on the OK button to accept the default settings.

A new document, titled Document*n* (where *n* indicates the number of new documents you have opened in this session) will open, as shown in figure 1.3. The specifications in the New dialog box have been applied to this document. The margins and the number of columns are indicated by the dotted lines, called *guidelines*.

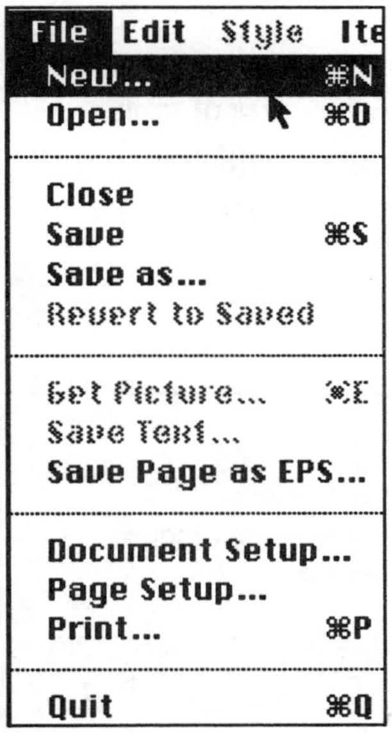

File
Edit
Style
Ite
New... ⌘N
Open... ⌘O
Close
Save ⌘S
Save as...
Revert to Saved
Get Picture... ⌘E
Save Text...
Save Page as EPS...
Document Setup...
Page Setup...
Print... ⌘P
Quit ⌘Q

Figure 1.1 The FILE menu.

New
Page Size
US Letter
A4 Letter
Tabloid
US Legal
B5 Letter
Other
Width: 8.5"
Height: 11"
Column Guides
Columns: 1
Gutter Width: 0.167"
Margin Guides
Top: 0.5"
Left: 0.5"
Bottom: 0.5"
Right: 0.5"
Facing Pages
Automatic Text Box
OK
Cancel

Figure 1.2 The NEW document dialog box.

NOTES

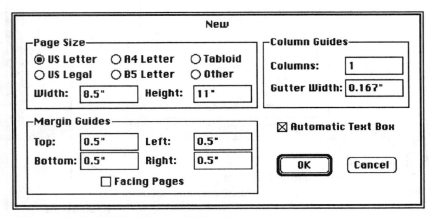

AN XPRESS DOCUMENT WINDOW

3. Examine the *document window* as it appears on your screen. Then examine figure 1.4. Though the *view size* of your document may be different from the figure, which is displayed in Fit In Window view, the components of the window will be the same.

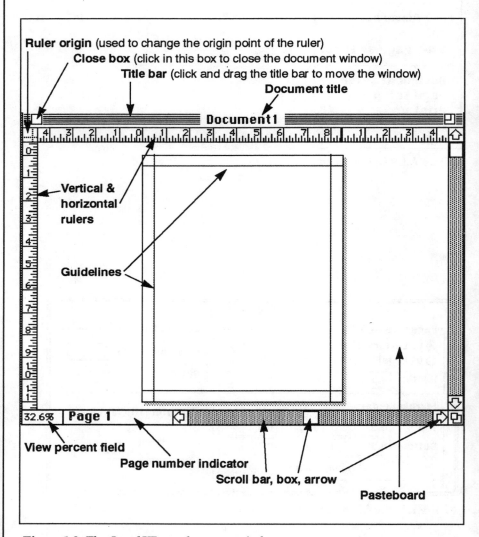

Ruler origin (used to change the origin point of the ruler)
Close box (click in this box to close the document window)
Title bar (click and drag the title bar to move the window)
Document title

Vertical & horizontal rulers

Guidelines

View percent field

Page number indicator

Scroll bar, box, arrow

Pasteboard

Figure 1.3 The QuarkXPress document window.

Quark XPress Menu Summary

Many XPress menus are *context sensitive*. This means that menu options change depending upon what is selected and with what tool.

The menus on this page display the menu options available when a text block is selected with the Contents Tool. If a picture box were selected with the Contents Tool, many options would change — most notably those on the STYLE menu.

As you work through the exercises in the Learning Guide, take care to notice which menu items are available and under what circumstances.

File Edit Style Ite

New...	⌘N
Open...	⌘O
Close	
Save	⌘S
Save as...	
Revert to Saved	
Get Picture...	⌘E
Save Text...	
Save Page as EPS...	
Document Setup...	
Page Setup...	
Print...	⌘P
Quit	⌘Q

Edit Style Item Page

Undo Item Change	⌘Z
Cut	⌘H
Copy	⌘C
Paste	⌘U
Clear	
Select All	⌘A
Show Clipboard	
Find/Change	⌘F
Preferences	▶
Style Sheets...	
Colors...	
H&Js...	

Style Item Page

Font	▶
Size	▶
Type Style	▶
Color	▶
Shade	▶
Horizontal Scale...	
Kern...	
Baseline Shift...	
Character...	⌘⇧D
Alignment	▶
Leading...	⌘⇧E
Formats...	⌘⇧F
Rules...	⌘⇧N
Tabs...	⌘⇧T
Style Sheets	▶

Item Page View Utili

Modify...	⌘M
Frame...	⌘B
Runaround...	⌘T
Duplicate	⌘D
Step and Repeat...	
Delete	⌘K
Group	⌘G
Ungroup	⌘U
Constrain	
Lock	⌘L
Send to Back	
Bring to Front	
Space/Align...	
Picture Box Shape	▶
Reshape Polygon	

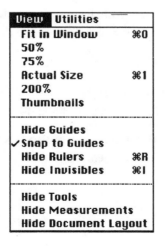

Page View Utili

Insert...	
Delete...	
Move...	
Master Guides...	
Section...	
Previous	
Next	
First	
Last	
Go to...	⌘J
Display	▶

View Utilities

Fit in Window	⌘0
50%	
75%	
Actual Size	⌘1
200%	
Thumbnails	
Hide Guides	
✓Snap to Guides	
Hide Rulers	⌘R
Hide Invisibles	⌘I
Hide Tools	
Hide Measurements	
Hide Document Layout	

Utilities

Check Spelling	▶
Auxiliary Dictionary...	
Edit Auxiliary...	
Suggested Hyphenation...	⌘H
Hyphenation Exceptions...	
Library...	
Font Usage...	
Picture Usage...	
Tracking Edit...	
Kerning Table Edit...	

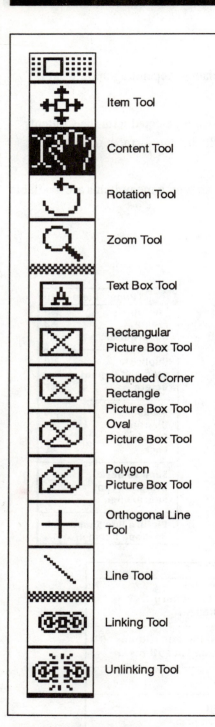

Figure 1.4 The QuarkXPress Tool palette.

Examine the QuarkXPress window on your screen. You will notice that there are smaller windows at the bottom and sides of the screen. These windows are QuarkXPress *floating palettes.* The palettes appear similar and function like normal Macintosh windows: they can be closed by clicking in the close box in the upper left-hand corner and moved by clicking on the top bar and dragging to a new location. A *floating* palette is always active and "floats" on the top layer above the document window.

The Tool Palette is a floating palette. In addition to clicking in the palette's close box, the Tool Palette may also be closed (*hidden*) or opened by pulling down the VIEW menu and selecting HIDE TOOLS or SHOW TOOLS respectively.

The Item Tool is used to select *page elements,* such as text boxes, picture boxes, and lines, and move, cut, copy, or resize them. XPress page elements cannot be cut, copied, or moved with any other tool. To quickly change to the Item Tool while using another tool (for example, the Content Tool) press the COMMAND (⌘) key.

The Content Tool, when inserted in a text block, is used to enter and import text, and when inserted into a picture block is used to import and manipulate pictures. The Content Tool may also be used to resize any page element (text and picture boxes or lines).

The Rotation Tool is used to rotate page elements.

The Zoom Tool is used to enlarge or reduce your view of the page in the document window. To enlarge the view, simply select the Zoom Tool and click on the document. To reduce the view, hold down the OPTION key before clicking the Zoom Tool on the document.

The Text Box Tool is used to create boxes in which to place text.

The Rectangle Picture Box Tool, as its name implies, is used to create boxes in the form of rectangles or squares in which pictures are placed.

The Rounded-corner Picture Box Tool is used to create picture boxes in the form of rounded rectangles.

The Oval Picture Box Tool is used to create oval or circular picture boxes.

The Polygon Picture Box Tool is used to create picture boxes in polygon shapes (3 or more sides).

The Orthogonal Line Tool is used to create perpendicular, straight lines.

The Line Tool is used to create lines at any angle.

The Linking Tool is used to link text boxes so that text flows and re-formats automatically from text box to text box.

The Unlinking Tool is used to break or change the text links between text boxes.

NOTES

THE MEASUREMENTS PALETTE

TEXT BOXES

The Measurements Palette is a floating palette located at the bottom of the QuarkXPress window. It can be accessed through the VIEW menu. The information displayed in the Measurements Palette varies, depending upon what item or group of items is currently active. Each value is displayed in an area called a *field.* All fields are "live." Entering new values in these fields changes the item or its contents interactively.

| X: 19p1 | W: 25p11 | △ 0° | ⬍ 14 pt | ▤ ▤ ▶ Times | ▶ 12 pt |
| Y: 1.241" | H: 8.519" | Cols: 1 | ⬌ 0 | ▤ ▤ P B I ⓞ ⑧ ⓠ U Ẅ ᴋ ᴋ ᴤ ᴣ ᴣ | |

Figure 1.5 The Measurements Palette when a text box is selected with the Content Tool.

The X coordinate indicates the item origin point from the left side of the page, and from the zero-point on the horizontal ruler, displayed in the current measurement system (inches, picas, etc.) of the horizontal ruler. A new origin point may be entered directly in the X field.

The Y coordinate indicates the item origin from the top of the page, and from the zero-point on the vertical ruler, displayed in the current measurement system of the vertical ruler. A new origin point may be entered directly in the Y field.

The W coordinate shows the width of the selected text box. To change the width, enter a value in this field.

The H coordinate shows the height of the selected text box. To change the height of a text box, enter a new value in this field.

The △ 0° symbol indicates the number of degrees the selected item has been rotated. To rotate a box or line, enter a value between 0° and 360° in .001° increments.

Cols: indicates the number of columns in the text box. Changing this value will change the number of columns in the active text box.

The ⬍ field shows the current *leading* (also called *line spacing*) of selected text. Leading may be changed by either entering a new value or clicking on the up/down arrows to change the leading in 1-point increments.

The ⬌ field displays the *kerning* or *tracking* values of selected text, and is modified in the same way as the leading field. Kerning and tracking are methods of controlling space between characters.

The next section of the Measurements Palette consists of icons. Clicking on the icons formats the current paragraph or selected text in the following ways:

NOTES

Left Align: Click on this icon to align a paragraph or section of selected text to the left.

Right Align: Click on this icon to align a paragraph or section of selected text to the right.

Center Align: Click on this icon to center a paragraph or section of selected text.

Justify: Click on this icon to justify a paragraph or section of selected text.

Typeface: To change the typeface, either enter the name of the new typeface directly into the field or select a typeface from the pop-up menu accessed by clicking on the triangle to the left of the current typeface name displayed.

Font Size: To change font size, either enter a new value into the field or select a size from the pop-up menu accessed by clicking on the triangle to the left of the size currently displayed.

Clicking on any of the remaining icons (displayed below) will affect the type characteristics at the cursor position or of selected text.

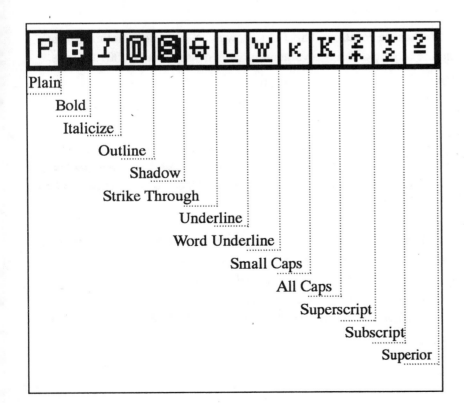

PICTURE BOXES

As you can see from figure 1.6, the Measurements Palette for picture boxes is similar to the palette for text boxes. Those fields that differ from the text box measurement fields and their uses are explained below:

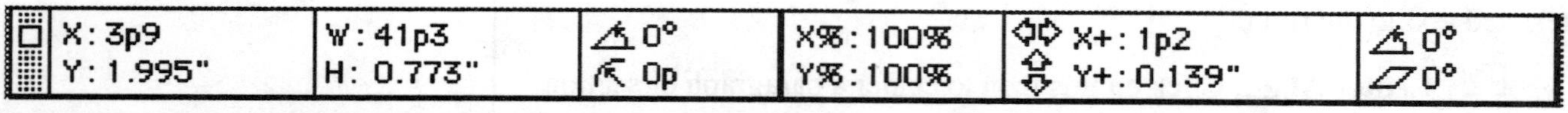

| ▥ | X: 3p9 | W: 41p3 | ◿ 0° | X%: 100% | ⬦ X+: 1p2 | ◿ 0° |
| | Y: 1.995" | H: 0.773" | ⬝ 0p | Y%: 100% | ⬦ Y+: 0.139" | ◹ 0° |

Figure 1.6 The Measurements Palette as it appears when a picture box is selected with the Content Tool.

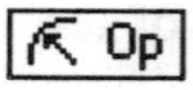

⬝ 0p **Corner Radius**: To change the corner radius of a rectangular or rounded-rectangle picture box, enter a new specification value.

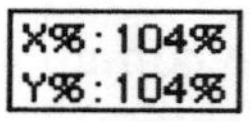

X%: 104% **Horizontal and Vertical scaling:** To change the horizontal
Y%: 104% scaling of a picture, enter a percentage value in the X% field. To change a picture's vertical scaling, enter a percentage value in the Y% field.

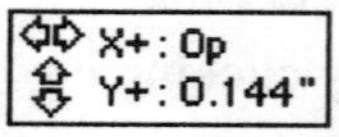

⬦ X+: 0p **Horizontal and Vertical Offsets:** To change the horizontal
⬦ Y+: 0.144" offset of a picture within a picture box, either enter a value in the X+ field or click on the left/right arrow to shift the picture horizontally in 1-point increments. The Y+ field and its up/down arrows correspond to the vertical offset of the picture and are used in the same manner as the X+ field.

◿ 0° **Picture rotation:** This field allows you to rotate a picture within its picture box by entering a value in increments as small as .001 degrees.

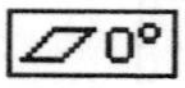

◹ 0° **Picture Skew:** This field allows you to skew a picture in its picture box by entering a value between 75° and -75°. This value may be entered in increments of .001°.

LINES

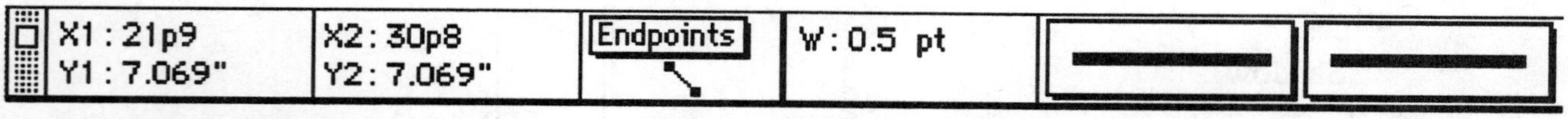

| ▥ | X1: 21p9 | X2: 30p8 | Endpoints | W: 0.5 pt | ▬▬▬▬ | ▬▬▬▬ |
| | Y1: 7.069" | Y2: 7.069" | ◿ | | | |

Figure 1.7 The Measurements Palette when a line is selected and the Endpoints mode is active.

The Line Measurements Palette shows the following modes in which to display the X and Y coordinates of a selected line: Endpoints, Left Point, Midpoint, and Right Point. To select the desired mode, point to the mode display and press the mouse button down to display the pop-up menu. Figure 1.7 shows the Measurements Palette with the Endpoints mode active.

When the Endpoints mode is in use, X1 and Y1 refer to the horizontal and vertical positions, respectively, of the left endpoint. X2 and Y2 refer to the horizontal and vertical positions of the right endpoint of the selected line. W indicates the weight or thickness of the line, displayed in points. All measurements may be changed by entering new values into the respective fields.

The last two items displayed on the Line Measurements Palette are line style pop-up menus (see figure 1.8). A new style may be applied to a line by selecting the line, then selecting from these menus.

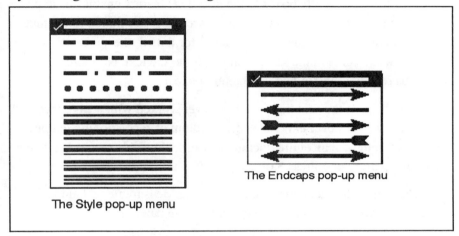

The Style pop-up menu

The Endcaps pop-up menu

Figure 1.8 The line pop-up menus.

When the Left Point mode is selected, X1 and Y1 refer to the horizontal and vertical position of the left endpoint. Two new fields display the angle and length of the line, instead of the right point position (see Figure 1.9).

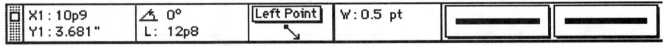

| X1 : 10p9 | ◹ 0° | Left Point | W : 0.5 pt |
| Y1 : 3.681" | L : 12p8 | | |

Figure 1.9 The Measurements Palette when Left Point line mode is selected.

When the Right Point mode is selected, the X2 and Y2 fields are active instead of the X1 and Y1 fields. These fields display the horizontal and vertical positions of the right endpoint.

Finally, when the Midpoint mode is selected, two new fields (XC and YC) display the horizontal and vertical positions of the line's midpoint. As before, the angle and length fields will be displayed.

GROUPED ELEMENTS

When a group of elements is selected, the Measurements Palette displays only the coordinates for the horizontal/vertical position of the upper left corner of the group and the angle of rotation, if applicable (see figure 1.10).

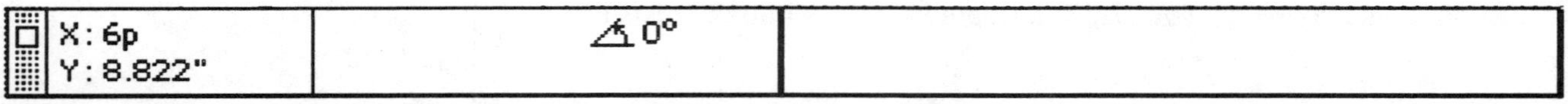

| ☐ X: 6p
 Y: 8.822" | △ 0° | |

Figure 1.10 The Measurements Palette when a group of elements is selected..

ANCHORED ELEMENTS

Quark XPress offers an exciting new feature in version 3.0: the ability to *anchor* text and picture boxes to the text. This feature enables us to place boxes into a text block so that these items are integrally linked to the text itself. If the text is subsequently edited or reformatted, the anchored elements will remain in the same relationship to the text. No more laborious repositioning of text and picture boxes!

Even if this is the first time you have ever worked with a page layout program and have never experienced the tedium of repositioning graphic elements throughout an entire document, you will be able to appreciate the anchoring feature of XPress 3.0.

When an anchored element is selected, the Measurements Palette display adds two new icons to the left side of the palette:

▦ Select this icon to align the top of the item with the text ascent. (This means to align it with the top of the text ascenders, such as the lower case letter *d*.)

▣ Select this icon to align the bottom of the item with the text baseline. (This means to align the anchored element with the imaginary line upon which the text sits. See pg. 67 for more information.)

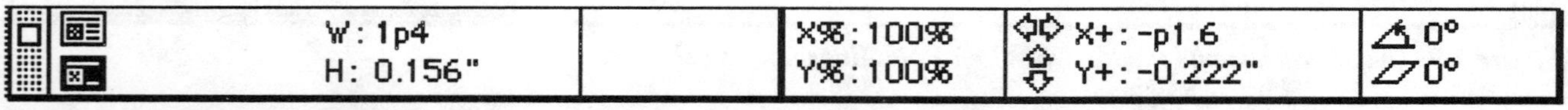

| ☐ ▦ ▣ | W: 1p4
 H: 0.156" | X%: 100%
 Y%: 100% | ⟷ X+: -p1.6
 ⇕ Y+: -0.222" | △ 0°
 ⟋ 0° |

Figure 1.11 The Measurements Palette as it appears when an anchored picture box is selected with the Content Tool.

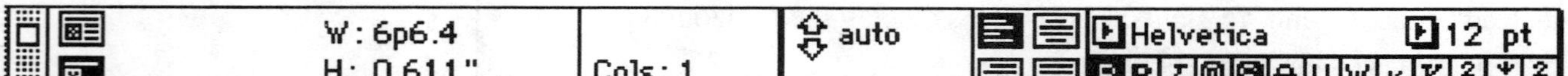

| ☐ ▦ ▣ | W: 6p6.4
 H: 0.611" | Cols: 1 | ⇕ auto | Helvetica · · · · 12 pt |

Figure 1.12 The Measurements Palette when an anchored text box is selected.

The X and Y coordinate fields are no longer displayed because the anchored element is treated as a text character. Other fields, such as scaling of pictures or leading and font/size options remain active in the palette. See figures 1.11 and 1.12 for examples of anchored element measurements.

There are two more QuarkXPress palettes: The Document Layout Palette, and the Library Palette.

The Document Layout Palette, as shown in figure 1.13, is used to display the page/document organization, to add and delete pages, to define and apply master pages, and to move quickly through your document.

The Library Palette (figure 1.14) is similar to a glossary. It is used to display and quickly retrieve graphics and/or text that the user has stored in a library file. You may create as many different libraries as you wish and may display more than one library at a time.

THE DOCUMENT LAYOUT AND LIBRARY PALETTES

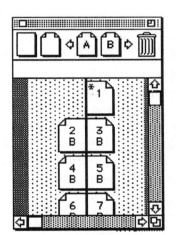

Figure 1.13 *The Document Layout Palette.*

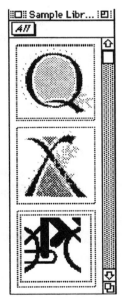

Figure 1.14 *The Library Palette.*

FILE / PAGE SETUP

Now that you are familiar with the XPress window, the menus and the floating palettes, you are ready to explore the PAGE SETUP menu option. The Page Setup dialog box, accessed under the FILE menu, allows you to specify printing controls such as paper size and printing effects.

☐ 1. Pull down the FILE menu and select PAGE SETUP.

Examine the Laserwriter dialog box that appears. The Page Setup dialog box, shown in figure 1.15, and the options it offers will vary according to the printer selected from the CHOOSER dialog box, selected under the APPLE menu.

PAPER SIZE

You may choose from among the standard paper sizes offered (these will vary with the printer) or type the measurements for a custom page. You may print at a size other than 100%, in a range from 25% to 400%, using the variable Reduce/Enlarge function.

ORIENTATION

You may choose to print using either a Horizontal (landscape) or Vertical (portrait) orientation.

GRAY SCREEN

The Gray Screen field is used to change the lines-per-inch (lpi) screen value of any RIFF / TIFF art in your document. The default value of 60 lpi is the value commonly used for newspapers. Most laserwriters are limited to a maximum of 75 lpi, but perform optimally at from 53 to 60 lpi.

PRINTER TYPE

You may change Printer Type, but usually you will want to keep the setting set to Laserwriter or Laserwriter II, if you have access to one of these types of printers.

PRINTER EFFECTS

Printer Effects — Usually you will want to keep all the Printer Effects items activated. They control the various aspects of print quality. For more information, click on the Help button.

OPTIONS

☐ 2. Click on the OPTIONS button to view the additional printing options that are available (figure 1.16). These options include: Flip, Invert, and font-related printer settings. Access them by clicking the OPTIONS button under the OK button (see figure 1.15). You can see the results of any changes you make by watching the little dog. Click on the Cancel button to return to the Page Setup dialog box without making any changes.

NOTES

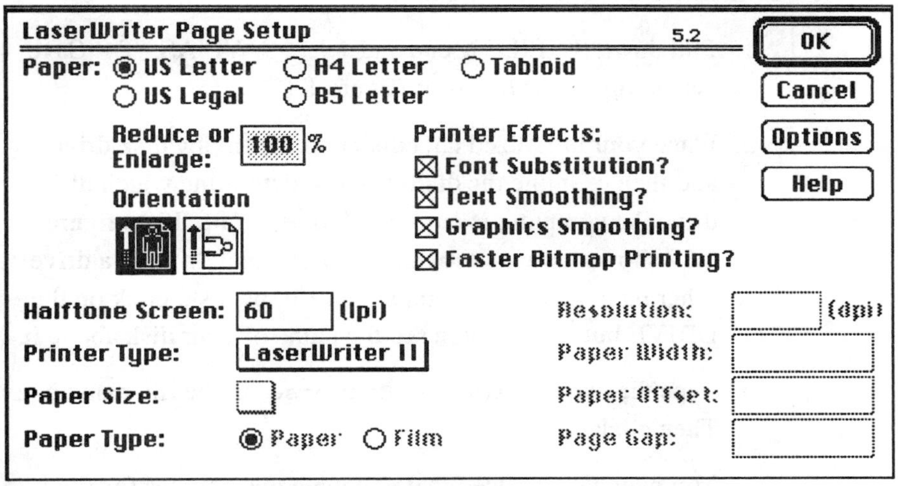

LaserWriter Page Setup   5.2   [OK]

Paper: ● US Letter   ○ A4 Letter   ○ Tabloid   [Cancel]
       ○ US Legal   ○ B5 Letter
                                                            [Options]
       Reduce or [100] %   Printer Effects:
       Enlarge: ⊠ Font Substitution?   [Help]
                                 ⊠ Text Smoothing?
       Orientation   ⊠ Graphics Smoothing?
                                 ⊠ Faster Bitmap Printing?

Halftone Screen: [60]   (lpi)   Resolution: [   ] (dpi)
Printer Type: [LaserWriter II]   Paper Width: [   ]
Paper Size: [ ]   Paper Offset: [   ]
Paper Type: ● Paper ○ Film   Page Gap: [   ]

Figure 1.15 The LaserWriter Page Setup dialog box.

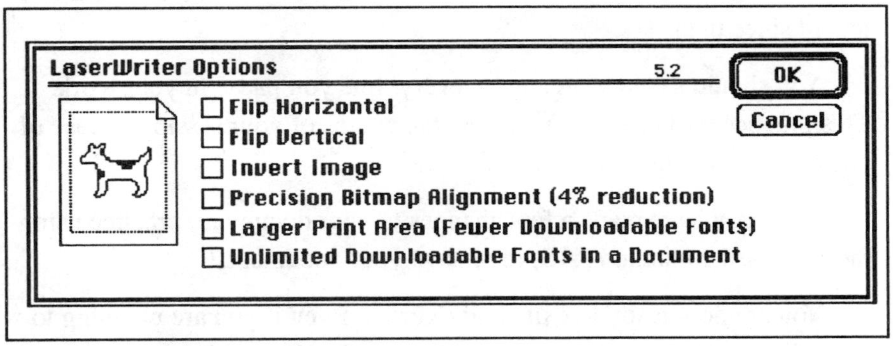

LaserWriter Options   5.2   [OK]

          □ Flip Horizontal   [Cancel]
          □ Flip Vertical
          □ Invert Image
          □ Precision Bitmap Alignment (4% reduction)
          □ Larger Print Area (Fewer Downloadable Fonts)
          □ Unlimited Downloadable Fonts in a Document

Figure 1.16 The LaserWriter Options dialog box.

FILE / SAVE AS

....USED TO SAVE A DOCUMENT TO DISK FOR THE FIRST TIME OR TO SAVE A PRE-EXISTING DOCUMENT UNDER A NEW NAME.

FILE / SAVE ⌘ S

...USED TO QUICKLY SAVE A DOCUMENT DURING THE SUBSEQUENT EDITING PROCESS.

FILE / QUIT ⌘ Q

☐ 3. Click OK to accept the Page Setup default settings and return to the document.

Next, you will save your document. The next few steps introduce you to the QuarkXPress Save As dialog box.

☐ 1. Pull down the FILE Menu and select SAVE AS. The Save As dialog box will appear (figure 1.17).

☐ 2. Place your initialized data disk into the floppy disk drive and then examine the dialog box to determine which disk drive the computer is currently "looking" at. If, as figure 1.17 shows, you are looking at the internal drive or a drive other than the one that holds your floppy disk, click on the DRIVE button until you see the name of your disk above it.

Type the name `Elements Exercise` in the file name box. Then click OK.

You may have noticed that you have two choices for file type: document and template. We have saved "Elements Exercise" as a document. You will learn more about documents and templates later in the Learning Guide.

After you have completed more of your document, or after you have edited it, you may use the SAVE command (also on the FILE menu). The SAVE IS or SAVE commands will not be accessible if your disk is locked or if you have recently saved and have not made any changes to your document since then.

You should save frequently — every time you pause in your work. This practice will protect you during the course of your session in case of power or system failure.

After you have made a few changes to your document, practice using the keyboard command (⌘S) to re-save your document.

You are now ready to exit QuarkXPress. Even if you are planning to immediately go on to the next exercise, you should practice quitting.

To return to the Macintosh desktop:

☐ 3. Pull down the FILE menu and select QUIT.

In the next lesson you will learn how to retrieve a previously created document.

The file names list box (note that your list will not be identical to this one)

The current folder is displayed on this pop-up menu

Save as

📁 **Quark Book**

🗋 Brochure2
🗋 Design Elements
🗋 DTP For Rest
🗋 Mac Hints
🗋 Newsletter Template
📁 OTHER EXERCISES

💾 **Cobra 70i**

Eject

Drive

Click on the Drive button to display the contents of other disks.

Save current document as:

Document1

Save

Cancel

◉ **Document**   ○ **Template**

Type the desired file name here, in the file name field to replace the temporary name displayed.

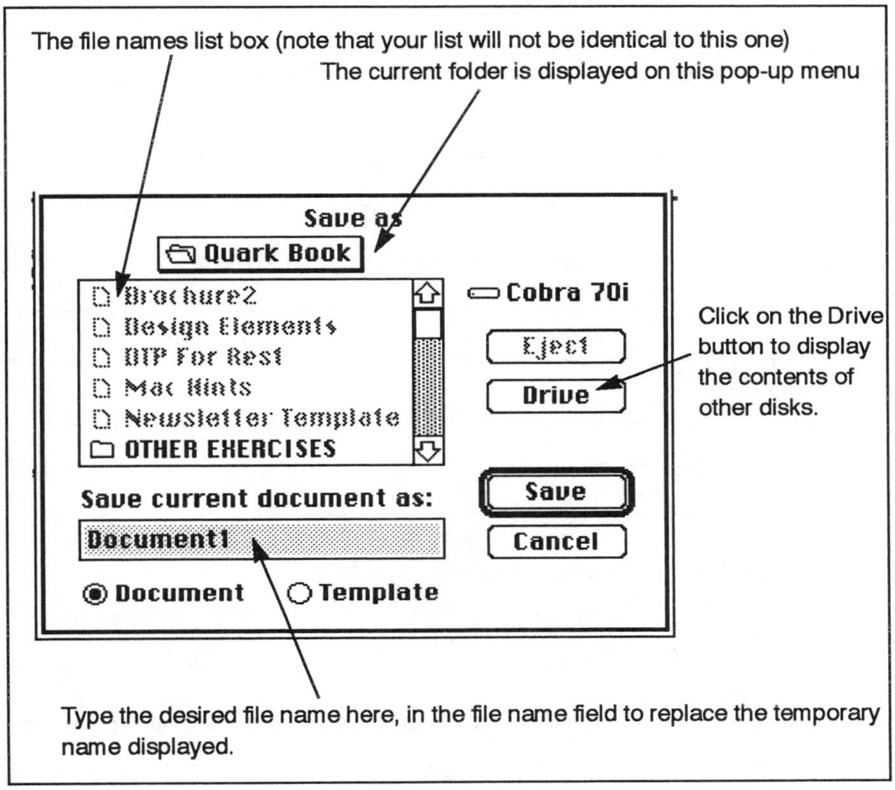

Figure 1.17 The Save As dialog box.

Study Questions

1. What is the purpose of the New document dialog box?

   _____

   _____

2. Name at least three differences between the QuarkXPress document window and a standard word processing program.

   _____

   _____

3. What are floating palettes? How many different palettes does XPress display?

   _____

   _____

4. On the Measurements Palette, what is an x-coordinate? a y-coordinate? a w-coordinate? an h-coordinate?

   _____

   _____

5. What are some of the text attributes that are displayed on the Measurements Palette?

   _____

   _____

6. On the Measurements Palette, what do X% and Y% refer to? When do these options appear on the palette?

   _____

   _____

7. What is a line point display mode? Name the four different modes.

   _____

   _____

8. What is the purpose of pop-up menus on the Measurements Palette?

   _____

   _____

9. What does it mean to "anchor" an element?

   _____

   _____

10. Describe how to save a document to your data disk and how to quit XPress.

   _____

   _____

Chapter Two

Creating and Using Page Elements

CHAPTER OBJECTIVES

STARTING XPRESS

OPENING YOUR ELEMENTS EXERCISE DOCUMENT

⌘ S

In completing the exercises in this chapter, you will learn to create and use the basic building blocks of electronic page layout — text boxes, picture boxes, rectangles, circles, and lines (graphic elements). For text or pictures to be placed in a document, you must first define an area to place the text or pictures. Of course, these area definitions can be altered at any time — that is the primary strength of desktop publishing. Changes to your layout can be made more quickly and easily than changes made through traditional paste-up methods.

In this chapter you will learn to do the following:

✔ Create text boxes and enter text directly from the keyboard.

✔ Create, select, move, resize, delete, copy and paste, and group XPress page elements:
> *text boxes*
> *picture boxes*
> *lines*

✔ Frame boxes (create borders around text or picture boxes in the shape of rectangles, rounded-rectangles, and ovals).

✔ Change line styles (shading, line endings, line types).

✔ Print your QuarkXPress document.

Ready to begin? Launch QuarkXPress, as before, by double-clicking on the application icon. When you see the QuarkXPress desktop displayed, complete the following:

☐ 1. Pull down the FILE menu and select OPEN (figure 2.1). You will see a dialog box (figure 2.2) that looks very much like the Save As dialog box.

☐ 2. Click on the DRIVE button until you see your disk icon displayed, select the file "Elements Exercise" from the file name list, and click OPEN. The blank document you created in chapter one will be displayed (you should see the title "Elements Exercise" in the center of the title bar as shown in figure 2.3).

To view the whole page, pull down the VIEW menu and select FIT IN WINDOW (⌘0).

NOTES

Figure 2.1   The FILE/OPEN command.

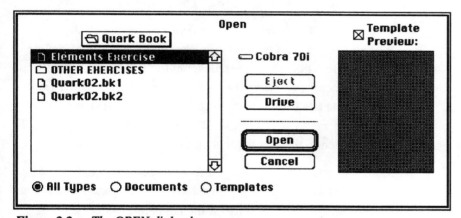

Figure 2.2   The OPEN dialog box.

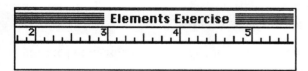

Figure 2.3   The "Elements Exercise" title bar.

NOTES

SELECTING THE DEFAULT TEXT BOX

ENTERING TEXT

CREATING AND MANIPULATING TEXT BOXES

When QuarkXPress creates a new document, it usually places a default text box (defined by the specifications you enter into the New dialog box) on the page. Since you are going to work with text boxes first, let's explore this one.

1. Click on the Content Tool to select it, and then click on the center of your page. You should see that the default text box which was defined and automatically created in the New dialog box, is now *selected* as shown in figure 2.4.

   When a text box is selected, the bold outline of the text box will be displayed along with handles at the corners and middle of each side of the box. The I-beam cursor will appear at the upper leftmost portion of the text box, ready for entry of keyboard or imported text. When the box is *not* selected, you will see only a light dotted outline of the box.

2. Select the Item Tool from the Tool Palette and click anywhere within the text box. You will see the bold outline of the text box and its handles, but the I-beam cursor will not be present. *You cannot enter or edit text with the Item Tool.* The box has been selected for modification (resizing or moving) not for text entry. Clicking on the Content Tool will again ready the box for text entry.

3. To enter text, make sure you have selected the text box with the Content Tool. Once you see the I-beam cursor in the text box, simply type directly on the keyboard. Enter the following information and compare your document with figure 2.5:

   Your name (press RETURN)
   Course title (press RETURN)
   Course number (press RETURN)

One of the most important features of any desktop publishing package is the ability to enter and import text into a document. Up to this point, you have been working with the automatic text box that was created according to the specifications defined in the New dialog box. Now you will learn how to create and modify additional text boxes.

4. To create a new text box, select the Text Box Tool from the Tool Palette. Click the mouse in the center of the larger text box. The cursor will change from an arrow to a crosshair.

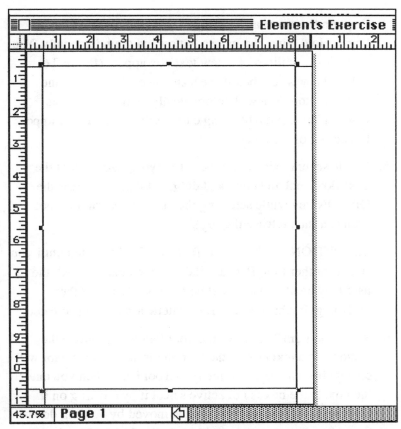

Figure 2.4   *The "Elements Exercise" window in Fit in Window view.*

Linda Peterson
Introduction to Desktop Publishing
CIS 116M

Figure 2.5   *A text box after name and course information have been entered into it.*

NOTES

USING THE OPTION KEY

MOVING A TEXT BOX

RESIZING A TEXT BOX

DELETING A TEXT BOX

⌘ S

Position the crosshair where you want the new text box to begin. Hold down the mouse button and drag diagonally. You will see the outlines of a new text box appear (figure 2.6). When the new text box is the size you desire, release the mouse button. You will automatically be returned to the Content Tool, and a blinking cursor will appear in the upper left corner of the text box.

5. Create several new text boxes of varying sizes: select the Text Box Tool and click and drag, but this time press the OPTION key while selecting the Text Box Creation Tool (you can then release the key).

The OPTION key keeps the Text Box Tool selected until you select another tool. Because the tool remains selected, the user may create several text boxes, one after the other, without going back to the Tool Palette after each is created.

6. Select the Item Tool from the Tool Palette and move the cursor into a text box. If the text box is active the cursor will change from an arrow to the Item Tool icon when you enter the box. If the box is not active select it by clicking on it. Once selected, the text box can be moved by holding down the mouse button and dragging it to the desired location. Then release the button. Figure 2.7 shows the box as it is being moved to its new location.

7. Select *either* the Content Tool or the Item Tool and move the cursor inside the text box. If the box is active the cursor will change from an arrow to the tool icon when you enter the box. If the box is not active, select it by clicking on it. Once the box is active, move the tool toward any of the eight handles. When you reach a handle, the cursor icon will change to a pointing hand called the *resizing pointer.*

Select any of the corner handles and drag (figure 2.8). Notice that the corner diagonally across from the handle remains anchored. Grabbing a middle handle constrains the resizing action to one direction only (up, down, left, right).

8. With the Item Tool, select a text box to delete. The text box can is deleted by pressing the DELETE key or by selecting CUT or CLEAR from the EDIT menu.

NOTES

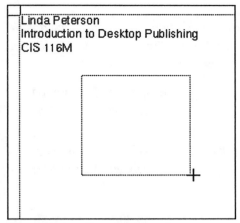

Figure 2.6   *Creating a text box.*

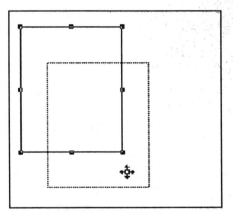

Figure 2.7   *Moving a text box*

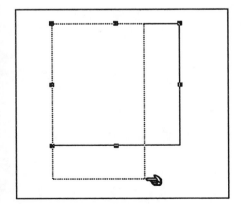

Figure 2.8   *Resizing a text box.*

COPYING AND PASTING A TEXT BOX

A box can only be deleted in this manner if it is selected with the Item Tool: you cannot delete a box or other page element in this way with the Content Tool.

☐ 9. Select the Item Tool and activate the text box. Pull down the EDIT menu, select COPY or CUT (see figure 2.9), and a copy of the text block will be placed on the clipboard. If you selected COPY, the original text box will remain on the page. If you selected CUT, the original text box will be removed from the page.

☐ 10. To paste the text box back into your document pull down the EDIT menu again and select PASTE (see figure 2.10). The box will be pasted onto the center of the screen area as shown in figure 2.11, and you may then move it to its desired location on the page.

PRACTICE

1. Create, move and resize text boxes until you feel comfortable with the these procedures.

2. Practice selecting, copying, cutting and pasting text boxes with the Item Tool.

3. Practice entering text into text boxes: click on a text box with the Content Tool and type a sentence that describes one of the procedures you are learning.

The next section will show you how to create and manipulate picture boxes.

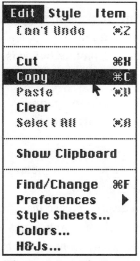

Figure 2.9 *The EDIT menu with COPY selected.*

Figure 2.10 *The EDIT menu with PASTE selected.*

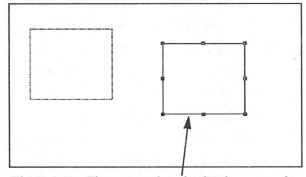

Figure 2.11 *The new text box that has been pasted on the document.*

CREATING AND MANIPULATING PICTURE BOXES

Picture boxes enable various graphics (line art, clip art, paintings, scrapbook pictures and scanned images) to be incorporated into a QuarkXPress document. The creation and manipulation of picture boxes is similar to that of text boxes.

☐ 1. To create a picture box, select any of the first three picture box tools (rectangle, rounded-rectangle, or oval) from the Tool palette.

Position the crosshair pointer where you want the new picture box to begin. Hold down the mouse button and drag diagonally. When the box is the size you desire, release the mouse button. Figure 2.12 shows a completed picture box. As before, you will automatically be returned to the Content Tool.

☐ 2. Create several new picture boxes: select a picture box tool and proceed as above, but this time, to keep the picture box tool selected, hold the OPTION key while selecting the tool. As with the Text Box Tool, this action allows you to continue creating picture boxes without returning to the Content or Item Tool between each box creation.

MOVING A PICTURE BOX

☐ 3. Select the Item Tool from the Tool Palette and then select one of the picture boxes. Once selected, the picture box can be moved by holding down the mouse button and dragging it to the desired location (figure 2.13).

RESIZING A PICTURE BOX

☐ 4. To resize a picture box, move the Item Tool pointer toward any of the eight handles. Just as with the text box, the icon changes to the resizing pointer when you reach a handle. Select any of the corner handles and drag to enlarge the box (see figure 2.14). Grabbing a middle handle will constrain the box to resizing in one direction only (up, down, left, right).

CREATING POLYGONS

Polygons are created with the Polygon Picture Box Tool. Instead of pressing and dragging to establish the size of the polygon, you will use a clicking action to establish each point of the polygon.

☐ 1. Select the Polygon Picture Box Tool and position the crosshair pointer on your screen. Click once to establish the first point. Move the mouse pointer to another position (do not hold down the mouse button) and click to establish the

⌘ S

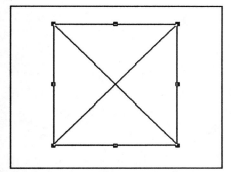

Figure 2.12   *A rectangle picture box.*

NOTES

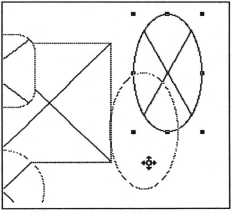

Figure 2.13   *An oval picture box as it is being moved.*

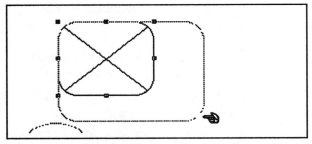

Figure 2.14   *A rounded rectangle picture box as it is being enlarged.*

second point. Continue clicking to create as many points/sides as you desire.

☐ 2. To complete the polygon, move the pointer over the first point you created. The cursor will change to the handle creation pointer (a small square with rounded corners). Click the mouse button once. The polygon will close (see figure 2.15).

Another way to close a polygon is to double-click when you establish the last point of the polygon. Create a triangle by selecting the Polygon Tool, click once, move the cursor, click again, move the cursor, *double-click*. This action will establish the last point and close the polygon simultaneously.

MOVING, RESIZING, AND RESHAPING POLYGONS

Polygons are moved in the same manner as other picture and text boxes. Resizing is also handled similarly, but with some differences which you will observe when you complete step 3 below. Polygons may be *reshaped*, and points may be added or deleted.

☐ 3. To resize a polygon, select it with either the Item or Content Tool. The handles which are displayed will define a rectangle. This is called the polygon's *bounding box*. A selected polygon is shown in figure 2.16.

Place the cursor over one of the handles and the resizing pointer will appear. Press the mouse button and drag in any direction. Notice that the polygon is enlarged or reduced *as a whole unit.*

To keep the polygon's original proportions, hold down the OPTION and SHIFT keys when you drag a bounding box handle.

☐ 4. To reshape a polygon, select the polygon and then pull down the ITEM menu and look at the RESHAPE POLYGON option. If a check mark appears next to it, then RESHAPE POLYGON is already active. If a check mark does not appear, select RESHAPE POLYGON to activate it. Handles will appear at the selected polygon's *vertices,* as shown in figure 2.17, instead of in the rectangular form of the bounding box.

☐ 5. To reposition a handle, move the cursor over the handle, press the mouse button and drag the handle to another

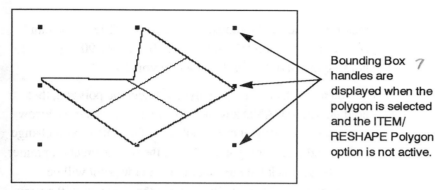

Bounding Box handles are displayed when the polygon is selected and the ITEM/ RESHAPE Polygon option is not active.

NOTES

Figure 2.15   A newly created polygon.

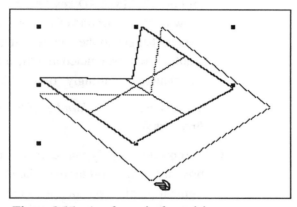

Figure 2.16   A polygon in the resizing process.

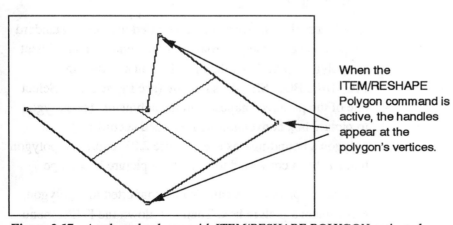

When the ITEM/RESHAPE Polygon command is active, the handles appear at the polygon's vertices.

Figure 2.17   A selected polygon with ITEM/RESHAPE POLYGON activated.

ADDING POLYGON
HANDLES

DELETING POLYGON
HANDLES

CONVERTING PICTURE BOX SHAPES

POLYGON TO STANDARD
BOX SHAPE

STANDARD BOX SHAPE
TO POLYGON

⌘ S

location. Release the mouse button (figure 2.18). You can constrain the handle's movement to 0°, 45° or 90° by holding the SHIFT key down while you drag.

6. To add a new handle to the polygon, select the polygon, then hold the COMMAND key (⌘) down while moving the arrow pointer over a segment of the polygon. The pointer will change to the handle creation pointer. When the handle creation pointer is displayed, click the mouse button. A new point will be established (see figure 2.19). You can then reposition the new handle by following the procedure in step 5.

7. To delete a handle from a polygon, select the polygon, then hold the COMMAND key (⌘) down while moving the arrow pointer over one of the existing handles. When the pointer changes to the handle deletion pointer, click on the handle. It will be deleted and the attached line segment will also change accordingly (figure 2.20).

    You may only delete handles if the polygon has more than three handles.

8. To reposition a polygon segment, select the polygon and then move the arrow pointer over the line segment. When the line segment pointer appears, press the mouse button and drag the line to its new location. Figure 2.21 shows a polygon as a line segment is being repositioned. Remember, you may constrain the movement by holding down the SHIFT key while dragging.

9. A polygon picture box can be converted to another standard shape, such as rectangle, rounded-rectangle, or oval. Select the polygon, pull down the ITEM menu and then the PICTURE BOX SHAPE submenu (see figure 2.22). Select one of the pictured shapes from the submenu. The polygon to picture box conversion will be sized according to the polygon's bounding box size. Figure 2.23 displays a polygon that has been converted to a standard picture box shape.

10. A standard picture box can also be converted to a polygon. First, select a picture box. Then pull down the ITEM menu and select the polygon shape from the PICTURE BOX SHAPE submenu. You can then resize and/or reshape the box as a polygon.

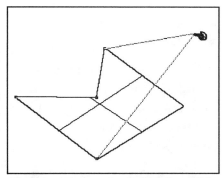

Figure 2.18 *A polygon handle as it is repositioned.*

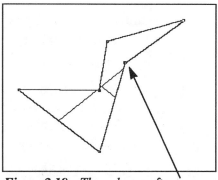

Figure 2.19 *The polygon after a handle has been added and repositioned.*

NOTES

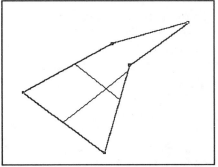

Figure 2.20 *The polygon's shape after a handle has been deleted.*

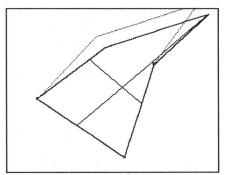

Figure 2.21 *The polygon when a segment is being repositioned.*

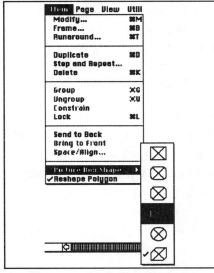

Figure 2.22 *The ITEM/PICTURE BOX SHAPE and submenu.*

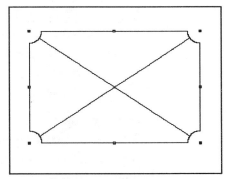

Figure 2.23 *A polygon converted to an inverted rounded-rectangle picture box.*

DELETING, COPYING, AND PASTING PICTURE BOXES

FRAMING BOXES

⌘ S

All picture boxes, whether polygonal or standard, are deleted, cut, copied, and pasted in the same manner as the text boxes.

☐ 1. To delete a picture box, select it with the Item Tool and press the DELETE key, or select CUT or CLEAR from the EDIT menu. Remember, a box may only be deleted if it is selected with the Item Tool: you cannot delete a page element in this way with the Content Tool.

☐ 2. To paste a picture box that has been cut or copied, simply pull down the EDIT menu and select PASTE. The box will be pasted onto the center of the screen area and may then be moved to its intended location.

All boxes — text or picture — may be framed with a decorative border. To place a frame around a box,

☐ 1. Select the box with *either* the Content or Item Tool, pull down the ITEM menu (figure 2.24) and select FRAME (⌘B).

☐ 2. The Frame dialog box will appear as shown in figure 2.25. The dialog box title displays an example of the current frame selection. If there is currently no frame on the selected box, the first frame style on the list is automatically selected. If the box already has a frame style applied to it, then that style is selected instead.

☐ 3. Scroll the Frame Style window and select a frame style. (New frame styles can be produced using Quark's Frame Editor, an application that is included in the QuarkXPress software package. If a QuarkXPress reference manual is available to you, consult it for more information.)

☐ 4. Next, type in specifications (in points) for the frame size. The size of a frame is the width of its line(s), from inside to outside. As a general rule, the more complex a frame is, the wider it must be in order to print clearly. For example, the second frame style choice—that of two solid lines—would look like one solid line if a frame size of only 1 point were specified. To print clearly, a frame size of 4 or more points would be desirable. The more complex styles should be made even wider — more than 12 pts. Click OK to apply the frame style and return to the document window.

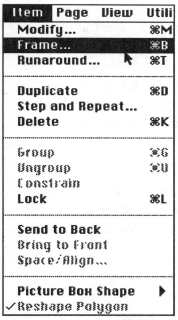

Figure 2.24   The ITEM/FRAME command.

An example of the selected frame is displayed here.

Enter point size for the frame in the width field.

The Frame Style window.

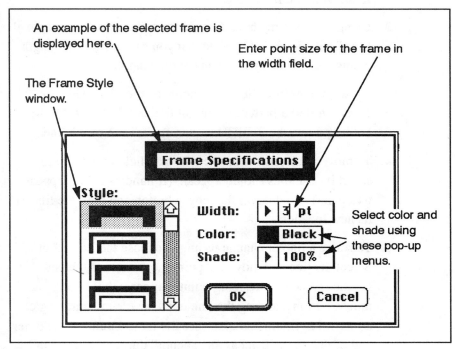

Select color and shade using these pop-up menus.

Figure 2.25   The Frame Specifications dialog box.

CREATING AND MANIPULATING LINES

5. You can assign any color or shade to a frame (the default color is black). To apply a color to a frame, select a box and choose FRAME from the ITEM menu. Then, select the color from the pop-up menu in the FRAME dialog box. To change the shade, either type in the new percentage (default setting is 100%), or use the scroll box to increase or decrease the percentage. Click OK to return to your document and see the effects of your frame choices.

Lines are excellent graphic elements to add to your document. They may be used to separate text and add emphasis or visual interest to a page. Arrows can be used for emphasis, giving direction to the text flow, or for labeling parts of pictures, charts, etc.

1. To create a straight line on your page, select the Orthogonal Tool by clicking on it with the mouse.

2. Click at the desired starting *(origin)* point, hold down the mouse button and drag the line to desired length. Release the mouse button. The line will blink once and then handles will appear at each end (figure 2.26). You will automatically be returned to the Item Tool.

3. Using the same method, draw another line using the Diagonal Line Tool (figure 2.27). Note that you can change the length or angle of the line while you are drawing it.

   Draw another line with the Diagonal Line Tool. This time constrain it to a perfectly straight line of 0°, 45° or 90°, by holding down the SHIFT key during creation of the line.

MOVING LINES

4. To move a line, select the Item Tool. Click on the line to select it. Handles should appear. (If handles do not appear, try again.) Hold down the mouse button and drag the line to its new location.

RESIZING LINES

5. To resize a line or change its angle, choose the Item Tool. Select the line and move the pointer over one of the end handles. When the resizing pointer appears, hold down the mouse button and drag the line to its new length and angle, as shown in figure 2.28. Release the mouse button. The other end of the line will act as an "anchor" during the resizing process.

⌘S

NOTES

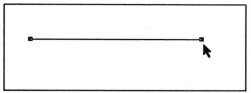

Figure 2.26 *A newly created orthogonal line.*

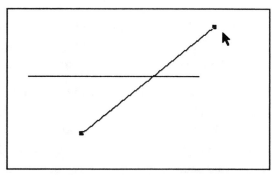

Figure 2.27 *A newly created diagonal line.*

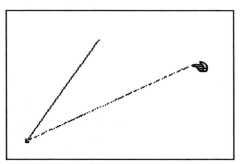

Figure 2.28 *A diagonal line as it is resized. Note that the user has also changed the angle of the line.*

DELETING/CUTTING LINES

COPYING LINES

CHANGING LINE STYLE USING THE STYLE MENU

⌘ S

6. To delete a line, select the line with the Item Tool. Press the DELETE key or select CUT or CLEAR from the EDIT menu.

7. Copying a line is done in the same manner as copying text and picture boxes. With the Item Tool, select the line to be copied. Pull down the EDIT menu and choose COPY. Then select PASTE from the EDIT menu to place a copy of the line in the middle of your screen.

There are several ways to change a line's style — its thickness, shading, color, and line type. By completing the next few steps you will learn to edit line style both by using the menus and the Measurements Palette.

1. Select a line with the Item Tool. Then, pull down the STYLE menu and select the LINE STYLE submenu as shown in figure 2.29. The STYLE menu gives you a choice of line types (single, double, arrowhead, etc.), as well as widths, colors, and shades. (For now, leave the line style at the default — single — line setting.)

2. With the STYLE menu still pulled down, pull down the ENDCAPS submenu (figure 2.30). Note the different combinations of straight and arrow endcaps. Select one of the arrow endcap styles.

3. With the line still selected, pull down the STYLE menu again and look at the WIDTH submenu (figure 2.31). Select 6 points.

4. Pull down the STYLE menu again and pull down the SHADES submenu (figure 2.32) in the same manner. Select 40%.

You also have a choice of colors for the lines. If you wish to change colors, pull down the STYLE menu, bring down the COLORS submenu and make your selection.

Remember that a line must be selected for your choices to have effect.

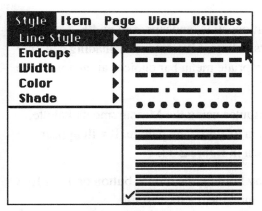

Figure 2.29   *The LINE STYLE menu.*

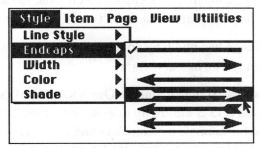

Figure 2.30   *The LINE ENDCAPS menu.*

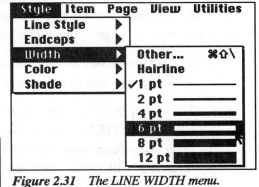

Figure 2.31   *The LINE WIDTH menu.*

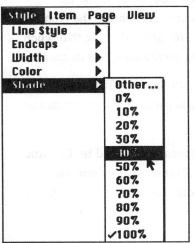

Figure 2.32   *The LINE SHADE menu.*

NOTES

CHANGING LINE STYLE USING THE MEASUREMENTS PALETTE

WORKING WITH GROUPED PAGE ELEMENTS

GROUPING ELEMENTS

MOVING A GROUP

CUTTING, COPYING AND PASTING GROUPED ELEMENTS

Four aspects of lines — position, style, endcaps, and width — can be changed using the Measurements Palette. Line color and shading can only be changed by selecting the appropriate menu bar choices at the top of the screen.

☐ 5. To change line attributes using the Measurements Palette, select a line and then examine the palette. It will appear similar to that shown in figure 2.33.

☐ 6. Change line style by holding the mouse button on the LINE STYLE pop-up menu. Select a dashed line.

☐ 7. Change the line's endcap by holding the mouse button on the endcaps pop-up menu. Select on of the arrow styles.

☐ 8. Change line width by double-clicking on the width field and then typing in a new figure.

Another new and exciting feature in QuarkXPress 3.0 that was not available in version 2.12 is the ability to *group* elements. This means that several elements, for example a picture box and text box, may be grouped and then manipulated as a unit. They may be cut and copied as a unit, yet moved and resized individually. Full editing capability is retained for each element. The next exercise will take you through the process of grouping, moving, resizing, and ungrouping a set of elements.

☐ 1. Create a picture box. Frame it. Then create a text box and a line, positioned as shown in figure 2.34.

☐ 2. Holding the SHIFT key down, select all of the elements. Pull down the ITEM menu and select GROUP or use the keyboard command (⌘G). Figure 2.35 shows the elements as they will appear after they are grouped. Note that when selected, a dashed line appears surrounding the elements.

☐ 3. To move the group, select it with the Item Tool and then move it just as you would any separate element: press and drag to a new location.

☐ 4. Cutting, copying, and pasting are all achieved in the same manner as before. The only difference is that you are working with a group of objects instead of only one object.

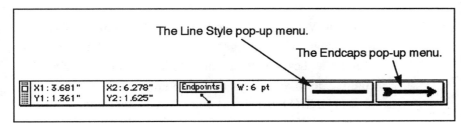

Figure 2.33 *The Measurements Palette when a line is selected.*

NOTES

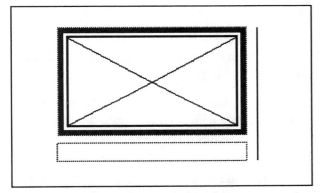

Figure 2.34 *Three elements before they are grouped.*

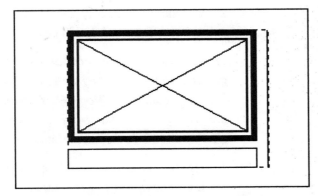

Figure 2.35 *After the items are grouped and selected, a dashed line surrounding the group appears.*

NOTES

MOVING ELEMENTS
WITHIN GROUPS

RESIZING ELEMENTS
WITHIN GROUPS

DELETING ELEMENTS
WITHIN GROUPS

⌘ S

Caution: When you delete, clear, or cut a group, you will see a dialog box appear with the message "This will delete several items and cannot be undone. OK to continue?" as shown in figure 2.36. If you delete or clear a group, you will not be able to UNDO the action if you change your mind. On the other hand, if you use the EDIT/CUT method, a copy of the group will be placed on the Clipboard. Although you cannot UNDO the cut, you can paste the group back onto the page.

5. To move an element within a group, activate the element with the Content Tool. In this case, select the bottom text box with the Content Tool. With the cursor directly over the text box, hold down the COMMAND key (⌘). The cursor will change to the Item Tool icon. Press the mouse button and drag the text box to a new location. Release the mouse button.

    The text box will remain a part of the group, even though it has been "relocated" within the group (see figure 2.37).

6. To resize an element within a group, select the element with the Content Tool and then resize it in the usual way. In this exercise select the picture box with the Content Tool. Move the cursor over one of the corner handles until the resizing pointer appears. Press and drag to resize the box, as shown in figure 2.38.

7. To delete an element within a group, select the element with the Content Tool and press ⌘K. In this exercise, delete the line. A dialog box appears, as shown in figure 2.39, informing you that an item contained in a group is about to be deleted and that the deletion cannot be undone.

    There is no menu command and no other way to delete a grouped element than by using the ⌘K keyboard equivalent. Also, you cannot CUT or COPY an element that is part of the group. You must ungroup the elements first and then CUT or COPY in the normal manner.

8. To ungroup the elements, select the group with the Item Tool. Pull down the ITEM menu and select UNGROUP. The elements can then be cut, copied or deleted individually.

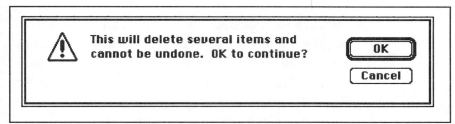

Figure 2.36   *The Group Deletion dialog box.*

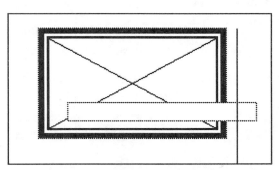

Figure 2.37   *The same group after one of the elements has been moved.*

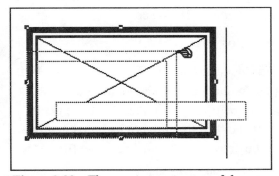

Figure 2.38   *The same group as one of the elements is being resized.*

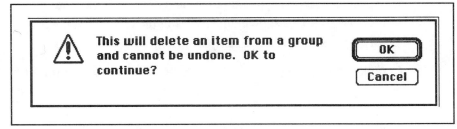

Figure 2.39   *The dialog box that appears when a grouped element is deleted.*

NOTES

PRINTING AN XPRESS DOCUMENT

APPLICATION PRACTICE

⌘ S

Note: Elements are grouped in sequential layers. In other words, if you group two elements together and then group that group with another element or group, these are "remembered" by XPress as two discrete groups. When you use the UNGROUP command, the elements are ungrouped in the reverse order in which they were grouped.

In this exercise, you will learn how to print a page (in this case a page with elements on it) to a laser printer.

☐ 1. Create a new XPress document and draw two or three text boxes, lines, etc. on the page.

☐ 2. Frame the boxes to place a printable border around them. (Remember, text and picture boxes do not automatically print borders. The dotted line you see on screen is there for your convenience, but will not print.)

☐ 3. Select CHOOSER from the APPLE menu to bring up the Chooser dialog box as shown in figure 2.40. Select the LaserWriter icon and select the printer name. (If you have more than one laser printer connected to your computer, you must select the printer you desire to use.)

Close the Chooser dialog box.

☐ 4. Pull down the FILE menu and select PRINT. The LaserWriter's Print dialog box will appear, as shown in figure 2.41. (The various options are described in the Reference Guide portion of this book and therefore are not included here.) Click OK to send the one copy of your document file to the printer.

Exercises:

1. Complete a "sampler" page of boxes and lines with different frames and styles, as shown on page 51 at the end of this chapter. Use a text box to label each sample.

2. Complete a page layout for a flyer, placing boxes and then framing these boxes.

NOTES

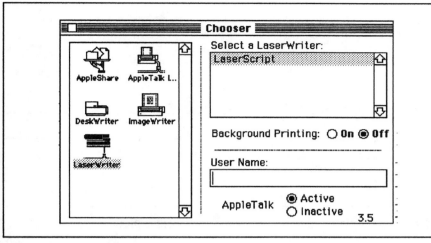

Figure 2.40   *The Chooser dialog box.*

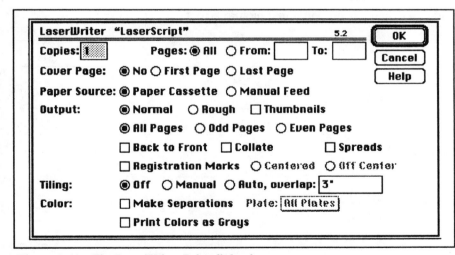

Figure 2.41   *The LaserWriter Print dialog box.*

1. What are "page elements"?

_____

_____

2. Describe the steps to create a text box and enter text from the keyboard.

_____

_____

3. When selecting one of the elements tools, what is the purpose of holding down the OPTION key?

_____

_____

4. Describe the difference between creating a polygonal picture box and a rectangular picture box.

_____

_____

5. List the steps to reshape a polygon.

_____

_____

6. Describe the procedures to add and delete handles on polygonal picture boxes.

_____

_____

7. What is a "bounding box"?

_____

_____

8. What is a box frame, and how is it created?

_____

_____

9. What are the different style options available for a line?

_____

_____

10. What is a "group"? How is it created?

_____

_____

11. If you want to move an element contained within a group, what should you do?

_____

_____

EXAMPLE

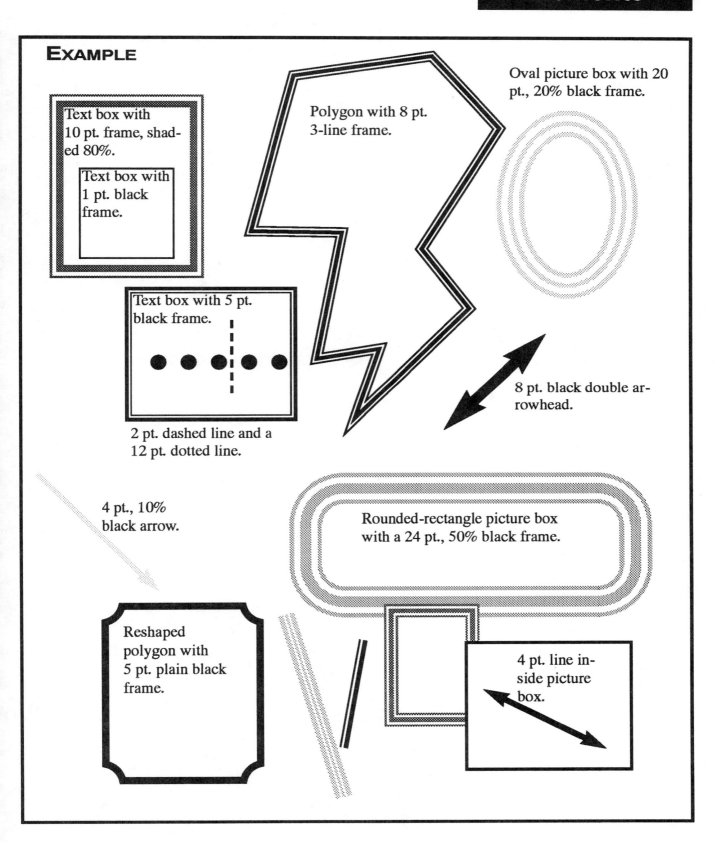

Text box with 10 pt. frame, shaded 80%.

Text box with 1 pt. black frame.

Polygon with 8 pt. 3-line frame.

Oval picture box with 20 pt., 20% black frame.

Text box with 5 pt. black frame.

2 pt. dashed line and a 12 pt. dotted line.

8 pt. black double arrowhead.

4 pt., 10% black arrow.

Rounded-rectangle picture box with a 24 pt., 50% black frame.

Reshaped polygon with 5 pt. plain black frame.

4 pt. line inside picture box.

Chapter Three

Building and Using a Memo Document

CHAPTER OBJECTIVES

EDIT / GENERAL PREFERENCES ⌘ Y

HORIZONTAL AND VERTICAL RULER MEASUREMENTS

⌘ S

Now that you are comfortable working with basic page elements, you are going to build a simple document — a memo. First, you will create a *template* for the memo. A template is simply a form that can be used over and over again. In the process of completing the exercises in this chapter, you will learn to:

✔ Change document preferences.

✔ Place and use guidelines.

✔ Lay out a page with lines and boxes.

✔ Save a template.

✔ Work with text: enter, select, change font size, type style, and alignment, and use tracking.

✔ Use the Lock to Baseline Grid feature.

1. If you quit QuarkXPress at the end of Chapter 2 or are starting a new session, launch the program.

2. Pull down the FILE menu and select NEW. When the New dialog box appears, enter 1-inch margins for all sides. Turn off the default text box placement by clicking the selection box next to Automatic Text Box. (Normally, it is set to on, but you won't need the large default text box to complete the memo.) Click OK.

Pull down the EDIT menu, select PREFERENCES as shown in figure 3.1, and then select GENERAL from the pop-up submenu. The dialog box as shown in figure 3.2 will appear

3. Examine the PREFERENCES dialog box. Note that the horizontal and vertical ruler measurement units are set to inches. (If yours are not set to inches, it means that someone has changed the default setting. Don't worry, just follow the next few steps.)

Pull down the HORIZONTAL MEASURE menu by clicking and holding the mouse on Inches. Select INCHES DECIMAL and release the mouse. Repeat this step with the VERTICAL MEASURE menu. When we return to the document the ruler will display inches in decimal increments instead of the traditional subunits.

NOTES

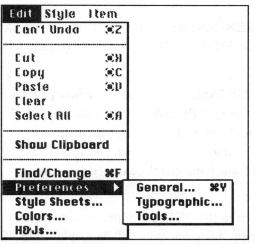

Figure 3.1 *The EDIT/PREFERENCES option.*

Preferences pop-up menus.

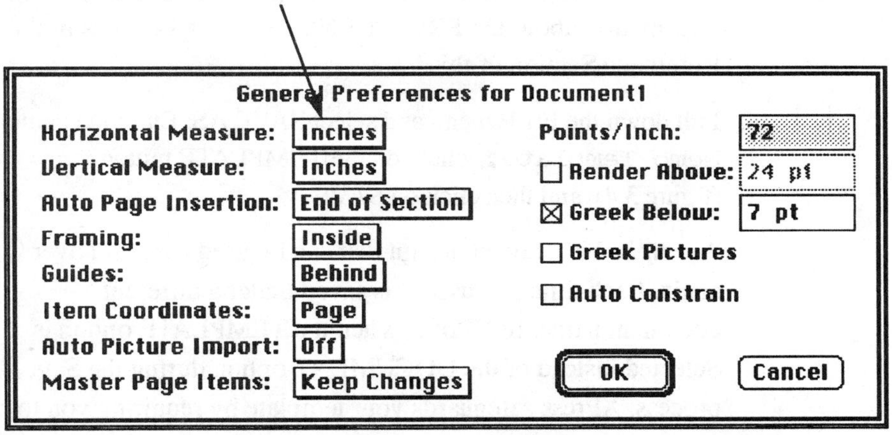

General Preferences for Document1

Horizontal Measure:	Inches
Vertical Measure:	Inches
Auto Page Insertion:	End of Section
Framing:	Inside
Guides:	Behind
Item Coordinates:	Page
Auto Picture Import:	Off
Master Page Items:	Keep Changes

Points/Inch: 72
☐ Render Above: 24 pt
☒ Greek Below: 7 pt
☐ Greek Pictures
☐ Auto Constrain

OK   Cancel

Figure 3.2 *The General Preferences dialog box.*

AUTO PAGE INSERTION

GUIDES DISPLAY

Saving the Template

⌘S

☐ 4. While the PREFERENCES dialog box is still open, press on the pop-up menu for AUTO PAGE INSERTION (figure 3.3) and select OFF.

#1   Usually, AUTO PAGE INSERTION will cause new pages to be inserted automatically at the end of the current section, if text overflows the text box of the page on which you are working. For this document we do not want XPress to insert pages automatically, and have therefore turned this feature off.

☐ 5. Select IN FRONT from the GUIDES submenu. As you are creating the document, the guidelines will be displayed in front of all text boxes and other page elements. Later, after completing the basic layout, you will probably want to change guidelines to BACK.

Click OK to return to the document. We will use other features of the PREFERENCES dialog box later. More information about the PREFERENCES dialog boxes is in the Reference Section of this book.

☐ 6. Pull down the FILE menu and select SAVE AS. Enter the name **Memo Template,** click on the TEMPLATE button (figure 3.4), and then click on SAVE.

#2

A *template* is a layout design that can be used over and over again. Each time it is used it is saved under a different document name. In XPress, when the TEMPLATE option is Selected instead of the DOCUMENT option during the Save process, XPress safeguards your template by requiring you to use the SAVE AS (instead of SAVE) feature each time you save. This safeguard prevents you from accidentally overwriting a document onto your memo template.

To save time during the rest of this exercise, you should save the memo template as a document, and only save it as a template when it is completed.

NOTES

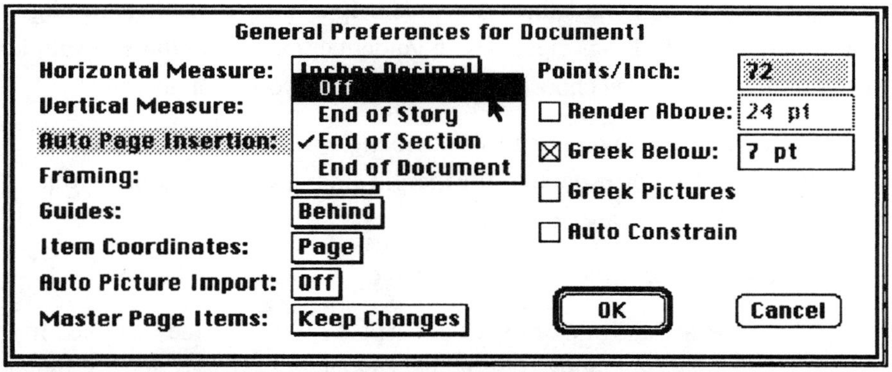

```
            General Preferences for Document1
Horizontal Measure:  Inches Decimal   Points/Inch:    72
                          Off
Vertical Measure:                      ☐ Render Above: 24 pt
                       End of Story
Auto Page Insertion:  ✓ End of Section ☒ Greek Below:  7 pt
Framing:                End of Document
Guides:        Behind                  ☐ Greek Pictures
Item Coordinates:  Page                ☐ Auto Constrain
Auto Picture Import:  Off
Master Page Items:  Keep Changes        ( OK )    ( Cancel )
```

Figure 3.3 *Turning AUTO PAGE INSERTION Off. Turning off the AUTO PAGE INSERTION feature prevents the automatic creation of new pages.*

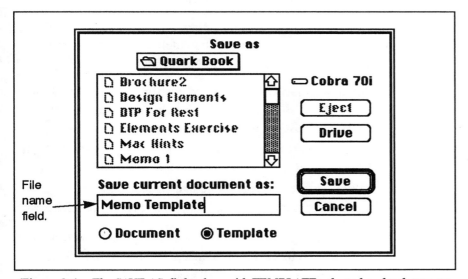

File
name
field.

Figure 3.4 *The SAVE AS dialog box with TEMPLATE selected and a document name entered in the file name field.*

Guidelines

PLACING AND USING GUIDELINES

Nonprinting guidelines are an important feature of most page layout software applications. Guidelines and grids help us plan, structure, and align our design elements. Grids created with guidelines can be complex or simple, many or few— how you choose to structure your layout is up to you.

When we first created our new document, we also specified four default guides that correspond to the margin settings. Look again at your page. The dotted lines are guidelines.

We can add more guidelines to our page:

☐ 1. Place the cursor over the vertical ruler (the ruler on the left), press the mouse button and drag a guideline to the 1.3–inch position as shown in figure 3.5.

☐ 2. Repeat the previous step, pulling a second guideline to the 2.2–inch position.

☐ 3. To place horizontal guidelines, place the cursor on the horizontal ruler at the top of the window, press the mouse button and drag to the following positions: 1.5", 1.6", 3", and 3.2".

☐ 4. To view the entire page, with guidelines, pull down the VIEW menu and select FIT IN WINDOW (figure 3.6).

VIEW / GUIDES OPTIONS

☐ 5. Pull down the VIEW menu and examine it. Notice that there are two menu options pertaining to guides. The first, HIDE GUIDES, allows you to view the page without displaying the guides — just as it will look when you print it (see figure 3.7). If you were to select HIDE GUIDES at this stage, you would see a blank page. Note that when the guides are hidden, the menu option is changed to SHOW GUIDES.

The second option, SNAP TO GUIDES, should have a check mark next to it. This option means that the *snap to* feature is turned on: page elements will snap to (align with) the guides when resized or created within the distance of a few pixels. If there is no check mark next to SNAP TO GUIDES, turn it on by selecting this option.

⌘ S

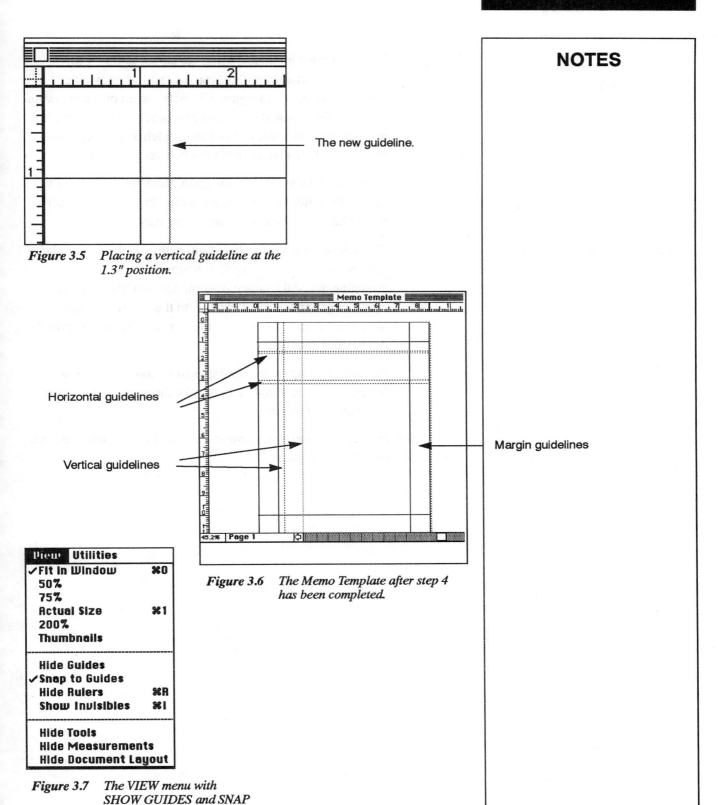

The new guideline.

Figure 3.5   *Placing a vertical guideline at the 1.3" position.*

Horizontal guidelines

Vertical guidelines

Margin guidelines

Figure 3.6   *The Memo Template after step 4 has been completed.*

View	Utilities
✓Fit In Window	⌘0
50%	
75%	
Actual Size	⌘1
200%	
Thumbnails	
Hide Guides	
✓Snap to Guides	
Hide Rulers	⌘R
Show Invisibles	⌘I
Hide Tools	
Hide Measurements	
Hide Document Layout	

Figure 3.7   *The VIEW menu with SHOW GUIDES and SNAP TO GUIDES activated.*

NOTES

Guidelines

REPOSITIONING
GUIDELINES

REMOVING GUIDELINES

☐ 6. To reposition a guideline, bring the cursor to the "white
#3 space" area outside the print margin and just above the
guideline as shown in figure 3.8. With the tip of the arrow on
the guideline, press the mouse button and move the line. You
will see the cursor change and the guideline will begin to
move. You may then position it wherever you wish.

If the line does not move, try again. Remember, in order to
"grab" the guideline, the cursor arrow tip should be directly
on the line when you press the mouse button.

☐ 7. To remove a guideline, simple move the line back onto the
#3 ruler of origin. For example, to remove a horizontal
guideline, place the cursor over the line in either the left or
right margin and move it back on to the horizontal ruler.
When you release the mouse, the line will disappear from the
document window.

Practice creating, repositioning, and removing guidelines.
When the memo template looks like the example in figure
3.6 remember to save it.

The next exercise will show you how to place and manipulate elements
(lines and text boxes) on the page.

⌘ S

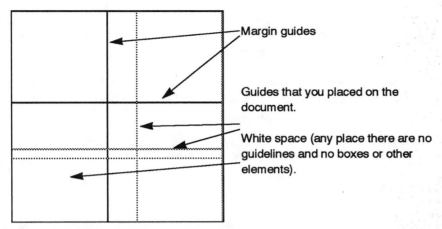

Margin guides

Guides that you placed on the document.

White space (any place there are no guidelines and no boxes or other elements).

Figure 3.8   *The "white space" in the margin area.*

PLACING PAGE ELEMENTS

CREATING AND PLACING A VERTICAL LINE

PLACING TEXT BOXES

⌘ S

☐ 1. Pull down the VIEW menu again and select 50%. This will allow you to view more of the document on screen.

Select the Orthogonal Tool and create a vertical line in the left margin of the document. Start it 1 inch from the top (at the 1–inch horizontal guide) and end it at 10 inches (the bottom horizontal guide — see figure 3.9). The line will snap to the guides. Then, with *either* the Item Tool or the Content Tool, select the line and move it to the right until it snaps to the 1" vertical guide .

☐ 2. With the line still selected, pull down the STYLE menu, and select the double line icon, or select the double line style from the pop-up menu on the Measurements Palette.

☐ 3. Pull down the STYLE menu again and select 6 PTS. from the WIDTH submenu, or type a 6 in the width section of the Measurements Palette. Figure 3.10 shows the memo document after the line style has been changed.

☐ 4. You will next place four text boxes on the page. To place the boxes, OPTION-SELECT the Text Box Tool (remember that pressing the OPTION key allows you to continue using the tool until you select something else).

Then create text boxes and place according to the example in figure 3.11. (The text boxes have been shaded in the illustration to make it easier for you to see. Yours will not be shaded.) Notice how using the SNAP TO GRID feature helps you place and align the boxes.

☐ 5. At this point, for the sake of convenience, you may wish to bring up the PREFERENCES dialog box again (select EDIT / PREFERENCES / GENERAL, or press ⌘ Y) and change the guides display to BACK.

Don't forget to save!

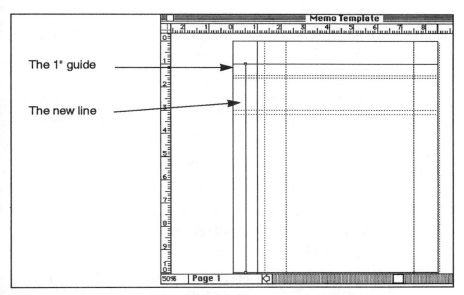

The 1" guide

The new line

Figure 3.9 Drawing a line in the margin area between top and bottom guides.

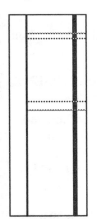

Figure 3.10 The line after style has been changed. (guides are in front).

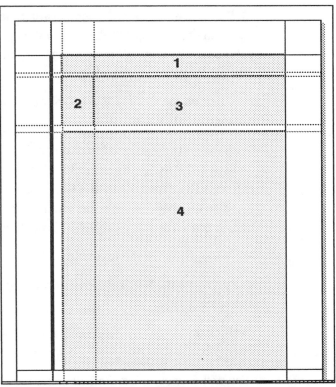

Figure 3.11 The "Memo Template" after text boxes have been placed.

CREATING THE MEMO HEADER

CHANGING TYPE SIZE BY MENU

CHANGING TYPE STYLE BY MEASUREMENTS PALETTE

CHANGING TYPE ALIGNMENT

CHANGING TRACKING

⌘ S

The next steps to completing your memo template involve entering a memo heading and other text that will not change from memo to memo.

1. Change the view back to Actual Size (or larger). Click on the Content Tool and then select the uppermost text box. This is where we will place the Memo header. The blinking cursor will appear in the upper left corner of the box.

2. Type: m e m o with a space between each letter.

3. Select the word by triple-clicking on it. Pull down the STYLE menu and select SIZE to bring up the submenu. With the mouse button still held down, select 24 points (figure 3.12).

4. With memo still selected, click on the ALL CAPS icon (K) on the Measurements Palette. The word memo will now appear in all caps: MEMO.

5. We will now change the alignment of the word MEMO. You may use one of two ways:

   a) Pull down the STYLE menu again. Select ALIGNMENT and then choose CENTERED from the ALIGNMENT submenu. The text will now be centered in the text box and will be 24 points in size, or

   b) Click on the CENTER ALIGNMENT icon (📃) in the Measurements Palette.

6. With the text still selected, pull down the STYLE menu again and select TRACK. When the TRACK dialog box appears (figure 3.13), type in 100 and then click OK. This action will increase the space between the letters of the word MEMO by one *en space* (or approximately 1/2 the letter width).

   #4

7. We will now make the text bold, either:

   a) Pull down the STYLE menu, the TYPE STYLE submenu, and select BOLD, or

   b) Click on the BOLD icon (B) on the Measurements Palette.

The memo header is complete and should resemble the example shown in figure 3.14. You will now complete the To/For section of the template.

Figure 3.12 *The STYLE menu with 24 point type selected.*

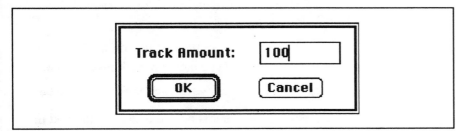

Figure 3.13 *The TRACK dialog box.*

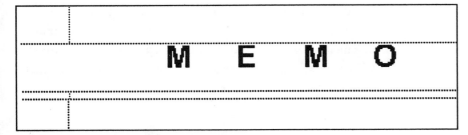

Figure 3.14 *The completed memo heading.*

THE "TO / FROM" BOX

SETTING A BASELINE GRID

LOCKING TEXT TO BASELINE GRID

⌘S

QuarkXPress offers precise typographical controls. In this next exercise, you are going to use only a few of these controls. The first is the LOCK TO BASELINE GRID feature. XPress allows us to define an invisible underlying grid in our document and enables us to lock the *baseline* of our text to this grid. (The baseline is illustrated in figure 3.15.)

The reason for defining and using the LOCK TO BASELINE GRID feature in this case is that we wish the memo form to be usable by anyone, even someone who does not know word processing or QuarkXPress very well. We want the name of the recipient to line up across from TO:, the name of the sender to line up across from FROM:, and so forth. LOCK TO BASELINE GRID is a technique for making sure that text is aligned vertically across text boxes.

1. Pull down the EDIT menu, choose PREFERENCES, and select TYPOGRAPHIC... from the PREFERENCES sub-menu. In the BASELINE GRID box type in specifications to start the grid at .5 inch, in increments of 24 points, as shown in figure 3.16.

2. With the Content Tool, select the text box on the left, directly under the header box. Type the memo address as shown.

   To:<return> From:<return> Subject:<return> Date:.

3. With the cursor still in the text box, select all of the text in the text box. (This can be accomplished quickly by pulling down the EDIT menu and choosing SELECT ALL, or by typing ⌘A.)

4. Pull down the STYLE menu and select FORMATS.... In the resulting FORMAT dialog box (figure 3.17), click to select the LOCK TO GRID option. Then click OK to return to the document. You will notice that the lines of text have moved further apart. The baseline of each line of text is now locked to the 24 point baseline grid.

5. Select the text block to the right of the address block. Following the same steps, bring up the FORMAT dialog box and select LOCK TO GRID. Text that is subsequently entered into this text block will be automatically locked to the baseline grid and will line up with the text in the block to its left.

6. Save your memo template *as a template*. It is now complete. If you wish, quit XPress at this time or go on to the next group of exercises.

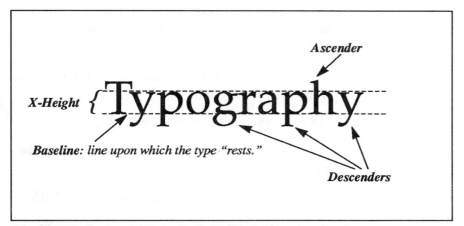

Figure 3.15 *The terminology of typography.*

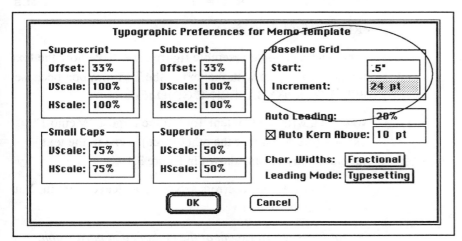

Figure 3.16 *The TYPOGRAPHIC PREFERENCES dialog box.*

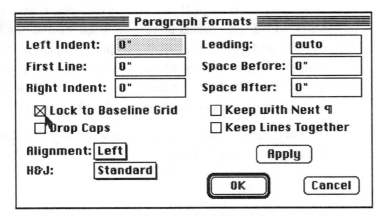

Figure 3.17 *The PARAGRAPH FORMATS dialog box with*
LOCK TO BASELINE GRID selected.

NOTES

WORD PROCESSING WITH QUARKXPRESS

ENTERING TEXT

In this next section, you will use your memo template, save it as a document, and print a memo.

☐ 1. If you closed the template after completing the last exercise, open "Memo Template" again.

SAVE AS a document under a new name: "Memo 1."

☐ 2. With the Content Tool, select the text box to the right of the address box. Enter the following

`Jim Cook,Production Supervisor <RETURN>`

(your name)`, Production Manager <RETURN>`

`Production Schedule for Text Publications`

`<RETURN>`*(today's date)*

Your heading should resemble figure 3.18. Note how the text in this box lines up with the text in the To/From box because of the LOCK TO BASELINE GRID feature.

☐ 3. Now click with the Content Tool in the largest "Memo 1" text box (the one under the other three). Type in the text (including any errors) shown in figure 3.19.

If you make additional errors as you type, leave them in. You will correct them later.

WRAPPING TEXT

Do not press return except at the end of each paragraph.

As with most word processing programs, the word processing function of Quark XPress includes *automatic line wraparound*. This means that if you reach the end of a line, the next word will automatically be placed on the next line. Automatic line wraparound facilitates corrections. If you were to press RETURN at the end of each line, the text will not reformat correctly when you need make changes.

Do not concern yourself with line endings — your entry will not look exactly like the example.

⌘ S

TAB-Delete To Remove

M E M O

To: Jim Cook, Production Supervisor

From: Linda Peterson, Production Manager

Subject: Production Schedule for Text Publications

Date: April 18, 1990

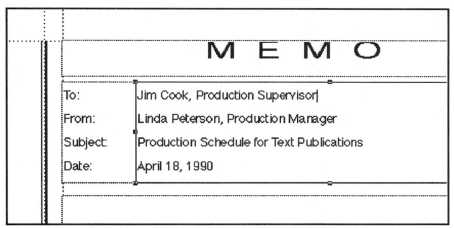

Figure 3.18 The "Memo 1" address heading after it has been typed in.

Jim, I'm very concerned about the prolonged delay we are currently experiencing as a result of the integration of desktop publishing technology into the text prodction process. As we discused at the last management meeting, we were all aware that the changeover would cause some slowdown initially, but I had hoped that we would be up to speed by now.

What is the problem? Rumors have it that some of the older employees (meaning those with more seniority) are having difficulty adjusting to the change. In adition, since many are learning the new software and systems "on-the-job," there are numerous errors that need to be cleaned up.

I would like you to contact Judy Tellard in HRD. She is the person who handles trainning and also contract and temporary recruiting. I think we need to find out what it would take to get these people trained . . . and quickly!

You have my approval to hire or contract temporary desktop publishing specialists - people that already know the software and can help us get back on schedule. In addition, I want you to hire additional, temporary office assistance. We need to get you out from under that mountain of paperwork on your desk and back on the floor. If we don't get our production schedule back under control, we're in for some tongue lashing from the board. Call me as soon as you have your strategy planned, and we'll discuss it.

Figure 3.19 Enter this text into the "Memo 1" document.

NOTES

USING THE CHARACTER SPECIFICATIONS COMMAND

4. With the cursor still in the text box, select all of the body text of the memo by pulling down the EDIT menu and choosing SELECT ALL (⌘A).

5. Next, pull down the STYLE menu and select CHARACTER. The CHARACTER SPECIFICATIONS dialog box will appear as in figure 3.20. Scroll the font list and select Times.

#7

We will not be changing anything else at this time, but take a few minutes to examine the CHARACTER SPECIFICATIONS dialog box. Choosing CHARACTER allows us to make several changes at one time, without having to pull down separate menus for each change. These specifications include:

Font—choices on the pop-up menu change the font (typeface).

Size—choices on the pop-up menu offer preset sizes, or you can type custom sizes into the size field. Fractional point sizes may be used, in increments of .25 points. For example, we could enter 13.25 points as a point size.

Color—changes the color of text (pop-up menu). These colors include defaults that come with QuarkXpress.

Shade—choices on the pop-up menu specify a color saturation percentage. You can also enter a custom percentage.

Style—the list contains options to alter the appearance of characters. These styles can be used in combination. Selecting PLAIN deselects all other styles.

Horizontal Scaling—this effect compresses or expands characters, actually distorting them rather than changing distance between them. It changes the width of the letters.

Track Amount—this effect changes the space between letters. A positive number increases the letter space and a negative number decreases the letterspace. Tracking and kerning values are entered in the range of -100 to 100, where 1=1/200 of an *em-space*. An em-space is equal to two zeros. The actual width varies the font being used.

Baseline Shift—This effect enables us to shift text up or down from its position in a line of text in increments as fine as .001 point.

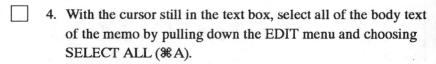

NOTES

The pop-up FONT menu

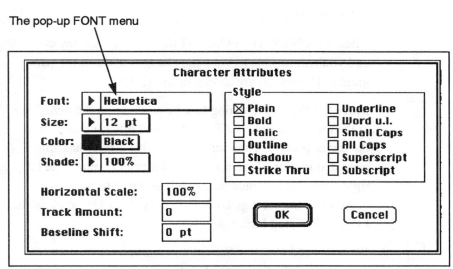

Figure 3.20 *The Character Attributes dialog box. In this exercise you will only change the font.*

71

DISPLAYING INVISIBLE CHARACTERS

FORMATTING A PARAGRAPH FOR INDENTS AND SPACE AFTER

OBSERVING THE FORMAT RULER

⌘ S

6. With the text still selected, pull down the VIEW menu and select SHOW INVISIBLES. This feature displays all spaces, tabs, and returns (see figure 3.21). These invisible characters do not print when you print your document, but displaying them on screen can be useful for editing.

7. Make sure all the text is still selected. Choose FORMATS from the STYLE menu. The FORMAT dialog box will appear. Enter the formatting changes as follows (also see figure 3.22):

   First Line Indent: .25 "

   Leading: 15 pt

   Space After: .1"

   Click on APPLY. The FORMAT dialog box will stay open and you will be able to view the changes made to the paragraphs. The results are shown in figure 3.23.

8. Move the FORMAT dialog box by clicking on the *active bar* at the top of the FORMAT window and dragging the bar to the lower portion of the screen. Note that a ruler has appeared at the top of the text box. This ruler displays the left, right, and first line indents, as well as any tabs that have been set. If the settings are satisfactory, click OK to close the FORMAT dialog box.

9. We now need to delete the extra paragraph return between each paragraph. To accomplish this, place the cursor before the first character of each paragraph (starting at the second paragraph), and press the DELETE key once. The extra returns will be deleted and the paragraphs below will move up one line.

   Repeat this process until all extra returns have been deleted.

Remember to save your document again. You may now move on to the next section where you will learn to use Quark's powerful spelling checker.

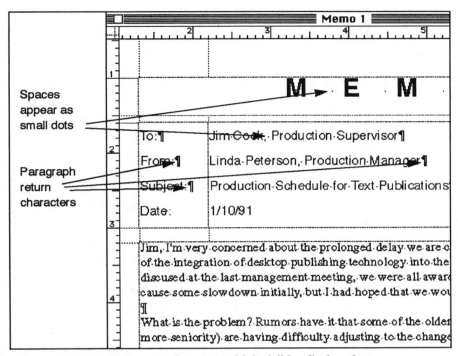

Figure 3.21 *The "Memo 1" document with invisibles displayed.*

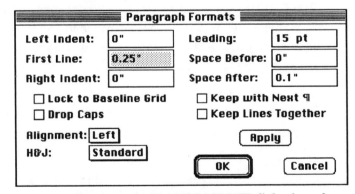

Figure 3.22 *The PARAGRAPH FORMATS dialog box after changes have been made to the FIRST LINE, LEADING, and SPACE AFTER specifications.*

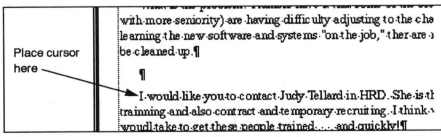

Figure 3.23 *To delete a return, place the cursor before the first character of a paragraph and press the DELETE key.*

USING THE CHECK SPELLING FEATURE

1. If you quit QuarkXPress at the end of the previous exercise, launch the program again and open the "Memo 1" document.

2. Place the cursor at the top of the largest text box. Pull down the UTILITIES menu, select CHECK SPELLING, and then select STORY from the submenu (figure 3.24). In QuarkXPress, a *story* is defined as all the text in one text box or a group of *linked* boxes (if the text flows from one box to the next).

3. A WORD COUNT dialog box will appear that tells you how many words are in the story, how many unique words there are (that is, words used once) and how many "suspect" words there are (words that the spelling checker needs to ask about).

   Note: The number you see in your dialog box may vary slightly from those that are shown in figure 3.25, depending upon the number of input errors.

   Click OK to continue the process.

4. The CHECK STORY dialog box will now appear (figure 3.26) listing the first suspect word at the top. If there is more than once instance of this word, it will display the number of times that the word exists.

   Click on the LOOKUP button. A word (or words) will appear in the middle text area. These words are possible replacements for the suspect word and are supplied by the XPress Dictionary on your hard drive.

   Select the correct spelling of the word and then click on the REPLACE option, which has been activated.

5. The next suspect word will appear in the dialog box. Repeat the process, selecting REPLACE when appropriate.

   Names (such as "Tellard") and acronyms (such as "HRD") may be skipped by clicking the SKIP button at the appropriate time. You may also add these words to a special user dictionary that you create. We will not cover that procedure in this exercise. Refer to the Reference Guide, pages 279–280, for more information about user dictionaries.

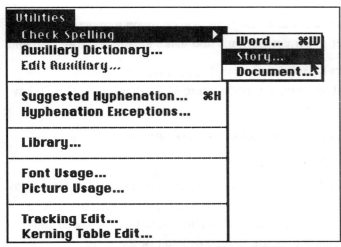

Figure 3.24 The UTILITIES / CHECK SPELLING menu.

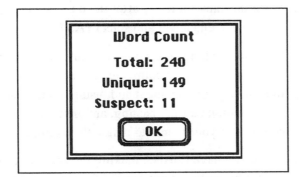

Figure 3.25 The WORD COUNT dialog box.

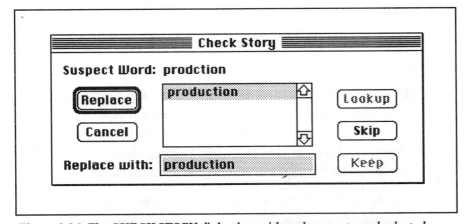

Figure 3.26 The CHECK STORY dialog box with replacement word selected.

FINISHING THE MEMO

...SELECTING, DELETING, REPLACING, MOVING, AND COPYING TEXT

We will now use the text editing features, common to most word processors, in order to correct grammar and make the memo more readable.

☐ 1. Select the word "currently" in the first paragraph by double-clicking on it (see figure 3.27). Press the DELETE key to delete it.

☐ 2. Select the words "the integration of," delete, and replace with "integrating."

☐ 3. Select the word "initially" in the second sentence. Be sure to include the space before the word, but not the comma after it. This is accomplished by clicking before the space and dragging the mouse to the last letter of the word.

☐ 4. Pull down the EDIT menu and select CUT.

☐ 5. Place the cursor directly after the d in "would," pull down the EDIT menu again and select PASTE.

☐ 6. Continue making corrections to your memo by comparing each sentence of the completed memo (at the end of this section) with your document and, using the techniques of selecting, deleting, cutting, pasting, and inserting, change the contents of your memo to match the example.

☐ 7. When you have finished making the changes to your memo, print it by pulling down the FILE menu, selecting PRINT, and clicking OK in the print dialog box.

Congratulations! You have just completed your first page layout project. Don't forget to save it!

APPLICATION PRACTICE

⌘S

Exercises:

1. Build your own design for a memo or letterhead template and save it as a template. Reopen and save the document under a new name. Enter text into your document – assume you are writing a memo to a friend or your instructor. Practice character and paragraph formatting, text editing, and spell checking.

2. Create a stationery set (letterhead, envelope, and business card) for personal or business use. Use only lines, framed boxes, and text.

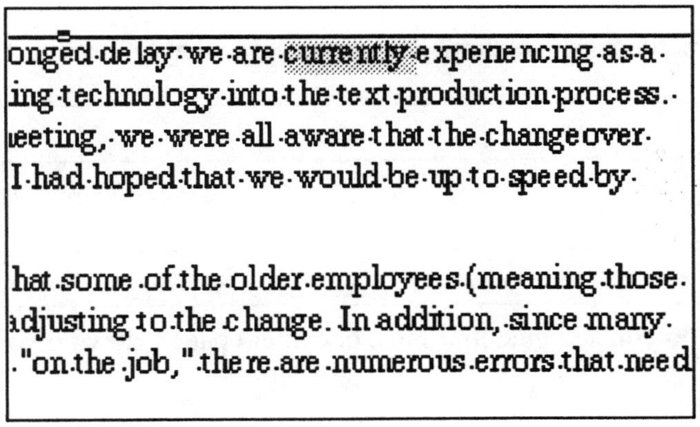

onged·delay·we·are·currently·experiencing·as·a·
ing·technology·into·the·text·production·process.·
eeting,·we·were·all·aware·that·the·changeover·
I·had·hoped·that·we·would·be·up·to·speed·by·

hat·some·of·the·older·employees·(meaning·those·
adjusting·to·the·change.·In·addition,·since·many·
·"on·the·job,"·there·are·numerous·errors·that·need

Figure 3.27 Selecting a word.

NOTES

1. What options does XPress offer for automatic page insertion? Why might you want to turn this feature off?
   _____
   _____

2. What is a *template?*
   _____
   _____

3. What purpose do *guidelines* serve? How do you add guidelines to a document page? How do you remove them?
   _____
   _____

4. What does *tracking* on the Style Menu do to selected text?
   _____
   _____

5. What is a *baseline?* In what dialog box can we change the XPress baseline grid?
   _____
   _____

6. Why might you want to *lock text to a baseline grid?*
   _____
   _____

7. What does *character* option on the Style Menu allow us to do?
   _____
   _____

8. What are *invisibles* and why would you want to display them?
   _____
   _____

9. How is a *story* defined in QuarkXPress?
   _____
   _____

10. Describe the operation of the QuarkXPress *spelling checker.* How is it different from the spelling checker in the word processing program you usually use?
    _____
    _____

M E M O

To: Jim Cook, Production Supervisor

From: Linda Peterson, Production Manager

Subject: Production Schedule for Text Publications

Date: January 10, 1991

Jim, I'm very concerned about the prolonged delay we are experiencing as a result of integrating desktop publishing technology into the text production process. As we discussed at the last management meeting, we were all aware that the changeover would initially cause some slowdown, but I had hoped that we would be up to speed by now.

What is the problem? Rumors have it that some of the older employees (meaning those with more seniority) are having difficulty adjusting to the change. In addition, since many are learning the new software and systems "on-the-job," there are numerous errors that need to be cleaned up.

I would like you to contact Judy Tellard in HRD. She is the person who handles training and she also handles contract and temporary recruiting. I think we need to find out what it will take to get these people trained…and quickly!

In the meantime, you have my approval to hire or contract temporary desktop publishing specialists — people that already know the software and can help us get back on schedule. In addition, I want you to hire additional temporary office assistance. We need to get you out from under that mountain of paperwork on your desk.

If we don't get our production schedule back under control, we're in for some tongue lashing from the board. Call me as soon as you have your strategy planned, and we'll discuss it.

Chapter Four

Integrating Pictures and Text

CHAPTER OBJECTIVES

THE CATALOG PROJECT

USING A MULTI-COLUMN GRID

⌘S

You are now ready to begin using one of the most exciting aspects of desktop publishing — the ability to electronically integrate text and pictures in a document. Just as you would manually lay out and paste up pictures and text to create a finished camera-ready publication, you will lay out and "paste up" your electronic documents.

In this chapter you will create two projects: a catalog page, and a two-column document (see pages 110-111). In the process you will learn to:

✔ Use a more complex grid for page layout.

✔ Import pictures using two different methods.

✔ Edit picture style, scaling, and placement.

✔ Modify specifications for picture and text boxes.

✔ Control picture/text runaround.

✔ Use more complex typographic controls.

1. Launch QuarkXPress and open a new document (FILE/NEW or ⌘N). Set up the page guides for the catalog's 8-column grid with 1-pica gutters between columns by entering the following specifications in the NEW dialog box (shown in figure 4.1).

   a) Page Size: US Letter (the default)

   b) Margins: Top 0.75", Bottom 0.75", Left 4p6, Right 4p6

   c) Column Guides: 8

   d) Gutter Width: 1p (the default). If you are using inches as the default horizontal measurement, the gutter width of 1p will be displayed as its equivalent, 0.167", as shown in figure 4.1.

   e) Turn off the Automatic Text Box by deselecting it and then click OK to create the document.

2. Pull down the EDIT menu and select PREFERENCES/ GENERAL. Enter specifications in the PREFERENCES dialog box as follows (figure 4.2):

   a) Change the Vertical Measure to inches, and the Horizontal Measure to picas.

   b) Change the GUIDES to in front.

   c) Click OK to return to the QuarkXPress document.

NOTES

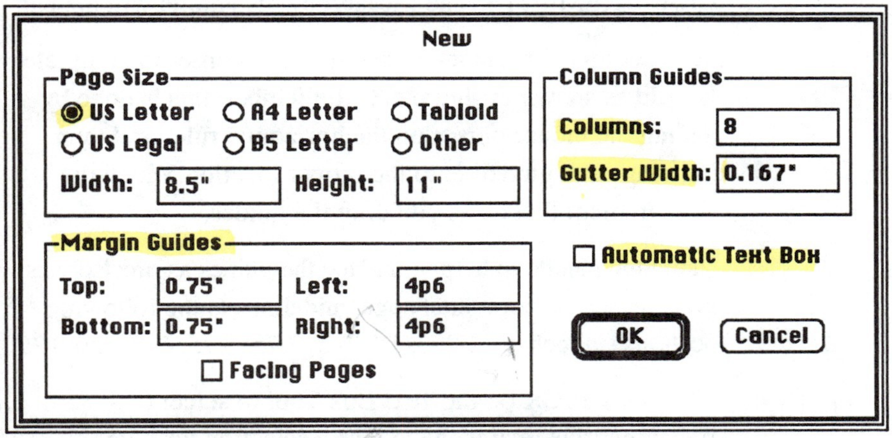

Figure 4.1 *The New dialog box, with eight column guides specified.*

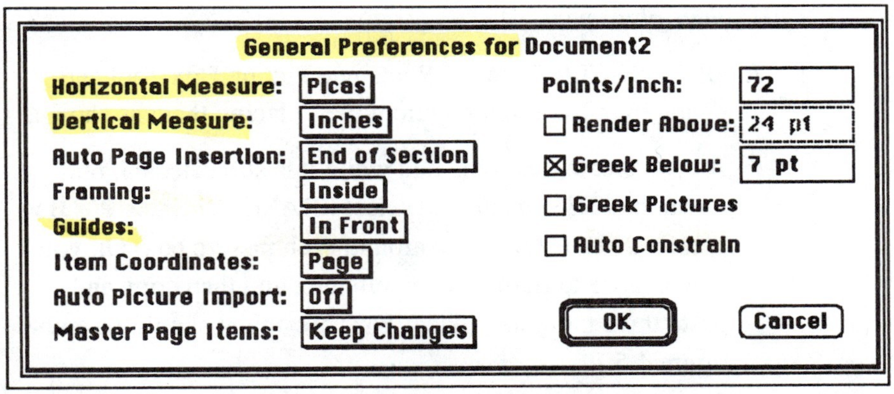

Figure 4.2 *The GENERAL PREFERENCES dialog box with specifications as listed in step 2.*

Placing horizontal guidelines

Placing text boxes

Placing picture boxes and applying a frame

⌘S

3. <mark>SAVE the document as "Catalog 1."</mark>

4. If the Measurements Palette does not appear at the bottom of your screen, pull down the VIEW menu and select SHOW MEASUREMENTS. The Measurements Palette will appear.

5. Next, set up the horizontal page guides in order to complete the grid as shown in figure 4.3. Remember, this is done by placing the mouse cursor on the horizontal ruler and then dragging each guideline to the proper location. Watch the Measurement Palette as you drag the guides.

   Using the palette to help you place the guides as precisely as possible, set the horizontal page guidelines to the following locations (in inches): 1.375, 1.5, 3.5, 3.75, 5.75, 6, 8, and 8.25.

6. OPTION-CLICK on the Text Box Tool to select it (remember this retains the tool as a selection until you purposefully select another tool) and create nine text boxes, placed as shown by the shaded boxes in figure 4.4.

   As you create the boxes, use the snap-to-grid feature to help you align and size the boxes.

   Note: your text boxes will not be shaded. The boxes in figure 4.4 have been shaded to make it easier for you to see their placement.

7. OPTION-CLICK on the Rectangle Picture Box Tool and create four 4-column picture boxes, placing them as shown.

   As you create each box, and while it is still selected, pull down the ITEM menu and select FRAME <mark>(or press ⌘-B)</mark> to <mark>place a .5 pt.</mark> black frame around <mark>each picture box.</mark> Or, you may choose to frame one picture box and then copy and paste three more into place. Your document should resemble figure 4.5

   Select EDIT/PREFERENCES/GENERAL and change guides to BACK so that they won't visually get in your way for the rest of this exercise.

You have now completed the layout for your catalog document. Next, you will learn how to import pictures into the picture boxes. But before you go on to the next steps, be sure to save your document again!

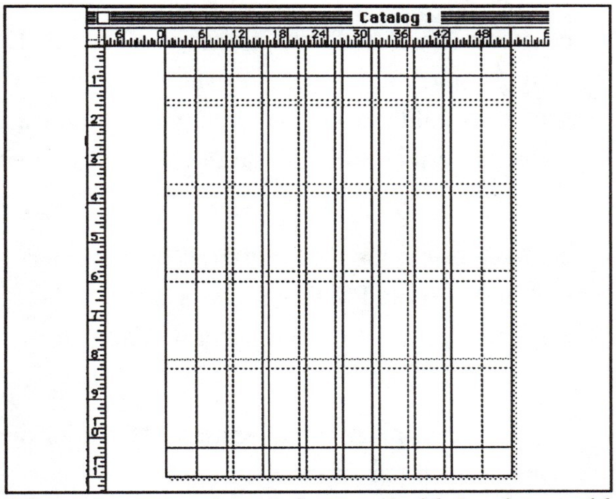

NOTES

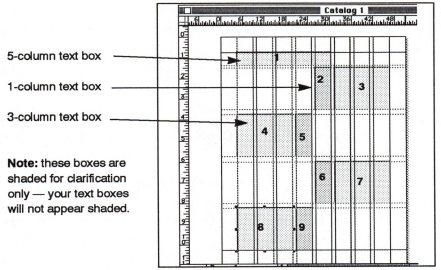

Figure 4.3 *"Catalog 1" document with 8-column grid.*

5-column text box

1-column text box

3-column text box

Note: these boxes are shaded for clarification only — your text boxes will not appear shaded.

Figure 4.4 *After the text boxes have been placed.*

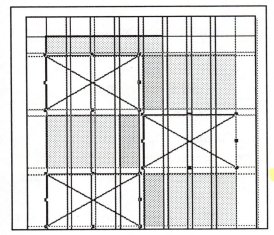

Figure 4.5 *"Catalog 1" after picture boxes have been placed and framed.*

Importing Pictures

The get picture method

Scaling Pictures in Three Ways

Scaling a picture using keyboard commands

⌘ S

The following exercise requires use of MacPaint (bit-mapped) or PICT format clip art. It is not necessary to match the pictures as shown in the example. You may use any clip art available to you, or even create your own artwork, but follow the methods as described to integrate the artwork into your QuarkXPress document(s).

1. With the Content Tool, select the first picture box on the left side of the page. Pull down the FILE menu and select GET PICTURE (⌘-E). The Get Picture dialog box will appear (figure 4.6).

   Insert a disk that contains clip art, or navigate to the folder on your hard disk where the clip art is stored.

   (If you do not have access to other clip art, there are two pictures that come with the QuarkXPress program, named Yesteryear Cyclist.PICT and Bikers.PAINT, that will work for this exercise. They are located in the Sample Pictures folder which may be located in the QuarkXPress folder on your hard drive.)

2. Select the document that contains the picture you wish to import, and click on OPEN. The picture will appear in the picture box.

   If the document you choose contains more than one picture, the picture you want to display might not be centered in the picture box. In this case, move the Content Tool pointer to the center of the picture box and click. Notice that the cursor turns into the hand (scrolling) icon. With the hand you can position the picture in the box by pressing the mouse button and dragging the picture to its desired location.

3. In the example shown in figure 4.7, the image is too large for the picture box and must be scaled down to size. XPress offers several ways to scale pictures: keyboard commands, the Measurements Palette, and the ITEM/MODIFY dialog box. We will use a different method for each picture.

   Scaling with Keyboard Commands: If you have not already done so, select the picture box with the Content Tool. Then simultaneously press ⌘ – OPTION-SHIFT and tap the < key. This action reduces the picture proportionally, in 5% increments. Continue to tap the < key until the picture reaches

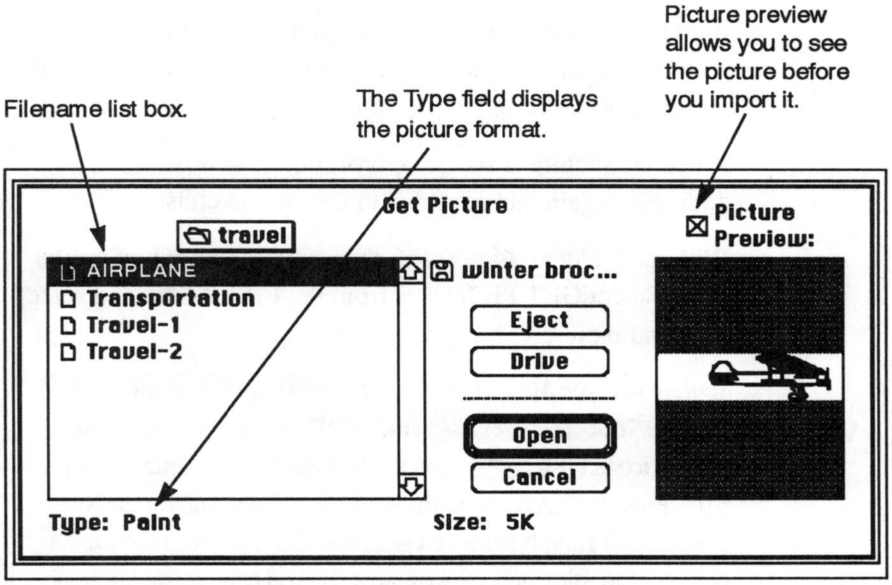

NOTES

Filename list box.

The Type field displays the picture format.

Picture preview allows you to see the picture before you import it.

Get Picture

⛁ travel

[] AIRPLANE
D Transportation
D Travel-1
D Travel-2

⬆ 🖫 winter broc...

Eject
Drive

Open
Cancel

⬇

☒ Picture Preview:

Type: Paint   Size: 5K

Figure 4.6 The Get Picture dialog box.

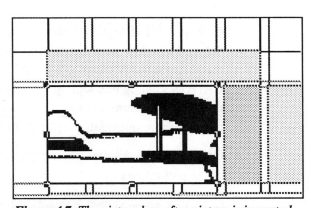

Figure 4.7 The picture box after picture is imported.

SCALING A PICTURE
USING THE
MEASUREMENTS PALETTE

SCALING A PICTURE
USING THE ITEM
MODIFICATION DIALOG
BOX

⌘ S

the appropriate size. In figure 4.8, the picture was reduced to 50% of its original size by using the keyboard command 10 times.

If you wish to enlarge the clip art picture using keyboard commands, tap the > key. The picture will be enlarged in 5% increments.

When the picture is scaled appropriately, save your document again and continue to the next exercise.

4. With the Content Tool, select the second picture box on the page. Select GET PICTURE from the FILE Menu and select a second picture to import.

Scaling with the Measurements Palette: Select the picture with the Content Tool. Then, highlight the 100% next to the horizontal scaling icons (X%:100%) on the Measurement Palette and type: 50%. Press the TAB key to move to the vertical scaling measure (Y%:100%) and type: 50% again, then RETURN to reduce the picture proportionately (see figure 4.9). You can enlarge or reduce pictures disproportionately by entering different percentages in the horizontal and vertical fields.

OR

Using the ITEM/MODIFY dialog box to scale a picture: Select the picture with the Content Tool, pull down the ITEM menu and select MODIFY. The PICTURE BOX SPECIFI-CATIONS dialog box will appear (figure 4.10). Take a moment to examine the various choices offered in this dialog box (for more information refer to the Reference Guide):

Origin Across — shows the starting position of the left side of the picture box

Origin Down — shows the starting position of the top side of the box

Width

Height

Box Angle — controls box rotation

Corner Radius — controls size of the corner radius of rounded corner picture boxes

NOTES

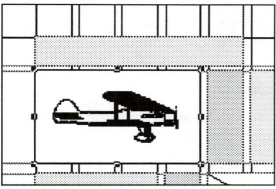

Figure 4.8 *Image reduced to* **50%** *of original size.*

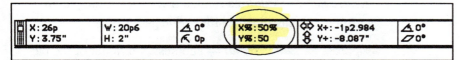

Figure 4.9 *The picture scaling fields on the Measurements Palette.*

The Scale Across and Scale Down fields.

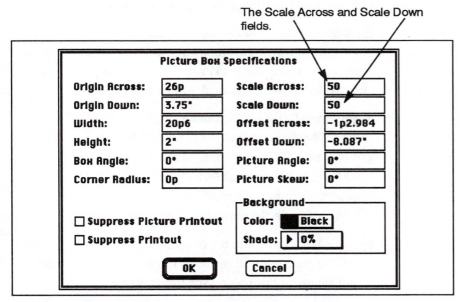

Figure 4.10 *The PICTURE BOX SPECIFICATIONS dialog box.*

Scale Across — scales the picture horizontally, from 10% to 1000% of the original size.

Scale Down — scales the picture vertically from 10% to 1000% of the original size.

Offset Across — controls horizontal position of the picture within the box

Offset Down — controls vertical position of the picture within the box.

Picture Angle — controls the angle of rotation of the picture within the box (can be positive or negative).

Picture Skew — controls slanted distortion of the picture within the box (can be positive or negative).

Suppress Picture Printout — suppresses printout of the picture, but will still print the frame and/or any background color (to speed the printing of page proofs).

Suppress Printout — suppresses printing of the picture and its box (to speed the printing of page proofs).

Background Color and Shade — specifies the background color against which the picture and any text is placed. If you enter 100% white, the background will be opaque. If you enter NONE, the background will be transparent.

a) Press the TAB key six times to move to the SCALE ACROSS field or double-click in the field to highlight it . Enter 50%. TAB once more to move to the SCALE DOWN field and enter 50% again. You may enlarge or reduce pictures disproportionately by entering different percentages in the horizontal and vertical fields.

b) Click OK to return to the document window. The clip art will be reduced to fit the box. You may need to reposition the picture at this point. (See figure 4.11.)

☐ 5. Save your QuarkXPress document. Next you will learn how to copy and paste pictures directly into picture boxes using the Clipboard and Scrapbook methods.

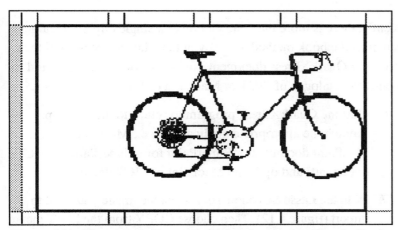

Figure 4.11 *The second picture, after it has been reduced but before it has been repositioned.*

NOTES

PASTING PICTURES USING THE CLIPBOARD / SCRAPBOOK METHOD

CAPTURING THE IMAGE

PASTING IMAGES INTO THE SCRAPBOOK

RETRIEVING PICTURES FROM THE SCRAPBOOK AND PASTING INTO AN XPRESS DOCUMENT

⌘ S

Frequently, there is more than one picture in a single clip art document. The Clipboard/Scrapbook method allows you to isolate an image and then paste it into your QuarkXPress document. You may also use this method to create an on-disk catalogue of PICT or MacPaint (bit-mapped) pictures.

☐ 6. Quit the QuarkXPress program to return to the desktop. Launch the appropriate application (i.e., MacPaint for a MacPaint document or SuperPaint for a SuperPaint or PICT document) and open the MacPaint or PICT document.

☐ 7. With the Lasso Selection Tool select the image you want to import (figure 4.12). Then choose COPY from the EDIT menu.

Note: If you use the rectangular selection tool in MacPaint, the background surrounding your selection will be opaque. If you use the lasso, the background will be transparent.

☐ 8. Select SCRAPBOOK from the ⬤ APPLE menu. The Scrapbook window will be displayed as shown in figure 4.13. Then select PASTE from the EDIT menu. The image will be pasted into the scrapbook (figure 4.14).

An alternative to the Scrapbook method is to open a new document in your application and then paste and save the picture by itself on the new page. Then instead of using the Clipboard method (described next) to import the picture, you would used the GET PICTURE method.

☐ 9. Close the Scrapbook window and repeat steps 7 and 8 for each image you wish to use. If needed, you may open other art documents and continue pasting into the scrapbook.

☐ 10. Quit the art application and return to the desktop when you have finished selecting pictures.

☐ 11. Launch QuarkXPress and open your "Catalog 1" document.

☐ 12. Open the SCRAPBOOK (from the ⬤ APPLE menu) and scroll to the image you wish to use. The scroll bar at the bottom of the Scrapbook is used to "page" through and locate images.

☐ 13. Select COPY from the EDIT menu. Then close the Scrapbook.

☐ 14. Select the third picture block with the Content Tool.

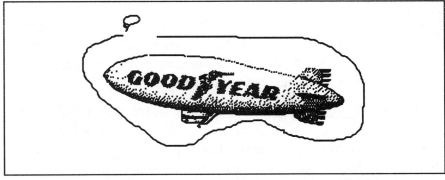

Figure 4.12 *Using the Lasso Tool in a paint, paint-draw, or Tiff-editing program to select a bitmapped picture.*

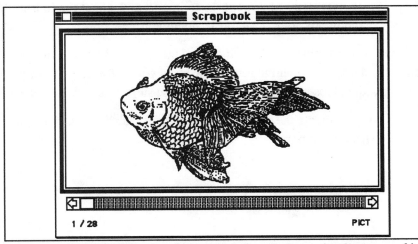

Figure 4.13 *The Scrapbook as it appears before the image has been pasted in. Note: The Scrapbook in your system may not appear exactly like this example.*

Figure 4.14 *The Scrapbook after the image is copied and pasted into it.*

NOTES

AUTOMATIC CENTERING OF
PICTURES WITHIN THEIR
BOXES

15. Select PASTE from the EDIT menu. The picture will appear in the block, and may then be positioned and scaled as desired. See figure 4.15 for an example of the third picture box after the picture has been placed and scaled.

16. To automatically center the picture, type ⌘-Shift-M. If necessary, scale the picture to an appropriate size using either the keyboard commands (⌘-Option-Shift-< or >), the Measurements Palette method, or the Picture Box Specifications dialog box (ITEM/MODIFY).

17. Repeat steps 12 through 16 to import and adjust the fourth picture of your "Catalog 1" document.

Whew! You just absorbed a great deal of information! Save your document and take a moment to review the steps you followed in order to import and adjust those four pictures. Write those steps in the space below.

Next, you will create the catalog "numbering" system and position the numbers in shaded text boxes.

⌘ S

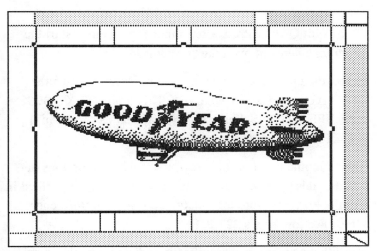

Figure 4.15 The third picture after it is imported into "Catalog 1."

NOTES

CREATING NUMBERED GRAPHIC ELEMENTS

☐ 1. If you quit QuarkXPress after importing pictures, start the program again and open the "Catalog 1" file.

☐ 2. Select the uppermost 1-column text block. Pull down the ITEM menu and select MODIFY. This time a TEXT BOX SPECIFICATIONS dialog box will appear as shown in figure 4.16.

☐ 3. Take a moment to familiarize yourself with the options offered in this specifications dialog box. These are described in brief below. For more information, consult the Reference Guide section, pages 227-228.

As with the picture box specifications dialog box, this specifies origin across, origin down, width, and height. It also offers the following options:

Box Angle — controls the rotation of the text box

Columns — allows you to specify up to 30 columns within each text box

Gutter — creates the space between columns

Text Inset — forces the text to stand away from the edges of the text block, creating a border of white space

Suppress Printout — suppresses printout of the text and frame of the box when printing the document

First Baseline — offset (specifies the placement of the first line of text in relationship to the top of the text box), and Minimum (places the first baseline at Cap Height, Cap+Accent, or Ascent)

Vertical Alignment — aligns text to the top, center, or bottom of the text box, or justifies it within the box

Background Color and Shade — This option applies to the color of the background behind the text and not to the text itself.

VERTICALLY ALIGN THE TEXT AND APPLY A BACKGROUND SHADE

☐ 4. Press on VERTICAL ALIGNMENT to bring up the pop-up menu and select BOTTOM.

☐ 5. Enter 50% in the BACKGROUND SHADE box and then click on OK to return to your document.

⌘ S

NOTES

Text Box Specifications

		First Baseline
Origin Across:	26p	Offset: 0"
Origin Down:	1.5"	Minimum: Ascent
Width:	4p4.5	
Height:	2"	Vertical Alignment
Box Angle:	0°	Type: Top
Columns:	1	Inter ¶ Max: 0"
Gutter:	1p.024	Background
Text Inset:	1 pt	Color: Black
☐ Suppress Printout		Shade: ▶ 0%

OK   Cancel

Figure 4.16 THE TEXT BOX SPECIFICATIONS *dialog box.*

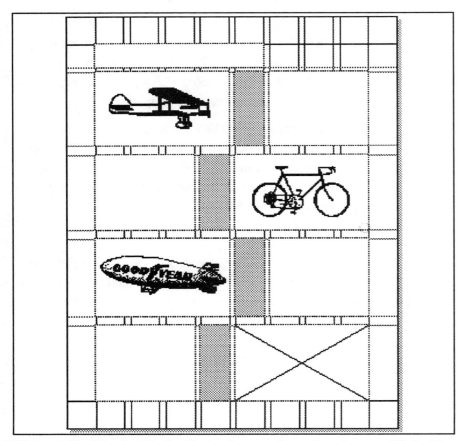

Figure 4.17 "Catalog 1" after the 1-column text boxes have been modified with a 50% background shade and a bottom alignment.

MODIFYING TEXT STYLE

HORIZONTALLY ALIGNING
THE TEXT TO CENTER

6. Repeat steps 2–5 using ITEM/MODIFY to give the three remaining 1–column text boxes a 50% background shading of black and an alignment to bottom (see figure 4.17).

7. Select the top most 1-column text block again with the Content Tool. Type: 1

#6

8. Highlight the typed 1, pull down the STYLE menu and select CHARACTER to bring up the Character Specifications dialog box. Select Palatino font, bold, and enter 56 pts for the font size. Then click white for the color of the text (figure 4.18). Click OK to return to the document window.

9. Select FORMATS from the STYLE menu and choose CENTERED ALIGNMENT. Then Click OK. Or click on the centering icon on the Measurements Palette.

You have now completed the first numbered graphic element.

10. Repeat steps 7–9 for each of the remaining 1-column text boxes, entering the numbers 2, 3, and 4 where appropriate. Figure 4.19 displays the "Catalog 1" document after the numbered graphic elements have been completed.

Tip: An alternate way to finish the remaining three boxes is to highlight the contents of the first box, select COPY from the EDIT menu, and then PASTE in each of the remaining boxes. Then, highlight and replace the number 1 with the appropriate number in each instance.

*OR Comm KEY C
PASTE Comm. V*

Save your document again. You are almost finished! To complete the "Catalog 1" project, you will next enter and format the picture descriptions for the catalog page, create a headline, save and print the document.

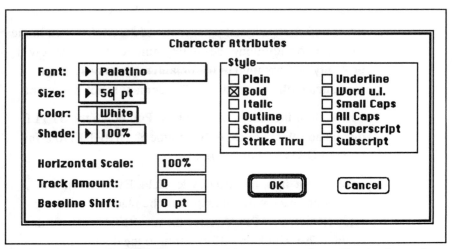

Figure 4.18 CHARACTER *dialog box, with font, size, color, and style changed.*

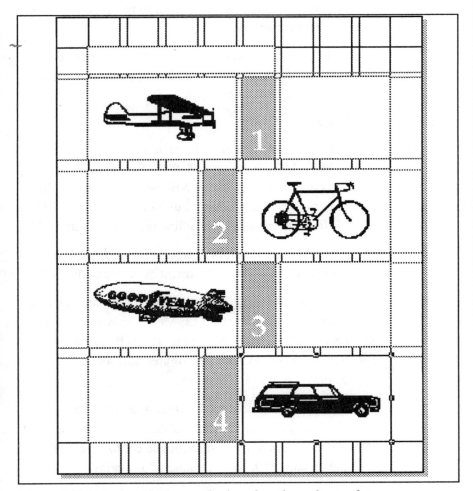

Figure 4.19 *"Catalog 1" after numbering of text boxes is complete.*

ENTERING AND FORMATTING BODY TEXT

CREATING AUTOMATIC SPACE AFTER A PARAGRAPH

CREATING THE HEADLINE

CREATING AN AUTOMATIC RULE AFTER A PARAGRAPH

⌘ S

1. Enter two short original paragraphs of descriptive text in the first text box adjoining the catalog number 1. (The text will probably be formatted in the default settings of 12 point Helvetica with auto leading.) The content is not important.

2. Select all of the text in the text box. Pull down the STYLE menu and select FORMATS (or type ⌘-SHIFT-F) to bring up the FORMATS dialog box.

3. Enter 16 pt into the Space After field. By doing this, a 16 pt. line space will automatically be placed after every return. Click on APPLY to see the results (also shown in figure 4.20). Click on OK to return to the document.

4. Repeat steps 1–3 for each of the remaining text boxes.

5. To enter the headline, place the cursor in the uppermost text box and enter the words:

   Travel by Land and Air. *(If you have used other pictures, you may wish to enter a more appropriate title of the same approximate length.)*

   Press the RETURN key.

6. Highlight the headline text, pull down the STYLE menu and select CHARACTER (or type ⌘-SHIFT-D) to bring up the Character Specifications dialog box. Select Palatino, bold, 24 points, and enter the value: 120% in the HORIZONTAL SCALE field (to expand the headline type). Then click OK.

7. With the text box still selected, select ITEM / MODIFY (⌘M) and select a vertical alignment of bottom. Click OK.

8. To cause a rule to appear below the title, make sure the text is selected, pull down the STYLE Menu again and select RULES (⌘-SHIFT-N). Click in the RULE BELOW field. The dialog box will expand (see figures 4.21 and 4.22) to include other options and features. #7

9. Type: 2 in the width field for 2 points, and enter: 1p (1 pica) in the offset field. Click APPLY to see the results. Click OK to return to the document and compare with the example on page 110. Save"Catalog 1" and print it.

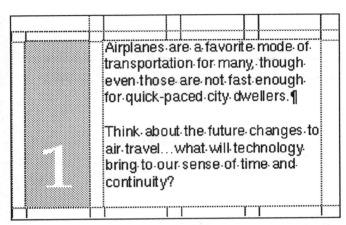

Figure 4.20 *The text box with invisibles showing after 16 pt. Space After Paragraph has been applied.*

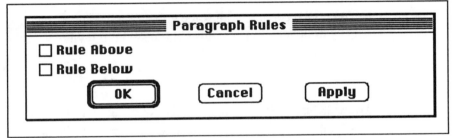

Figure 4.21 *The Paragraph Rules dialog box before an option has been selected.*

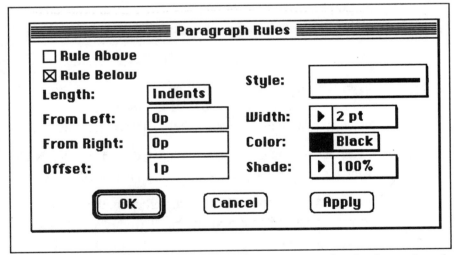

Figure 4.22 *The Paragraph Rules dialog box after Rule Below has been selected. Width and Offset specifications have been changed as instructed in step 9.*

NOTES

THE PICTURE RUNAROUND PROJECT

The next portion of this chapter of the Learning Guide will show you how to create a two-column document, import text from a word processor document, and manipulate picture and text runaround to achieve several different effects. Before beginning this section, you will need to make a few preparations. Please do the following:

✔ Be sure to have a one-page text document on disk for importing. To accomplish this, launch a word processing application, type in a paragraph or two, then copy and paste repeatedly until the page is full. Save as "Text.doc."

Or, if you wish and if it is available to you, you may use the "Sample ASCII" text document located in the Sample Text folder (inside the QuarkXPress folder) on your hard drive.

✔ Also be sure to have a disk with some clip art on it, such as the clip art used in the previous exercise, or create your own pictures using a paint application.

DEFINING A TWO-COLUMN TEXT BOX

1. Launch QuarkXPress and open a NEW document. In the NEW dialog box, enter left and right margins of 1". In the COLUMN box enter 2, and select the AUTOMATIC TEXT BOX option: this will cause the default text box to be a 2-column box instead of a 1-column box in the main text box.

2. Save as "Picture Proj 2."

3. Drag a horizontal guideline down to the 1.5" position.

4. Select the Text Box Tool and draw a text box across the top of the document, snapping to the 1.5" guideline. Enter your name and the title of the document as shown in figure 4.23.

5. Select the Rectangle Picture Box Tool, draw a box that is 3" wide by 2" deep, and center it between the two columns.

USING STEP AND REPEAT TO DUPLICATE AND PLACE OBJECTS

⌘ S

6. With the picture box still selected, pull down the ITEM menu and select STEP AND REPEAT (figure 4.24). Specify 2 steps, with a horizontal offset of 0" and a vertical offset of 2.5". Figure 4.25 displays the Step and Repeat dialog box. Click OK. This action will cause the box to be duplicated two times, 2.5" apart (vertically) and perfectly aligned horizontally, as shown in figure 4.26.

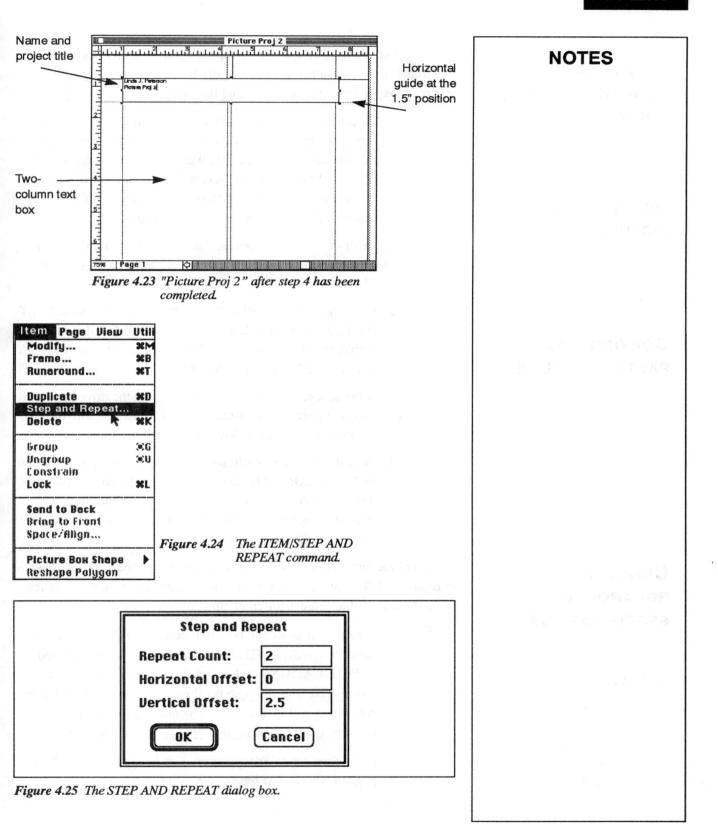

Name and project title

Horizontal guide at the 1.5" position

Two-column text box

Figure 4.23 *"Picture Proj 2" after step 4 has been completed.*

Figure 4.24 *The ITEM/STEP AND REPEAT command.*

Figure 4.25 *The STEP AND REPEAT dialog box.*

NOTES

IMPORTING TEXT WITH THE GET TEXT COMMAND

IMPORTING A PICTURE

COPYING AND PASTING PICTURES

CHANGING RUNAROUND SPECIFICATIONS

RUNAROUND ITEM

⌘ S

Now that you have completed the basic layout for your document, you will import the text you prepared previously for this exercise. Importing text is as easy as importing a picture and the procedure is similar.

☐ 1. Select the Content Tool, click its cursor into the large text box and then select GET TEXT from the FILE menu. Locate the text file you created ("Text.doc") or another appropriate file and click OPEN. The text will automatically flow into the text box, around the picture boxes and into the two columns defined by the text box (see figure 4.26).

Justify the text by choosing SELECT ALL from the EDIT menu and then clicking on the justification icon ▤ on the Measurements Palette.

☐ 2. Click the Content Tool in the top picture box and select GET PICTURE from the FILE menu. (If GET PICTURE is not active, then either the picture box is not selected, or you have not used the Content Tool to select it.)

If the disk containing the clip art is not in the drive, you will need to insert it at this time. Import a clip art picture by selecting it from the dialog box.

☐ 3. With the picture box still selected, pull down the EDIT menu and select COPY. This command copies the clip art picture onto the Clipboard. Now, click the Content Tool in the second picture box and EDIT/PASTE. Repeat this procedure in the third (lowest) picture box.

All of the picture boxes will now be identical in appearance as shown in figure 4.27. The next part of this exercise will show you how to change the text runaround to achieve different effects.

☐ 4. Select the first picture box, pull down the ITEM menu and select RUNAROUND (⌘T). Examine the RUNAROUND SPECIFICATIONS dialog box that appears as shown in figure 4.28. This dialog box allows you to control the mode which text will flow around or within a page element and the distance it will stand off (be *offset*) from the element.

Note: Runaround Specifications can be applied to all XPress page elements: text boxes, lines, and picture boxes.

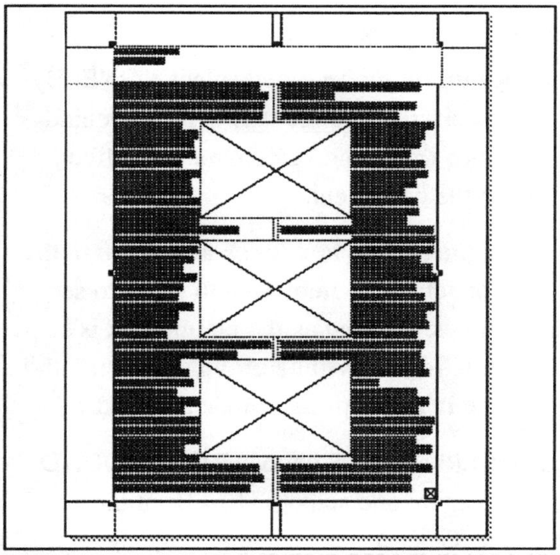

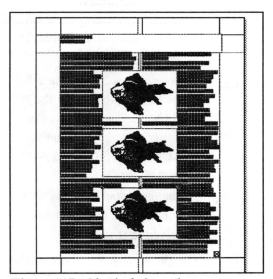

NOTES

Figure 4.26 "Picture Proj 2" after text has been imported.

Figure 4.27 Identical picture boxes.

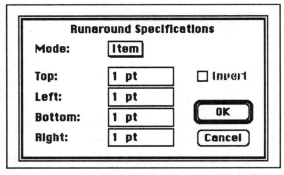

Figure 4.28 The RUNAROUND SPECIFICATIONS dialog box.

VIEWING THE EFFECTS
OF A RUNAROUND

RUNAROUND AUTO IMAGE

RUNAROUND MANUAL
IMAGE

⌘ S

Press on the MODE pop-up menu—which, by default will display ITEM as the current mode— and select NONE. By doing this, you are specifying that the text will run behind the picture box. In other words, no runaround is in effect. Click OK to return to the document.

Important: Deselect the picture box (click anywhere in the document's margin) or select the Item Tool in order to see the effects of the changes. As long as the picture box is selected with the Content Tool, it will be brought forward and will appear to have the item runaround mode selected.

5. With the picture box still selected, choose RUNAROUND from the ITEM menu again and select ITEM from the MODE pop-up menu. Type: 3 pt in each of the Text Outset fields (top, left, bottom, and right) to specify a 3 pt. distance between the text and the picture box frame. Click OK. See figure 4.29 for an example of how the text flow should appear after the runaround has been set.

6. Select the second picture box with the Content Tool. Choose RUNAROUND from the ITEM menu, and select AUTO IMAGE. The text now flows around the graphic image, rather than the picture frame. The TOP field in the RUNAROUND SPECIFICATIONS dialog box change to read "Text Outset." The default text outset is 1 pt. You can change distance if you wish. Then click OK to return to the document. Deselect the picture box to see the results of your selection (figure 4.30).

7. Select the third picture box with Content Tool. Once again, choose RUNAROUND from the ITEM menu, but this time select MANUAL IMAGE from the MODE menu. Again, if you wish, type in a text offset distance. Click OK to return to the document.

Choosing Manual Image creates a dotted-line polygon shape around the contours of the picture. This is called a *runaround polygon* and contains handles which you can position to precisely control the flow of text around the picture. Figure 4.31 shows the text flow after the shape of the runaround polygon has been manipulated.

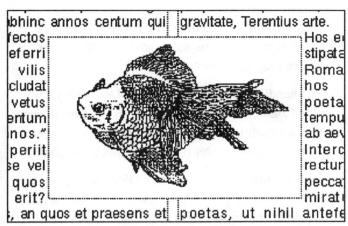

Figure 4.29 Text flow when runaround has been set to ITEM, with a 3 pt. outset.

Figure 4.30 Text flow when runaround has been set to AUTO IMAGE.

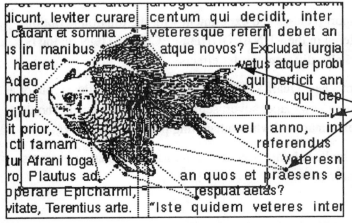

When text runaround is set to Manual Image, a runaround polygon will appear. The handles and segments may be individually moved to change the shape of the runaround.

Figure 4.31 Text flow when runaround has been set to MANUAL IMAGE.

NOTES

ADDING AND DELETING
RUNAROUND HANDLES

a) To move a handle — and therefore the runaround line connected to it — press on the handle with the mouse pointer and drag to a new location.

b) To add a handle, hold down the COMMAND (⌘) key, place the Content or Item Tool cursor over a line segment (not over a handle), and click when the cursor changes to the handle creation pointer (a small rounded-rectangle).

c) To delete a handle, hold down the COMMAND (⌘) key, place the Content or Item Tool cursor over a handle, and click when the cursor changes to the handle deletion pointer (the same small rounded-rectangle icon with an "x" through it).

☐ 8. Adjust the text runaround so that when printed it obviously has a Manual Image Runaround Mode applied to the picture box. Save the document again and print it.

Exercises:

1. Write a letter to a friend and import clip art pictures.

   a) Open a new QuarkXPress document, using a 2-,3-, or 4-column text box.

   b) Create at least three picture boxes with different shapes — experiment!

   c) Import pictures and experiment with the runaround options offered in the RUNAROUND SPECIFICATION dialog box, and also different border effects.

2. Construct a new QuarkXPress document that copies the layout of a magazine or newspaper advertisement. The advertisement should utilize text runaround when integrating pictures and text.

3. Create a multi-column, one-sided flyer for a personal or business advertisement.

ADDITIONAL PRACTICE

1. What is the purpose of a *grid?*

   _____

   _____

2. Describe the steps to *import, scale,* and *position* a picture (you may choose any method you wish).

   _____

   _____

3. What are the three different methods of picture scaling, as shown in this chapter? What are the advantages and disadvantages of each method?

   _____

   _____

4. Why might you choose to use the *Scrapbook method* of storing and importing pictures?

   _____

   _____

5. How do you change the *vertical alignment* of text?

   _____

   _____

6. What does it mean to *scale text horizontally?* In what dialog box(es) is this option offered?

   _____

   _____

7. List the steps to place a *rule above or below* a paragraph of text.

   _____

   _____

8. List the steps to *import word processor text* into an XPress document.

   _____

   _____

9. What does the *Step and Repeat* command allow us to do?

   _____

10. List and describe the effects of the four different *text runaround modes.*

    _____

    _____

Travel by Land and Air

Airplanes are a favorite mode of transportation for many, though even those are not fast enough for quick-paced city dwellers.

Think about the future changes to air travel…what will technology bring to our sense of time and continuity?

In many European communities, the bicycle is the main mode of travel, especially in the Netherlands where the terrain is level.

Bicycles are not only a cheap form of transportation, but also a source of much-needed exercise.

Ah, the Good Year Blimp! A symbol of times past, of parades and football games!

What were the inventors thinking when they designed this giant fish-shaped balloon? Were they thinking that this new technology would carry us into the future?

The large family station wagon, now a remnant from the gas-guzzling 60's has given way to smaller, more efficient vehicles.

Will we see a return to larger cars (with more efficient engines) or do you think that the trend toward smaller will continue indefinitely?

Si meliora dies, ut vina, poemata reddit, scire velim, chartis pretium quotus arroget annus. scriptor abhinc annos centum qui decidit, inter perfectos veteresque referri debet an inter vilis atque novos? Excludat iurgia finis, "Est vetus atque probus, centum qui perficit annos." Quid, qui deperiit minor uno mense vel anno, inter quos referendus erit? Veteresne poetas, an quos et praesens et postera respuat aetas?

"Iste quidem veteres inter ponetur honeste, qui vel mense brevi vel toto est iunior anno." Utor permisso, caudaeque pilos ut equinae paulatim vello unum, demo etiam unum, dum cadat elusus ratione ruentis acervi, qui redit in fastos et virtutem aestimat annis miraturque nihil nisi quod Libitina sacravit.

Ennius et sapines et fortis et alter Homerus, ut critici dicunt, leviter curare videtur, quo promissa cadant et somnia Pythagorea. Naevius in manibus non est et mentibus haeret paene recens? Adeo sanctum est vetus omne poema. ambigitur quotiens, uter utro sit prior, aufert Pacuvius docti famam senis Accius alti, dicitur Afrani toga convenisse Menandro, Plautus ad exemplar Siculi properare Epicharmi, vincere Caecilius gravitate, Terentius arte. Hos ediscit et hos arto stipata theatro spectat Roma potens; habet hos numeratque poetas ad nostrum tempus Livi scriptoris ab aevo.

Interdum volgus rectum videt, est ubi peccat. Si veteres ita miratur laudatque poetas, ut nihil anteferat, nihil illis comparet, errat. Si quaedam nimis antique, si peraque dure dicere credit eos, ignave multa fatetur, et sapit et mecum facit et Iova iudicat aequo.

Non equidem insector delendave carmina Livi esse reor, memini quae plagosum mihi parvo Orbilium dictare; sed emendata videri pulchraque et exactis minimum distantia miror. Inter quae verbum emicuit si forte decorum, et si versus paulo concinnior unus et alter, iniuste totum ducit venditque poema.

Si meliora dies, ut vina, poemata reddit, scire velim, chartis pretium quotus arroget annus. scriptor abhinc annos centum qui decidit, inter perfectos veteresque referri debet an inter vilis atque novos? Excludat iurgia finis, "Est vetus atque probus, centum qui perficit annos." Quid, qui deperiit minor uno mense vel anno, inter quos referendus erit? Veteresne poetas, an quos et praesens et postera respuat aetas?

"Iste quidem veteres inter ponetur

Chapter Five

Creating a Brochure

CHAPTER OBJECTIVES

CREATING A BROCHURE

Now that you have learned the basics about integrating text and graphics, you are ready to move on to a more complex project: a two-sided, two-fold brochure. In completing this project, you will learn to:

- ✔ Work with different page sizes and orientations.
- ✔ Use a master page.
- ✔ Insert and delete pages.
- ✔ Modify tool preferences.
- ✔ Use more precise typographical controls, including leading, drop caps, kerning and tracking, raised caps, horizontal and vertical justification, and left indents.
- ✔ Use the Measurements Palette more extensively.
- ✔ Use tabs and rules to create a table.
- ✔ Group and rotate page elements.
- ✔ Shade bitmapped pictures.
- ✔ Use shaded polygons as graphic elements.

Assume that you have been asked to create a one-color, two-fold brochure for the Association of Story Tellers. The purpose of the brochure is to announce a special exhibit at the local art center. In addition to the art display, the Association will be sponsoring performances by renowned story tellers.

Although you will be *proofing* the brochure by printing it on your laser printer, you plan to output final camera-ready copy on an *imagesetter* at a local service bureau. It will then be printed, cut and folded. Though the final page size is 8 1/2" by 11", you will need to create a larger electronic page in QuarkXPress and then place crop and fold lines on it for use by the printer.

1. Launch QuarkXPress and select FILE/NEW, entering the following specifications in the NEW dialog box (also shown in figure 5.1):

   Page Size: 12" wide by 9.5" tall. (This will place the paper in a horizontal, not vertical, orientation.)

   Margin guides: Top .5"; Bottom .5"; Left .75"; Right .75". (The margins on both sides of the document will be identical, so do not select the Facing Pages option.)

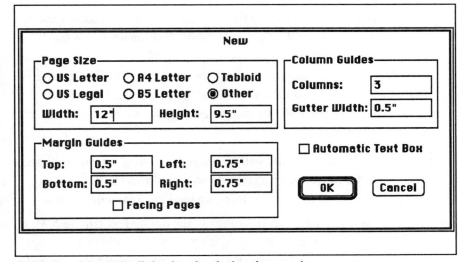

Figure 5.1 *The NEW dialog box for the brochure project.*

**TURNING OFF THE
AUTOMATIC PAGE
INSERTION FEATURE**

**VIEWING THE
DOCUMENT**

**INSERTING A
SECOND PAGE**

**USING MASTER
PAGES**

⌘ S

Automatic Text Box: No—make sure this option is deselected.

Columns: 3, with a gutter width of .5".

2. Click OK. Your new document will appear on screen.

3. Turn off the automatic page insertion feature by pulling down the EDIT menu, selecting PREFERENCES/ GENERAL and selecting OFF from the Auto Page Insertion pop-up menu. Click OK to return to the document.

4. SAVE AS "Phantasy Brochure."

5. To view the entire page as shown in figure 5.2, pull down the VIEW menu and select FIT IN WINDOW, or type ⌘0.

Another way to move from full size to Fit in Window view is to hold down the Option key and click anywhere on the document page. Option-clicking functions as a toggle *on an XPress document to move between Fit in Window and Actual Size views. To return to Actual Size view, hold down the Option key and click the mouse pointer on the document page again.*

6. Since the brochure will be printed on two sides, you will need to insert another page. To do so, pull down the Page menu, and select INSERT to bring up the Page Insert dialog box.

Examine the default settings in the dialog box (figure 5.3). If you accept these settings, one page will be added after page 1, based on master page A. (Master pages will be explained a little later.)

7. Click OK to accept the default page insertion settings. One page will automatically be inserted after page 1.

You will now need to place the guides and the cut and fold lines to be used when setting up the brochure. Rather than repeating the procedure of placing guides and lines on both pages, you will place these elements on the document's master page.

A *master page* is an underlying page that is a basis for document formatting. Any elements (boxes, lines, headers, footers, page numbering, etc.) placed on a master page will appear on all pages of the document to which that master page has been applied. Master page A is created from the specifications you entered in the NEW dialog box. QuarkXPress is capable of handling 127 master pages per document!

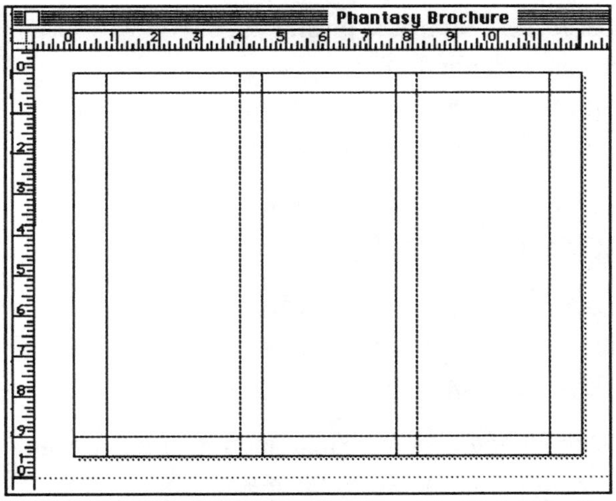

Figure 5.2 The "Phantasy Brochure' in Fit in Window view.

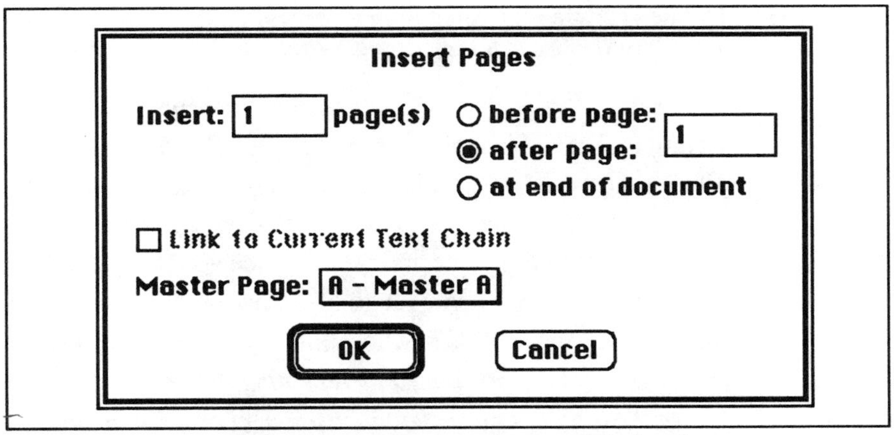

Figure 5.3 The INSERT PAGES dialog box showing default values.

NOTES

8. To view Master Page A, pull down the PAGE menu, select the DISPLAY submenu and then select Master Page A. If necessary, select FIT IN WINDOW view from the VIEW menu to examine the characteristics of a master page (figure 5.4):

   a) In the upper left corner of the master page, you will see the broken link symbol, indicating that the auto page insertion has been turned off. If the link is not broken, it indicates that the page insertion feature is active.

   b) In the lower left corner of your document window, the page number indicator will read "Master A."

   c) In other respects, the page will be identical to page 1 of your document—the 3-column and margin guides will be in place as specified in the New dialog box.

The next few steps will show you how to change the ruler origin point, place master guides, cut lines, and fold marks on the master page.

CHANGING THE RULER ORIGIN POINT

You will change the ruler origin point to display the final 8 1/2" by 11" printed page size. The electronic page you specified is 12" by 9 1/2". The top and bottom margin guides (placed at .5" from the edges) actually indicate the final page size. The left and right page margins were set at .75" in order that the 3-column guides, with .5" gutters would divide the *final* page size into three equal-sized columns.

1. Before changing the ruler, drag a vertical guide to the .5" and 11.5" positions, and horizontal guides to the .75" and 8.75" positions to define the document's print area (figure 5.5).

2. Return to Actual Size view. Change the ruler's origin point by placing the mouse pointer in the ruler origin box in the upper left corner of the window, press and drag to the intersection of the top margin (.5") guide and the .5" guide you just placed (see figure 5.6). When you let go of the mouse, the 0-point of the ruler will move to its new location. *If you make a mistake, the ruler may be repositioned by repeating this procedure. To return the 0-point to its original position, click once in the ruler origin point box.*

Next, you will place crop marks on the master page to show the actual size of the finished product. Normally, the default line size (thickness) for a new line is 1 pt. You want the crop lines to be of hairline width (.25pt), and would like XPress to automatically create lines of that thickness.

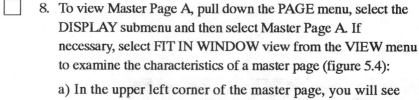

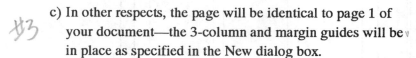

The link symbol indicates whether auto page insertion is on or off.

The page indicator field displays "Master A."

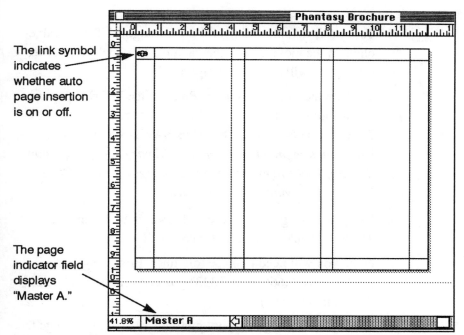

Figure 5.4 Screen display of Master Page A.

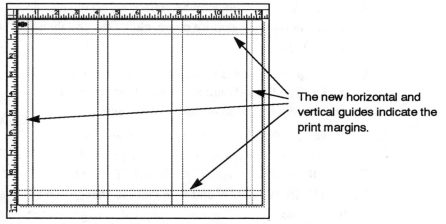

The new horizontal and vertical guides indicate the print margins.

Figure 5.5 Vertical guides placed to indicate print margins.

The new zero-point

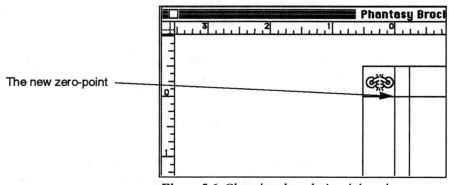

Figure 5.6 Changing the ruler's origin point.

NOTES

MODIFYING TOOL PREFERENCES

PLACING CROP / FOLD MARKS

⌘ S

3. To modify default settings for the Orthogonal Tool, double-click on the tool icon (on the palette). The Tool Preferences dialog box will appear (see figure 5.7).

   Click on the MODIFY button. Press on the WIDTH pop-up menu and select HAIRLINE. Click OK to return to the Preferences dialog box. Then click SAVE to keep the changes. *Note: Though preference options will vary depending upon the tool, Tool Preferences may be changed for all XPress Tools by following these procedures.*

4. Using the page guides, draw crop lines as indicated in figure 5.8. The lines should not meet at the corner..

5. Next, you will need to place fold lines. First, drag vertical guides to the 3.666" and 7.333" positions (in the middle of the column gutters).

6. Modify the Orthogonal Tool preferences again to change the line to a dashed style:

   Double-click on tool, click on MODIFY, select the dashed style from the style pop-up menu, click OK, and then click SAVE.

7. Using the guides, draw the fold lines as indicated in figure 5.8 (The lines should be drawn short of the page border to avoid inclusion on the final document).

8. You have now finished creating the brochure master page. To return to the document and view the changes, pull down the PAGE/ DISPLAY and select DOCUMENT. Select VIEW/FIT IN WINDOW and note that the changes you made to Master Page A have been applied to page one (new guides, crop and fold lines are in place).

   To view the document as it will print, select HIDE GUIDES from the VIEW menu.

9. Pull down the PAGE menu, select GO TO, and enter page number 2. Click OK. View the changes to page 2. Following the same procedure, return to page 1.

   If you were to add more pages to this document, using Master Page A as a base, the new pages would also contain the crop and fold marks. The elements applied to document pages from master pages are referred to as *Master Elements*.

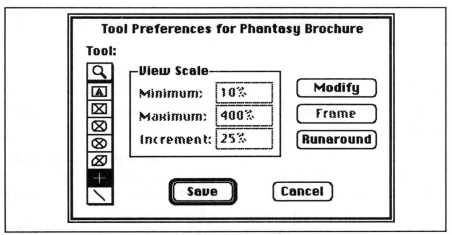

Figure 5.7 *The Tool Preferences dialog box with Orthogonal Line tool selected.*

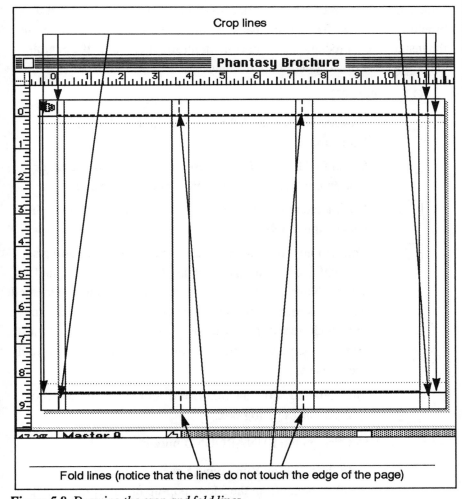

Figure 5.8 *Drawing the crop and fold lines.*

I-51
Occupational Coun.
I-50-CElebration 1pm
10/5/95

PLACING ELEMENTS ON THE DOCUMENT PAGES

⌘ S

You are now ready to begin placing text and pictures on your brochure document pages. Be sure to save your document before you begin.

Let's review the document structure you have created so far: the brochure has two pages, each representing one side of the brochure; each page has been divided into three equal panels; and the crop and fold marks have been placed.

To better visualize how you will place elements on the brochure panels, take a blank 8 1/2" by 11" piece of paper and fold it into thirds. Then unfold it, turn it so that it is wider than it is tall (*landscape orientation*), and look at how the panels are arranged. The first page of your XPress document represents the outside of the brochure. The right panel will be the cover, the middle panel will be used as a mailer (addressee, return address, stamp, and other pertinent postal information), and the left panel will be folded under the cover panel. It will also be the first panel seen when the brochure is opened. The second page of your XPress document represents the inside of the brochure and will contain information about the exhibit and a schedule of story-telling performances.

O.K., let's begin…

1. If necessary, launch XPress and open the "Phantasy Brochure" document.

2. Select FIT IN WINDOW view from the VIEW menu (or Option-click on the document) to see all of page 1.

3. Draw a rectangle picture box in the upper half of the right panel (figure 5.9).

4. You will now draw several text boxes, but before doing so, you will need to modify the default Text Box Runaround setting. Normally, the Runaround default for a newly created text box is set to Item. Since several of the text boxes used in this brochure will be placed over a graphic image, and must therefore be transparent, you will modify the Text Box Tool Preferences.

    a) Double-click on the Text Box Tool to bring up the Tool Preferences dialog box.

    b) Click on the RUNAROUND button.

    c) In the resulting Runaround Specifications dialog box, select None from the Mode pop-up menu (figure 5.10).

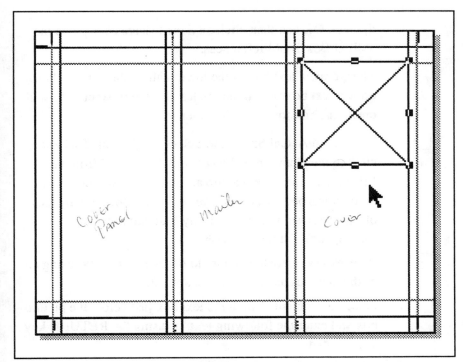

Figure 5.9 *The page after a picture box has been drawn in the right panel.*

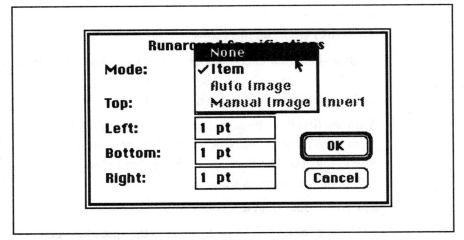

Figure 5.10 *The Runaround Specifications dialog box, accessed from the Tool Preferences dialog box.*

IMPORTING A PICTURE

ENTERING AND FORMATTING TEXT

DROP CAPS

LEADING

APPLYING A LEFT INDENT

d) Click OK and then click on Save to save changes to the Text Box Tool Preferences.

Then, draw a text box in the lower half of the panel. Also, draw a text box within the guides of the left panel. (We will create the box for the mailer later.)

5. Go back to Actual Size view. Select the Content Tool and click in the picture box. Select GET PICTURE from the FILE menu and import a clip art picture of your choice. A unicorn has been used in the example, but for the purposes of this exercise, you may use any MacPaint format (bitmapped) picture you wish.

6. If necessary, scale the picture to fit the picture box, using any of the methods as outlined in chapter 3.

7. Place the Content Tool in the text box just below the picture box and enter the following text, pressing the RETURN key as indicated:

```
Adventures <RETURN>
In <RETURN>
Phantasy <RETURN>
<RETURN><RETURN>
A Celebration of <RETURN>
Phantasy <RETURN>
& <RETURN>
Mythology <RETURN>
In Storytelling and the Arts
```

8. Highlight the first three lines and select CHARACTER from the STYLE menu. Change the font to Times, 36 pt., Italic and click OK to return to the document.

9. With the first three lines still selected, choose FORMATS from the STYLE menu. Click in the DROP CAPS option box to select it. The Formats dialog box will change to reflect this selection as shown in figure 5.11.

a) Change line count to 2.

b) Change leading to 18 pt. *Leading* is the space between lines of text, and is measured from the baseline of one line of text to the baseline of the line above it.

c) Click OK to return to document and see the changes.

NOTES

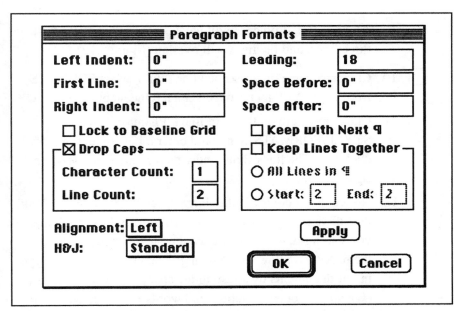

Figure 5.11 The FORMATS dialog box after Drop Caps has been selected.

Figure 5.12 The first three lines after completing step 9(c).

KERNING / TRACKING

USING THE MEASUREMENTS PALETTE TO CHANGE TEXT FORMATTING

⌘S

At this point, drop caps will have been applied to the first three lines, and the lines will overlap (figure 5.12).

10. Click anywhere on the second line ("In"), select FORMATS from the STYLE menu and enter a left indent of .5". Click OK.

11. Click anywhere on the third line ("Phantasy"), select STYLE/FORMATS again, and enter a Left Indent of .75". click OK. The lines should now be formatted as shown in figure 5.13.

12. Notice that there is a rather large space between the "A" and the "d" in the word Adventures. To remedy this problem, you will tighten the space between the letters by kerning them. XPress allows us to gain greater control over the type in our documents by adusting the space between letter pairs (*kerning*) or between letters and words in a selected group of more than two characters (*tracking*).

    To apply a kerning value:

    a) Click between the letters "A" and "d" to place the insertion point. Pull down the STYLE menu, select KERN, and enter a value of – 15 into the resulting dialog box as shown in figure 5.14,

    OR

    b) Select the value next to the tracking/kerning icon on the Measurements Palette and enter a value of -15 (see figure 5.15).

    The two letters will move closer together. You may desire to adjust these even further (closer or apart) and should feel free to adjust letter spacing to your taste.

    The title is now complete. Next you will format the subtitle.

13. Highlight the remaining lines. Using the Measurements Palette, change the type to 14 pt. Helvetica, with a leading value of 33 pt. by completing the following steps:

    a) If the typeface is currently Helvetica, go on to step b. If it is another typeface do the following: Press the mouse pointer on the typeface pop-up menu (the small triangle to the left of the current typeface name) and select Helvetica.

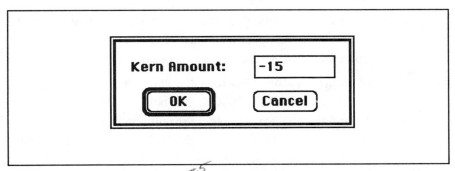

NOTES

Figure 5.13 *The first three lines after adjusting Left Indent settings.*

Figure 5.14 *The Kern dialog box. Kerning is used to adjust the space between two adjacent characters.*

Figure 5.15 Changing the kerning value on the Measurements Palette from 0 to -15. To change the kerning value in increments of 10, click on the left or right arrow to the left of the value field.

DRAWING A SHADED POLYGON

SENDING ONE ELEMENT BEHIND ANOTHER

⌘ S

b) Press the top (up) arrow on the leading icon until it displays a value of 33 pt.

c) Press the mouse pointer on the typesize pop-up menu (the small triangle to the left of the current type size) and select 14.

d) Click on the Right Align icon (▤).

The front panel is now complete except for the shaded polygon, which you will create next.

14. Select the Polygon Tool and create a polygon as shown in figure 5.16. For the purposes of this exercise, don't worry if the polygon is not the *exact* dimensions as the example — it only needs to be approximate.

15. With the Item Tool, double click on the polygon to bring up the Picture Box Specifications dialog box and select the color Black with a shading value of 30%. Click OK.

16. With the polygon still selected, pull down the ITEM menu and select SEND TO BACK. The polygon will be sent behind the text box. Deselect the polygon by clicking on the margin area of the document. Since the text box Runaround Mode has been modified to None, the text box will be transparent and you will be able to see the text run across the shaded polygon (figure 5.17).

You have now completed the front panel of the brochure. Before going on the complete the left panel, review the previous steps and make note of the different XPress features you used in order to complete the first panel.

Save the brochure again. You may either quit XPress at this point, or go on to create the next panel.

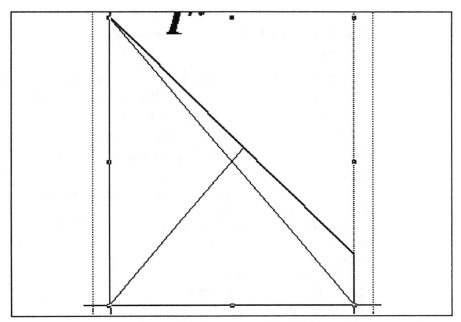

Figure 5.16 Create a polygon similar to this one in the lower portion of the panel.

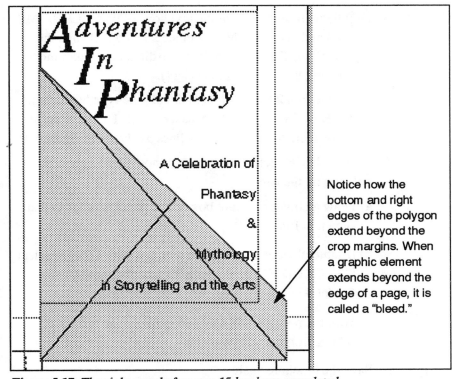

Notice how the bottom and right edges of the polygon extend beyond the crop margins. When a graphic element extends beyond the edge of a page, it is called a "bleed."

Figure 5.17 The right panel after step 15 has been completed.

NOTES

CREATING THE SECOND PANEL

1. If necessary, launch XPress and open the Phantasy Brochure document.

2. Place the Content Tool in the text box on the left panel and enter the following text. Press RETURN at the end of each line and between paragraphs as shown, and do not worry about formatting at this point. Figure 5.18 shows you what the panel should look like when you complete this step.

   ```
   <RETURN>
   Don't Miss <RETURN> Adventures in Phantasy!
   Presented by <RETURN>
   The Association of Story Tellers <RETURN>
   on exhibit at <RETURN>
   <RETURN>
   The Mercury Art Center <RETURN>
   1525 Main Drive <RETURN>
   Mercury, CA 92345 <RETURN>
   (123) 445-7890 <RETURN>
   Free Admission! <RETURN>
   Open 9 am to 5 pm <RETURN>
   Monday — Saturday
   ```

3. Highlight all of the text in the text box (EDIT/SELECT ALL or ⌘A) and, using the Measurements Palette, change the type to 18 pt. Times with a 36 pt. leading, and center the text by clicking the centering icon (▤).

4. Select the first 2 lines of text and, bold the type by clicking on the Bold (**B**) icon on the Measurements Palette. Repeat this procedure to bold the other lines as shown in figure 5.19.

5. To complete the left panel, you will now place a shaded polygon on the panel:

   a) Draw a polygon picture box on the panel, similar to that shown in figure 5.20.

   b) Double-click on the polygon with the Item Tool (or select ITEM/MODIFY) and enter a 30% background shading. Click OK.

   c) With the polygon still selected, pull choose SEND TO BACK from the ITEM menu.

6. Save the brochure again.

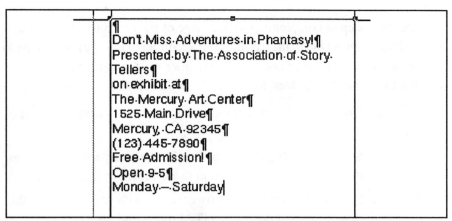

Figure 5.18 *The left panel after the unformatted text has been entered (invisibles are displayed).*

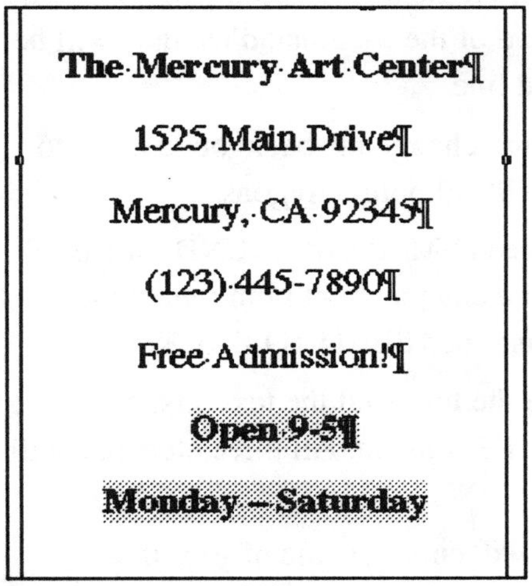

The·Mercury·Art·Center¶

1525·Main·Drive¶

Mercury,·CA·92345¶

(123)·445-7890¶

Free·Admission!¶

Open·9-5¶

Monday — Saturday

Figure 5.19 *Bolding the text.*

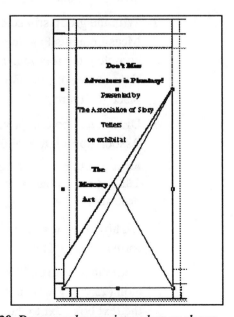

Figure 5.20 *Draw a polygon picture box as shown.*

CREATING THE THIRD PANEL

USING POLYGONS TO MAKE A LOGO

GROUPING AND ROTATING ELEMENTS

CHANGING RUNAROUND OUTSETS

⌘S

The next step to completing the first page of the brochure is to create the middle panel — the mailer. In order to accomplish this, you will need to create and place the logo, draw a text box, enter and format the return address information, and then rotate and place the boxes.

☐ 1. Draw a small text box (approx. .75" x .75") with a hairline frame.

☐ 2. Select the Polygon Picture Box Tool and draw two polygons inside the text box similar to those shown in figure 5.21.

☐ 3. Holding the SHIFT key down, select both polygons with the Item Tool, pull down the ITEM menu and select GROUP (⌘G). See figure 5.22. You will notice that when you now select either polygon with the Item Tool, both polygons will be highlighted and, instead of the usual handles, they will be surrounded with a dashed line.

☐ 4. Select ITEM/MODIFY and change the backgound color to enter 100% black. This will fill both polygons.

☐ 5. Select the text box, choose ITEM/RUNAROUND, SELECT Item Runaround Mode, and enter a Right Item runaround value of 3 pt. Click OK and then SEND TO BACK.

☐ 6. Shift-click to select both the logo and the text box, and select GROUP from the ITEM menu. All three elements will now be grouped as one.

☐ 7. With the group still selected, enter a value of -90° in the Measurements Palette rotation field (△0°). Press Enter to complete the rotation. Then place the group in the upper right corner of the middle panel, using the guides to help place it (figure 5.23).

☐ 8. Draw a text box, approximately 1" tall by 2" wide. Enter the Association's return address:

```
Association of Story Tellers
1855 San Thomas Way
Mercury, CA
```

☐ 9. Highlight the text and, using the Measurements Palette, format as 9 pt. Helvetica with 20 pt. leading.

☐ 10. With the text box still selected enter -90° next to the rotation icon (△0°). Press enter to complete the rotation, and place the text box next to the logo box (see figure 5.24).

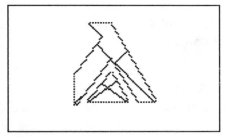

Figure 5.21 *Two polygons*

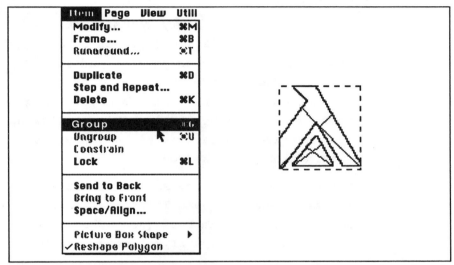

Figure 5.22 *The ITEM/GROUP command and the resulting group when selected with the Item tool.*

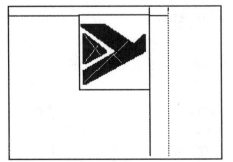

Figure 5.23 *The "logo" after it has been shaded, grouped, rotated, and placed.*

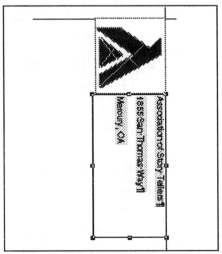

Figure 5.24 *The "logo" and rotated text box.*

CREATING THE FOURTH PANEL

You have now completed the middle panel of the first page and are ready to start on the second page. Before continuing, be sure to save the brochure again.

The second page represents the inside of the brochure. It will contain more information about the Adventures in Phantasy Exhibit and a schedule of story telling performances. You will begin with the left panel:

☐ 1. Scroll to page 2. Draw a text box within the guides of the left panel, and enter the following:

```
The Association of Story Tellers invites
you to view a special collection of
mythology, phantasy adventure, and legend
as portrayed through the ages in story
telling and the arts. Daily story telling
performances enliven the exhibits, allowing
you to travel to faraway places only your
imagination can take you. <RETURN>

Featured story telling artists include
Tamorra Brunwick, Sean Tinwell, Tiffany
Sowell, and William Earl (see schedule of
performances for specific times). <RETURN>

Don't miss this exciting collection of art
on exhibit at the Mercury Art Center. Bring
the whole family and enjoy a journey into
magic lands where anything can and does
happen!
```

☐ 2. Select all of the text (⌘A) and format as 12 pt. Times, with 14 pt. leading.

☐ 3. Select FORMATS from the STYLE menu and enter a Space After of .125". This action will add .125" — in addition to the leading — after each paragraph return. Figure 5.25 displays the panel as it should appear at this point.

RAISED CAPS

⌘S

☐ 4. Select the first character of each paragraph and change the type size to 20 pts. Because you previously set the leading to an absolute value of 14 pts., the space between lines will remain constant even though the first character is larger. If you did not specify an absolute leading value, leaving it on the default setting of Auto, there will be more space between

The association of storytellers invites you to view a special collection of mythology, phantasy adventure, and legend as portrayed through the ages in story telling and the arts. Daily story telling performances enliven the exhibits, allowing you to travel to faraway places only your imagination can take you.

Featured storytelling artists include Tamorra Brunwick and Sean Tinwell, Tiffany Sowell, and William Earl (see schedule of performances for specific times).

Don't miss this exciting collection of art on exhibit at the Mercury Art Center. Bring the whole family and enjoy a journey into magic lands where anything can and does happen!

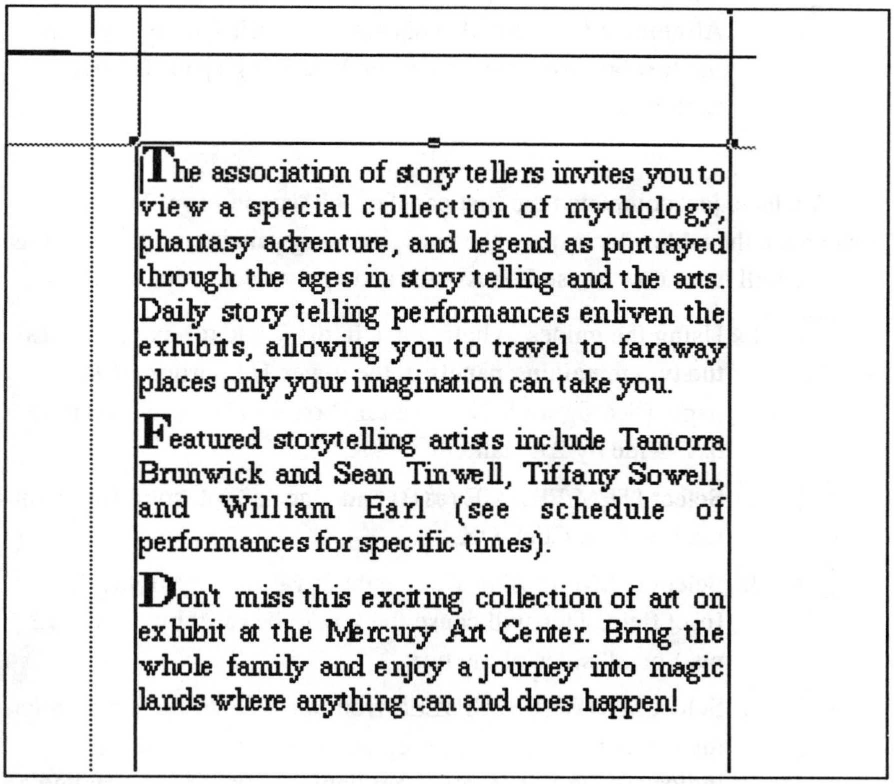

Figure 5.25   The inside left panel after it has been formatted (through step 4).

the first and second lines than between subsequent lines. See figure 5.26 to view the completed panel.

☐ 5. Lastly, select ITEM/MODIFY and change the Vertical Alignment to Justified. This action justifies all text within the text box from top to bottom by adding space between each line.

CREATING A TABLE

You have just completed the first panel of the second page. You will now create the table which spans the two remaining panels, and through this exercise will learn how to use XPress tabs and apply rules to lines of text.

☐ 1. Using the guides to help place it, draw a text box that spans the two remaining panels in the lower 1/3 portion of the page. (See figure 5.27.) The text box will be approximately 6.8" wide by 2.8" tall.

USING TEXT BOX INSET VALUES

☐ 2. Select ITEM/FRAME (⌘B) and place a 2 pt. solid frame on the text box. Click OK.

☐ 3. Select ITEM/MODIFY and enter a value of 1p in the Text Inset field. This will cause the text to be inset by 1 pica (12 pts.) on all sides of the box.

☐ 4. Select SHOW INVISIBLES from the VIEW menu and enter the following text, typing returns and tabs only where indicated. Do not worry about how it looks or is formatted at this point (see figure 5.28):

```
Schedule of Performances <RETURN>
<RETURN>
Performers <RETURN>
<TAB> Tamorra Brunwick <TAB> Sean Tinwell
   <TAB> Tiffany Sowell <TAB> William Earl
   <RETURN>
Monday <TAB> 10:30 am <TAB> 1:00 pm <TAB>
   1:45 pm <TAB> 4:00 pm <RETURN>
Tuesday <TAB> 4:00 pm <TAB> 2:45 pm <TAB>
   1:00 pm <TAB> 10:30 am <RETURN>
Wednesday <TAB> 10:30 am <TAB> 1:00 pm <TAB>
   1:45 pm <TAB> 4:00 pm <RETURN>
Thursday <TAB> 4:00 pm <TAB> 2:45 pm <TAB>
   1:00 pm <TAB> 10:30 am <RETURN>
Friday <TAB> 10:30 am <tab> 1:00 pm <TAB>
   1:45 pm <TAB> 4:00 pm <RETURN>
Saturday <TAB> 10:00 am <TAB> 11:00 am <TAB>
   1:00 pm <TAB> 3:00 pm
```

⌘S

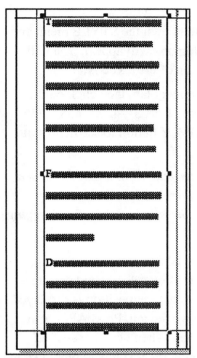

Figure 5.26 *The completed panel with vertical justification applied to the text box.*

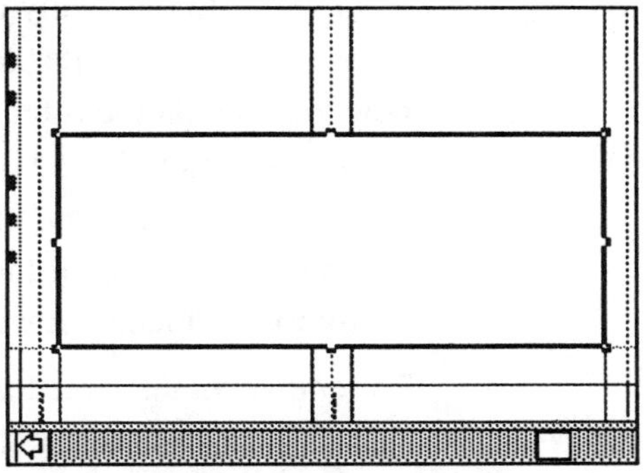

Figure 5.27 *The two-column text box with frame applied.*

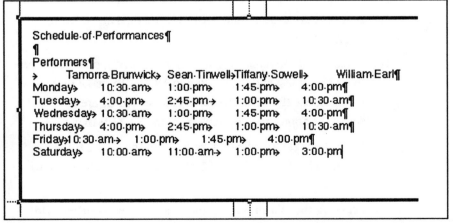

Schedule·of·Performances¶
¶
Performers¶
→ Tamorra·Brunwick→ Sean·Tinwell→Tiffany·Sowell→ William·Earl¶
Monday→ 10:30·am→ 1:00·pm→ 1:45·pm→ 4:00·pm¶
Tuesday→ 4:00·pm→ 2:45·pm→ 1:00·pm→ 10:30·am¶
Wednesday→ 10:30·am→ 1:00·pm→ 1:45·pm→ 4:00·pm¶
Thursday→ 4:00·pm→ 2:45·pm→ 1:00·pm→ 10:30·am¶
Friday→10:30·am→ 1:00·pm→ 1:45·pm→ 4:00·pm¶
Saturday→ 10:00·am→ 11:00·am→ 1:00·pm→ 3:00·pm

Figure 5.28 *Schedule of Performances text before it has been formatted and with Invisibles displayed.*

PLACING TABS

MOVING, REMOVING, AND CLEARING TABS

5. Select all of the text (⌘A), pull down the STYLE menu and select TABS... The Tabs dialog box will appear. You will also see a ruler appear at the top of the text box.

6. Click to select the Center alignment tab, then click on the ruler to position tabs as follows: 1.5", 3", 4.45", and 5.75" (see figure 5.29). Press the APPLY button to see the results of the tab positioning (figure 5.30).

   If the Tabs dialog box obstructs your view, it may be moved just as you would move any other Macintosh window by pressing the mouse pointer in the title bar area and dragging to a new location.

7. If you wish to move any of the tabs to adjust positioning, press the mouse pointer on the tab to select it and drag to a new location on the ruler. Note that the position is displayed in the Position field as you move the tab. Press APPLY to view the results of your changes. When you are satisfied with the positioning of the text in the text block, press OK to return to the document window.

   To remove an unwanted tab, press and drag it down off the ruler. When you release the mouse, the tab will disappear.

   To clear all of the tabs from the ruler at one time, hold down the OPTION key and click on the tab ruler.

8. Select the table title and, using the Measurements Palette, format it as bolded, 14 pt. Helvetica, aligned Center.

9. Select "Performers" and format as 12 pt. Times, Bold, aligned Center.

10. Select all of the *remaining* text in the text box, change the type to 12 pt. Times, and the leading to 18 pts. To make these changes, use the Measurements Palette (see figure 5.31) or select the appropriate options from the STYLE menu.

11. With the text still selected, pull down the STYLE menu again and select RULES. Click in the Rule Below box to select it.

   Press on the Width pop-up menu and select Hairline width (figure 5.32).

   Click APPLY to see the results (figure 5.33). Click OK to return to the document window.

FORMATTING RULES BENEATH PARAGRAPHS

⌘ S

NOTES

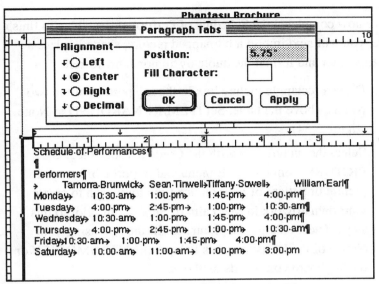

Figure 5.29 Setting tabs for the performances schedule.

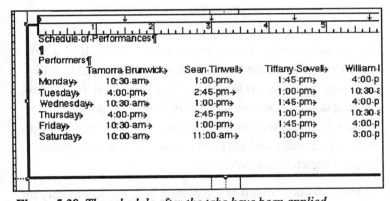

Figure 5.30 The schedule after the tabs have been applied.

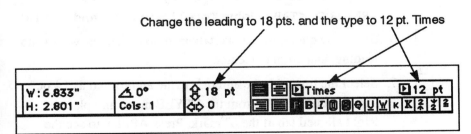

Figure 5.31 Changing the text format using the Measurements Palette.

IMPORTING AND SHADING A BITMAPPED PICTURE

You have now completed the Schedule of Performances table. To finish the brochure, you will next import a bitmapped picture, shade it, place a text box on top, enter and format the quote by author John Torrell.

☐ 1. Draw a rectangle picture box in the top portion of the two panels, above the table. Set ITEM/RUNAROUND to None (figure 5.34).

☐ 2. Select the picture box with the Content Tool, select GET PICTURE from the FILE menu and import a bitmapped picture or pattern of your choice (you may wish to create your own artwork in MacPaint or SuperPaint prior to this step). Then, enlarge the picture to fill the box using your choice of the Measurements Palette, the ITEM/MODIFY or the keyboard commands methods.

☐ 3. To apply a shading to the image, pull down the STYLE menu and select 10% from the SHADE submenu.

Note how the STYLE menu changes options according to the mode or context in which you are operating. If you did not have access to the menu as shown in figure 5.35, make sure that the picture is selected with the Content Tool before pulling down the menu. If SHADE is not an accessible option, it means that the picture you have imported is not a bitmapped image and may not be shaded. If that happens, you should choose another image.

☐ 4. Draw a text box on top of the picture box, approximately the same size. The ITEM/RUNAROUND should already be set to None, since you changed the Text Box Tool Preferences previously, but you may quickly verify the setting by selecting RUNAROUND from the ITEM menu.

☐ 5. Enter: "Nothing ignites the spirit or sets imagination free as a story well told." <RETURN> <TAB> John Torell, writer and artist

☐ 6. Select the quote, format as italicized 36 pt. Times, with Auto leading, and align to Center.

☐ 7. Select the line with the author's name and format as 14 pt. Times. Select TABS from the STYLE menu and place a Right aligned tab at the 6" mark. Press APPLY to see the results. Adjust tab placement if necessary and click OK to return to the document window.

⌘S

NOTES

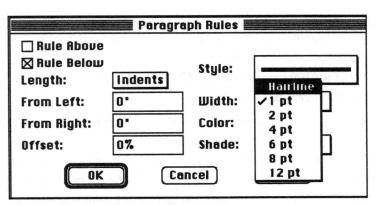

Figure 5.32 Selecting a Hairline rule.

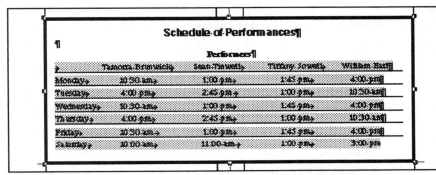

Figure 5.33 Schedule of Performances with rules applied after paragraph returns.

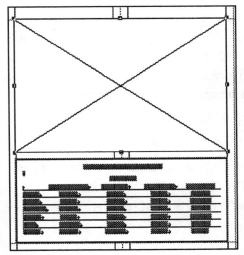

Figure 5.34 The two-column picture box with Runaround set to None.

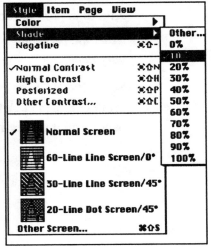

Figure 5.35 Changing the shade of a bit-mapped MacPaint formatted picture.

PRINTING A PROOF OF THE BROCHURE

PRINT TILING

PRINT REDUCTION

⌘S

8. Lastly, double-click on the text box with the Item Tool to bring up the Text Box Specifications dialog box and set the Vertical Alignment to Center. Click OK. Figure 5.36 displays the completed panels.

You have completed the Phantasy Brochure! Save once more. You will now prepare to print a proof of the brochure. Remember that the brochure document size is larger than a standard letter size sheet of paper, so in order to print it, you have two options: you may either tile it when it prints and paste the tiles together, or you may change the print size to a percentage less than 100%. To *tile* a document means to print a larger document in sections on smaller pieces of paper — like a mosaic. To understand how XPress is able to print large size documents, and for the purposes of this exercise, you will both tile the document and print at a reduced percentage.

1. To tile the brochure, select PAGE SETUP from the FILE menu and select a Portrait Orientation. Then, select PRINT from the FILE menu (⌘P). In the Print dialog box select Auto Tiling and enter a value of 1" in the overlap field (see figure 5.37).

   Click OK. The brochure will be printed onto 4 pages (2 for each side and may then be trimmed and pasted together.

2. To continue, you will now print the entire brochure on two pages, select PAGE SETUP from the FILE menu. Select the landscape orientation and enter a value of 80 into the Enlarge or Reduce field (see figure 5.38). This action instructs XPress to print the document at 80% of its normal size.

   Note: the percentage you choose to print a document may vary depending upon document and paper size.

   Select PRINT from the FILE menu, make sure that Tiling is set to Off, then click OK. The brochure will print on two pages, and it will be reduced to 80% of its original size.

In order to format your quote line endings like the example in this figure, press SHIFT-RETURN at the end of each line. This key character is called a soft return and does not create a new paragraph.

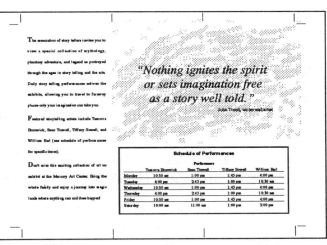

Figure 5.36 *The completed page. Hide Guides was selected from the View menu in order to view the page without displaying the guides.*

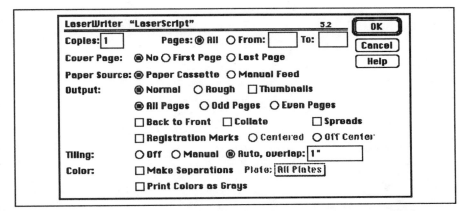

Figure 5.37 *The LaserWriter print dialog box with 1" Auto Tiling specified.*

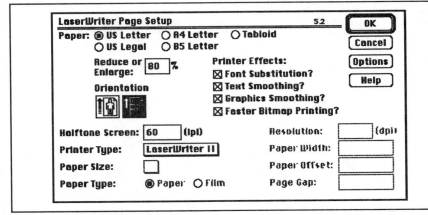

Figure 5.38 *The Page Setup dialog box with 80% value in the Reduce field and a landscape orientation specified.*

ADDITIONAL PRACTICE

Exercises:

1. Design an advertising flyer that contains a price list — necessitating the use of a table. Experiment with XPress tab types: left aligned, right aligned, centered, and decimal. In addition to a table, the flyer should contain text, graphic elements such as lines, boxes, and at least one picture.

2. Design and produce a folded business card template—two cards per letter size paper. Place crop and fold marks. Print at 100%.

3. Design and produce your own 2- or 3-fold brochure on either 8 1/2" x 11" or 8 1/2" x 14" paper. The electronic document should be larger than the final product and include crop/fold marks. Print the brochure at a reduced size to fit each side on one page.

1. In this chapter, what is the purpose of creating an electronic page that is larger than the final printed page? Can you think of any other reasons you might want to do this?

    _____

    _____

2. What is a *Master Page?* How many master pages is XPress capable of handling?

    _____

    _____

3. What is a *ruler origin box?* What can you use it for?

    _____

4. What are *drop caps* and how are they created?

    _____

    _____

5. Define the terms *leading, tracking,* and *kerning.* Why are these terms important to know?

    _____

    _____

6. List the steps to draw a filled polygon.

    _____

    _____

7. How do you rotate an element? Which elements can you rotate in QuarkXPress?

    _____

    _____

8. Why is it important to set an absolute leading specification when creating *raised caps?*

    _____

    _____

9. Why would you want to print a reduction of your document? How is this accomplished?

    _____

    _____

10. What is tiling? Describe the procedure for printing a tiled document.

    _____

    _____

Adventures
A **I**ⁿ **P**hantasy

A Celebration of

Phantasy

&

Mythology

in Storytelling and the Arts

Association of Story Tellers
1855 San Thomas Way
Mercury, CA 92345

Don't Miss

Adventures in Phantasy!

Presented by

The Association of Story

Tellers

on exhibit at

The Mercury Art Center

1525 Main Drive

Mercury, CA 92345

(123) 445-7890

Open 9 am to 5 pm

Monday – Saturday

The association of story tellers invites you to view a special collection of mythology, phantasy adventure, and legend as portrayed through the ages in story telling and the arts. Daily story telling performances enliven the exhibits, allowing you to travel to faraway places only your imagination can take you.

Featured storytelling artists include Tamorra Brunwick, Sean Tinwell, Tiffany Sowell, and William Earl (see schedule of performances for specific times).

Don't miss this exciting collection of art on exhibit at the Mercury Art Center. Bring the whole family and enjoy a journey into magic lands where anything can and does happen!

"Nothing ignites the spirit or sets imagination free as a story well told."

—John Torell, writer and artist

Schedule of Performances

	Performers			
	Tamorra Brunwick	Sean Tinwell	Tiffany Sowell	William Earl
Monday	10:30 am	1:00 pm	1:45 pm	4:00 pm
Tuesday	4:00 pm	2:45 pm	1:00 pm	10:30 am
Wednesday	10:30 am	1:00 pm	1:45 pm	4:00 pm
Thursday	4:00 pm	2:45 pm	1:00 pm	10:30 am
Friday	10:30 am	1:00 pm	1:45 pm	4:00 pm
Saturday	10:00 am	11:00 am	1:00 pm	3:00 pm

Chapter Six

Concepts for Multi-page Documents

In this chapter you will complete a simple 2-page newsletter and, in doing so, will incorporate many of the skills you have learned so far and add quite a few. Though the newsletter only contains two pages, we will approach the creation of the document as though it may contain more. Indeed, many newsletters vary from issue to issue. Properly organized and built, a newsletter template should be both efficient and flexible. It should be useful through many issues and allow for growth.

CHAPTER OBJECTIVES

The concepts contained in this chapter can be applied, not only to the publication of newsletters, but also to catalogs, books, and technical manuals. After completing this project you will have learned to:

- ✔ Use master pages to place repeating page elements and automatic page numbering.

- ✔ Use and apply XPress H&J (Hyphenation and Justification) settings.

- ✔ Create style sheets for copy, headlines, subheads, captions, and pull-quotes.

- ✔ Use text runaround for graphic elements (other than picture boxes).

- ✔ Rotate text / picture boxes.

- ✔ Link text boxes to control text flow.

CREATING THE NEWSLETTER TEMPLATE

1. Launch XPress and open a New document. In the New dialog box, select Facing Pages. Enter .5" for the top, bottom and outside margins, and .75" for the inside margin setting. (Note that the inside and outside margins used to be listed as the left and right margins.)

   Specify 3 columns in the Column Guides field, leaving the gutter at the default setting of 1 pica.

   If the Automatic Text Box option is selected, deselect it to turn it off. The New dialog box, with changed specifications, is shown in figure 6.1. Click OK.

2. In the General Preferences dialog box (⌘ Y) set the horizontal measure units to *Picas* and the vertical measure to *Inches*. Turn Auto Page Insertion *off* (figure 6.2).

3. Save the document as Newsletter Template.

NOTES

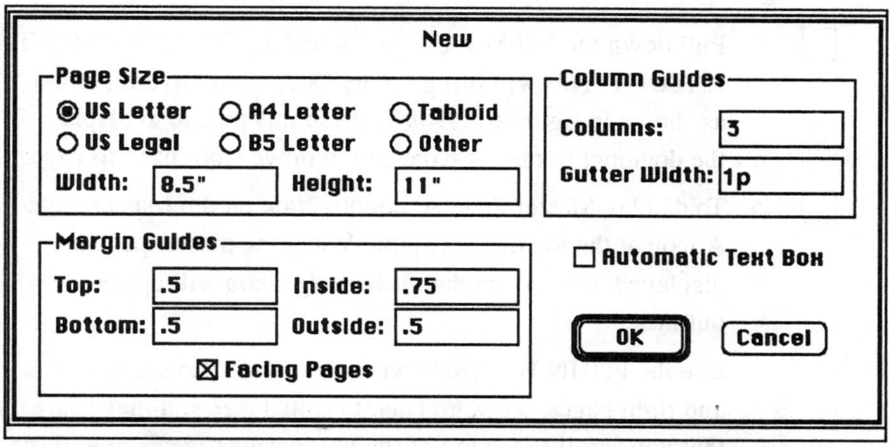

Figure 6.1 The New dialog box specifications for the "Newsletter Template."

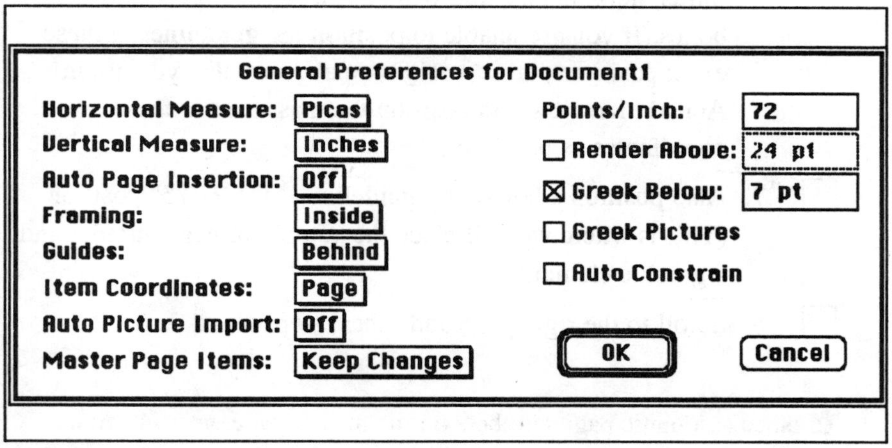

Figure 6.2 The General Preferences dialog box for the "Newsletter Template."

USING THE DOCUMENT LAYOUT PALETTE TO DISPLAY AND MODIFY MASTER PAGE A

GUIDELINES

AUTOMATIC PAGE NUMBERING

⌘S

Now that you have created the basic document, you will format Master Page A to include repeating elements: guidelines and automatic page numbering.

4. Pull down the VIEW menu and select SHOW DOCUMENT LAYOUT. This will bring up the Document Layout Palette as shown in figure 6.3. You will use this palette to display the document's master page and to move from page to page.

5. To display Master Page A, double-click on the Master Page A icon at the top of the palette. When the master page is displayed, the "A" on the master page icon will appear outlined.

   Use the FIT IN WINDOW view if you wish to see both left and right pages. Now, go back to actual size and make sure that you scroll to the top of the left master page. You will see L-Master A in the page box at the lower left corner of the window.

6. On the left page, pull down horizontal guidelines to the 3.333" and 6.666" positions. This step divides the page into thirds, horizontally, and will be used to help position text boxes.(If you are unable to position the guidelines at these exact positions, don't worry — make sure that you are in Actual Size view and position them as close to these coordinates as possible.)

7. Also position a horizontal guideline at the 9.875" position. (This is where we will place the automatic page number and a graphic element.)

8. Scroll to the right page and repeat steps 6 and 7.

To place automatic page numbers on the master page, you will first create a text box and then type the *Current Page Number* —COMMAND-3 (⌘3) into the box.

9. On the left master page, draw a text box to fit between the bottom margin and the 9.875" guide (it will be .625" tall) and approximately 2 1/2 picas wide (see figure 6.4).

   a) To make the text box transparent, select RUNAROUND from the ITEM menu (⌘T) and change the runaround mode to None.

NOTES

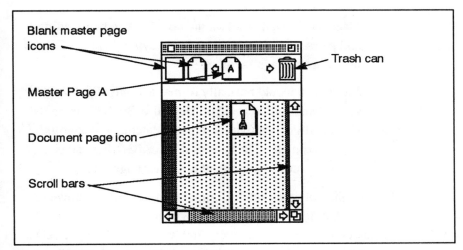

Blank master page icons

Master Page A

Document page icon

Scroll bars

Trash can

Figure 6.3 The Document Layout Palette.

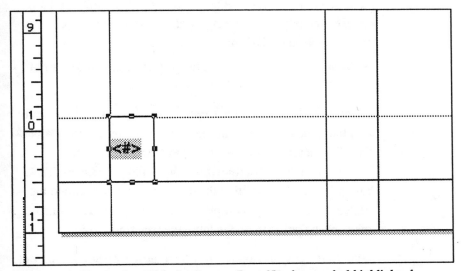

Figure 6.4 The text box with the Current Page Number symbol highlighted.

Sunday
@10PM
"Witches"

NOTES

FORMATTING THE AUTOMATIC PAGE NUMBER

b) Place the Content Tool on the box, click to begin editing and press ⌘3 . You will see a <#> symbol appear. This is the "Current Page" symbol.

c) Just as you would normally format text, highlight the <#> symbol and format as 12 pt. Helvetica Bold. Click on the Center Align icon (Measurements Palette) to center the text horizontally. Then, select ITEM/MODIFY and change the box's vertical alignment to Center (figure 6.4)

☐ 10. With the Polygon Picture Tool, draw a triangle as shown in figure 6.5. Its dimensions as shown on the Measurements Palette will be approximately 3p9 wide by .625" high. Select ITEM/MODIFY and fill with a 30% black shading. Click OK to return to the document.

☐ 11. With the polygon still selected, pull down the ITEM menu and SEND TO BACK. Select and group the polygon and text box.

☑ 12. To place a copy of these two elements on the right master page, select the group, choose COPY from the EDIT menu, scroll to the bottom of the right master page, and select PASTE from the EDIT menu.

Position the text box between the guides at the bottom right side of the page.

COPYING ELEMENTS FROM THE LEFT MASTER PAGE TO THE RIGHT MASTER PAGE

ROTATING ELEMENTS

Select the polygon with the Content Tool (if you try to select it with the Item Tool, you will select the entire group), and rotate it 180° by entering that value next to the rotation icon (△ 180°) on the Measurements Palette and pressing ENTER. You may need to reposition the text box in relationship to the rotated triangle. When complete, it should appear as a mirror image of the polygon on the left page (see figure 6.6).

☐ 13. Save your Template again. You have now finished laying out the master page for your newsletter.

☐ 14. To view your document again, double-click on the page 1 icon on the Document Layout Palette and select the FIT IN WINDOW view. Note that the guides and page number appear on page one exactly as positioned on the right master page (figure 6.7).

⌘S

NOTES

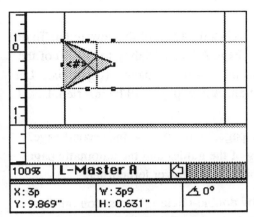

Figure 6.5 The shaded triangle.

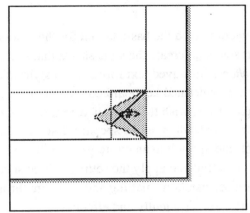

Figure 6.6 The triangle and page number after it has been copied to the right master page and rotated.

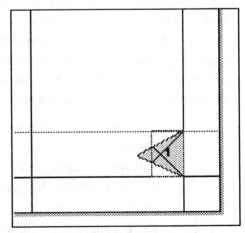

Figure 6.7 When page 1 of the document is displayed, the page number will display.

USING THE DOCUMENT LAYOUT PALETTE TO INSERT A PAGE

15. Next, you will need to insert page 2 of the newsletter. To do so, select the Master Page A icon and drag to the left of the spread dividing line and underneath page 1 (figure 6.8). Let go of the mouse button. A new page will be inserted, based on Master Page A.

Double-click on the page 2 icon to view the second page. Note the positioning of the guides and the automatic page number (2) that appears in the lower left corner.

Go back to Page 1 by double-clicking on its icon on the Document Layout Palette.

You have now completed the basic layout for the newsletter. Not so bad, eh? The next step is to create the style sheets that will be used in the newsletter. *Style sheets*, are saved text formats and styles that can be applied either by a user-defined keyboard command or from the STYLE menu. For example, if you wish the copy of your newsletter to be 12 pt. Palatino, with a specific leading, and a specific first line indent, you can save those settings and apply it to an entire paragraph or section very easily, without having to redefine and apply the settings. Style sheets help a document maintain consistent formatting and structure throughout, as well as help you to work more efficiently and effectively.

HYPHENATION AND JUSTIFICATION

Before you actually define the style sheets for the newsletter, we will need to explore XPress's Hyphenation and Justification feature because we will be using it within the style sheet definitions. Many programs offer limited options when it comes to hyphenation—it is either on or off. Likewise, when you specify a justified horizontal alignment of text, most programs give you little or no control over exactly how that justification is implemented. QuarkXPress 3.0, on the other hand, offers complete control over both of these features, as you will see.

1. Pull down the EDIT menu and select H&Js (this stands for Hyphenation and Justification settings). The H&J dialog box will appear (see figures 6.9 and 6.10). The name Standard will appear in the H&J name list and on the right are a number of options.

2. Click on the NEW button to create a new H&J specification setting. The Edit Hyphenation and Justification dialog box will appear (figure 6.11).

⌘ S

NOTES

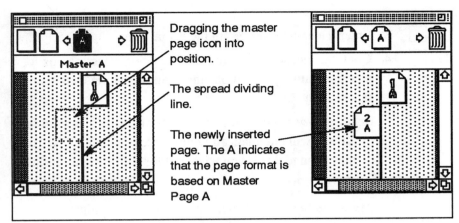

Figure 6.8 *The Document Layout palette while dragging the master page icon and after the page insertion is complete.*

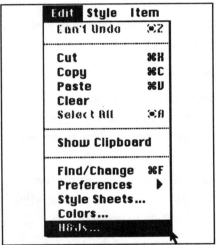

Figure 6.9 *Selecting the Hyphenation and Justification Command to create new settings.*

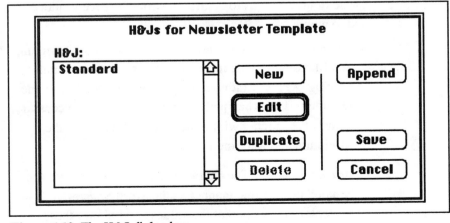

Figure 6.10 *The H&J dialog box.*

USING THE EDIT HYPHENATION AND JUSTIFICATION SETTINGS DIALOG BOX

☐ 3. Enter the name Hyphon in the Name field.

☐ 4. Click the mouse on the Auto Hyphenation selection box to activate Auto Hyphenation, and examine the fields within that section.

Smallest Word: The default setting for the smallest word that XPress will automatically hyphenate is 6 characters. You may change this if you wish, but for the purposes of this exercise, we will leave it at 6.

Minimum Before: This number refers to the minimum number of characters before XPress will hyphenate. In other words, a word such as "prefix" would be hyphenated after the "pre," but a word such as "replace" would not be hyphenated after the "re." You may wish to change the Minimum Characters Before setting to 2.

Minimum After: Leave this on the default setting of 2.

☐ 5. Tab to the Hyphens in a Row field and change from "unlimited" to 2. By doing this, you are specifying that XPress will not allow more than 2 lines in a row to end with a hyphen.

The Hyphenation Zone (set by default to 0) controls the distance and range from the right edge of the text box within which XPress will allow hyphenation to occur.

☐ 6. Examine the Justification Method fields in the dialog box. When a line of text is justified (aligned between indents) space is added or removed between words and characters. These fields allow us to control how much space is added and to where.

Word Spacing: The percentages in the Minimum, Optimum, and Maximum fields represent percentages of normal spacing. XPress first uses the percentage specified in the Optimum field when justifying text and then, if necessary, adjusts the spacing within the values specified in the Minimum and Maximum fields.

Character Spacing: The character spacing percentages are handled in the same manner as the Word Spacing percentages, except that the values entered into these

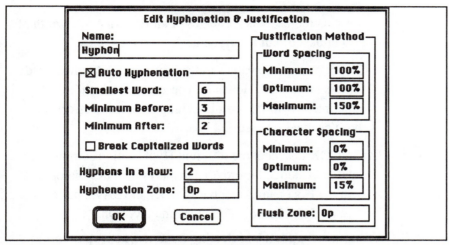

Figure 6.11 *Creating the H&J setting called HyphOn.*

NOTES

fields represent percentages of an En space (the width of a 0 in the current font/typeface).

Do not change the values in the Justification Method fields for this newsletter. However, you are encouraged to experiment with the various settings to see the effects of those changes on justified text.

☐ 7. Click OK to accept the different Hyphenation settings you entered in step 3. Figure 6.12 displays the H&J dialog box with the H&J names displayed. Click the SAVE button to save the H&J Setting with the name HyphOn.

✓ **H&J Settings are applied by selecting from the pop-up menu in the Formats dialog box** (figure 6.13). Save the Newsletter Template again.

DEFINING STYLE SHEETS

You are now ready to define style sheets for the document. When defining style sheets, it is important to think about the look, feel, and structure of your document. For example, since this is a three-column document, not a four- or five-column, you can use a larger type size than if the columns were narrower. For this newsletter, you will be defining styles for the article headlines, subheads, copy, an indented copy style, a sidebar copy (and indented style), continuation lines, and pull-quotes — a total of 8 styles.

The reason for creating style sheets, rather than just "manually" formatting many of these items, especially small-use items such as continuation lines or pull-quotes, is to maintain consistency from issue to issue of the newsletter. Once the template, including style sheets, is created it will be used as a basis for each subsequent issue. Formatting for all of the type will remain consistent and contribute to a recognizable identity for the publication.

☐ 1. Pull down the EDIT menu and select STYLE SHEETS (figure 6.14). The Style Sheets dialog box will appear (figure 6.15). Style sheets that are created when a document is active will apply only to that document. Since you are currently working within the active Newsletter Template, the style sheets will apply to the newsletter.

☐ 2. Click on the NEW button to bring up the Edit Style Sheet dialog box.

⌘ S

NOTES

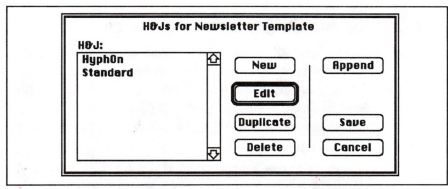

Figure 6.12 *The H&J dialog box after specifications for HyphOn are complete.*

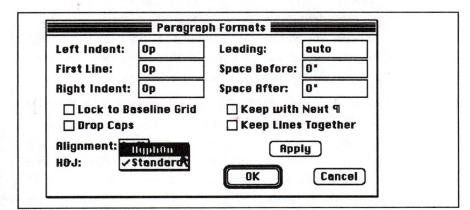

Figure 6.13 *H&J settings are applied by selecting the desired setting from the H&J pop-up menu in the Paragraph Formats dialog box.*

Figure 6.14 *The Edit/Style command.*

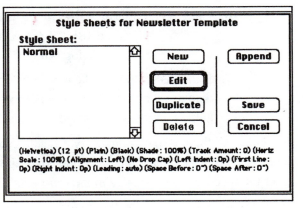

Figure 6.15 *The Edit Style Sheets dialog box as it first appears.*

ENTERING A STYLE NAME
AND KEYBOARD
EQUIVALENT

3. Enter the name: `Header` in the name field.

4. The next field, Keyboard Equivalents, allows you to define keyboard commands in order to quickly apply a style sheet. These equivalents always use a keypad number (or F-key if you use an extended keyboard) and may be a combination of a keypad number and another key such as the COMMAND or CONTROL keys.

   Tab to the Keyboard Equivalent field and press the SHIFT key, then—while holding the SHIFT key down—press the number 1 *on the keypad* (the numbers at the top of the keyboard will not work as keyboard equivalents for style sheets). The words "shift-keypad 1" will appear in the field (figure 6.16). **Do not try to type the letters "s h i f t" etc.** If you do, the computer will simply beep at you.

   Note: The *Based On* field is a pop-up menu that contains the names of all previously created style sheets for the active document. Style sheets can be based on other style sheets. If changes are subsequently made to the original (source) style sheet, then the same changes will automatically be made to the second style sheet.

5. Press the CHARACTER button to bring up the Character dialog box (figure 6.17). Format the characters as 14 pt. Helvetica Bold. Type 120% in the Horizontal Scale field, and enter 5 for the Track Amt. value. Click OK to accept the changes and you will be returned to the Edit Style Sheets dialog box.

6. Click on the FORMATS button. Enter .167" in the Space After field (figure 6.18). Click OK. Click OK again to return to the Style Sheets dialog box.

7. Click SAVE to save the new Header style sheet. Figure 6.19 displays the Style Sheet dialog box with the new style sheet name included in the style sheet list.

That's all there is to creating a style sheet! You will repeat steps 1–6 seven more times to create the remaining style sheets, *except* that you will enter the specifications as listed in the following chart.

⌘ S

NOTES

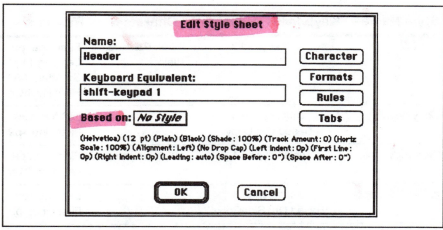

Figure 6.16 *The EDIT STYLE SHEET dialog box with the "Header" style name and keyboard equivalent entered.*

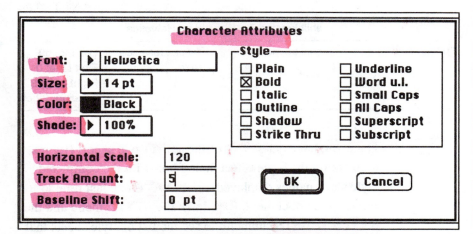

Figure 6.17 *The CHARACTER ATTRIBUTES dialog box.*

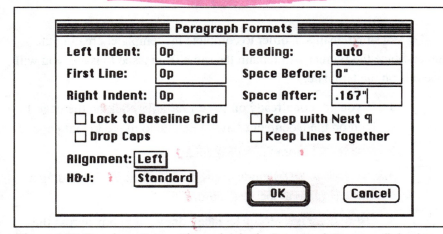

Figure 6.18 *Entering a Space After value in the Paragraph Formats dialog box will cause an additional space to be added to the end of each paragraph that is formatted with this style.*

DEFINING ALL OF THE STYLE SHEETS FOR THE NEWSLETTER TEMPLATE

Style Name	Keyboard Equivalent	Character	Formats
Copy	shift keypad 2	12 pt. Palatino Plain	First Line: p9 Leading 14 pt. Sp After: .056" H&J: HyphOn
CopyIndent	shift keypad 3 Based On: Copy		Left Ind: 1p6 First Line: -p9
SideCopy	shift keypad 4	10 pt. Helvetica	First Line: p9 Leading: 24 pt.
IndentSideCopy	shift keypad 5 Based On: SideCopy		Left Ind: 1p6 First Line: -p9
Subhead	shift keypad 6 Based On: Header	12 pt. Plain	First Line: 0 Sp After: 0 Leading: 24 pt.
ContLines	shift keypad 7	8 pt. Helvetica	
Pull-quotes	shift keypad 8	14 pt. Helvetica Bold	Left Ind: p9 First Line: 0 Right Ind: p9 Leading: 22 pt.

☐ 8. Once you have entered all of the above style sheets (figure 6.20 shows the Style Sheet dialog box with the completed style sheet names displayed), click SAVE one last time to return to the document. Pull down the STYLE menu and the STYLE SHEETS submenu to see the list of style sheets that may be applied to paragraphs of text (figure 6.21).

One last step remains in order to complete the template: creating the Banner. Since the Banner will remain the same from issue to issue, you will place this on the template.

☐ 1. If you are not already on page 1, double-click on the page 1 icon on the Document Layout Palette to move to that page.

☐ 2. Select 75% from the VIEW menu.

☐ 3. Drag a horizontal guide to the 1.625" position. Then drag a vertical guide to the 3p position (.5").

☐ 4. Using the guides for placement, draw a text box across the top of the page, starting at the 3p vertical guide (figure 6.22). The box should be 45p wide by 1.125" high.

NOTES

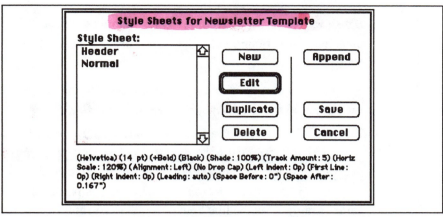

Figure 6.19 The Style Sheet dialog box after the Header style has been added.

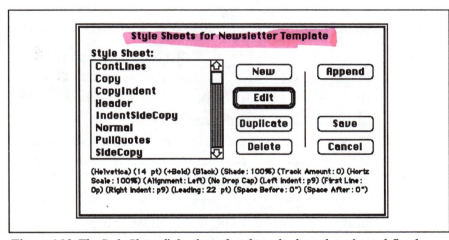

Figure 6.20 The Style Sheet dialog box after the style sheets have been defined.

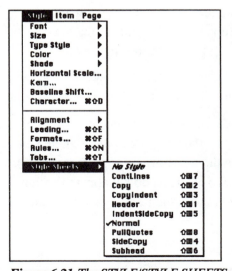

Figure 6.21 The STYLE/STYLE SHEETS command.

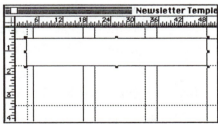

Figure 6.22 The banner text box placed on the top of page 1.

CREATING THE BANNER

USING A SOFT RETURN TO FORCE JUSTIFY A LINE OF TEXT

SHIFT RETURN
SOFT RETURN

⌘ S

Select RUNAROUND from the ITEM menu (⌘T) and change the text runaround to NONE in order to make the box transparent.

5. Enter: `Not Really News` into the text box. At the end of the line, hold the SHIFT key down and press RETURN.

   #8 The SHIFT-RETURN is a Macintosh *soft return* and will allow you to *force justify* the line of text — that is to align it with both the left and right indents. A soft return causes XPress to format and treat the following line as part of the same paragraph as the line containing the soft return.

   Highlight the text and, using the Measurements Palette, format as 56 pt. Bold, Italic, and Shadowed Palatino. Click on the Justified alignment icon on the Measurements Palette.

   Because you entered a SHIFT-RETURN at the end of the line of text, the line will force justify across the text box (figure 6.23). If you had pressed a normal (hard) return, or no return, the line would not justify.

6. Draw a triangle with the Polygon Picture Box Tool, starting at the 3p guide and extending to the letter "l" of the word "Really," as shown in figure 6.25.

   Select ITEM/MODIFY and fill the polygon with a black shading of 30%. Click OK, then send the polygon to the back (ITEM/SEND TO BACK).

7. With the Orthogonal Tool draw a straight line down the 3p vertical guide, from the upper margin guide to the lower margin guide. The line will be 10.5" long (figure 6.25).

   Change the width to 10 pt. and change the shade to 30% (under the STYLE menu). SEND TO BACK.

8. Change the View to 200%, scroll to the upper left corner of the page and make sure that the left edge of the triangle and the line meet properly so that there are no gaps (figure 6.26). If there are gaps, or the two elements do not appear to align properly, select the polygon with the Item Tool and adjust until they are aligned.

NOTES

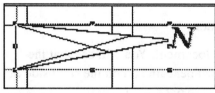

Figure 6.23 *The newsletter banner after it has been force-justified to align with both sides of the text box.*

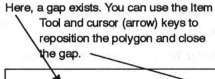

Figure 6.24 *Drawing a triangle with the polygon tool. The newsletter banner will temporarily run around the triangle until it is sent behind the text box containing the banner.*

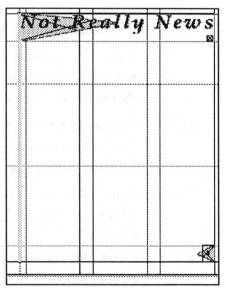

Figure 6.25 *The newsletter after vertical line has been added.*

Here, a gap exists. You can use the Item Tool and cursor (arrow) keys to reposition the polygon and close the gap.

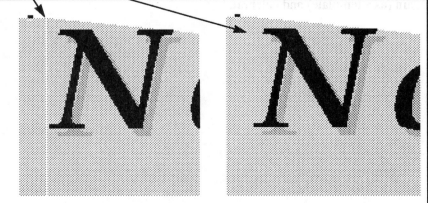

Figure 6.26 *Be sure that there are no gaps between the line and the polygon.*

FINISHING THE NEWSLETTER TEMPLATE

9. Next, you will need to place the folio information. Draw another text box beneath the newsletter banner and change the Runaround Mode to None.

   To precisely position the box, select MODIFY from the ITEM menu (with the box still selected) and enter the following values:

Origin across:	15p7
Origin down:	1.464"
Width:	32p5
Height:	0.21"

   Vertical alignment: Bottom

   Click OK to return to the document. You will see that the box has been positioned just beneath and on the right side of the banner, as shown in figure 6.27.

10. Click in the text box with the Content Tool and enter:

    ```
    A Classroom Publication <TAB> January 1990
    <TAB> Volume 1, No. 1
    ```

11. Highlight the text and format as 9 pt. Helvetica and track to 40 (you may use the right tracking/kerning arrow on the Measurements Palette to achieve the tracking).

12. Select TABS from the STYLE menu. Click on the ruler to enter a Centered tab at 18p and a Right tab at 32p. Click APPLY to see the results. If necessary, adjust the tabs to space the text as you desire (figure 6.28).

You have now completed the Newsletter Template. Save the template again (as a template) and celebrate!

⌘ S

NOTES

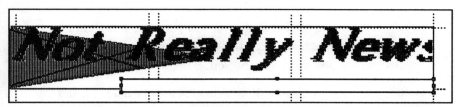

Figure 6.27   *Position of text box after using the Item/Modify command to resize and position it.*

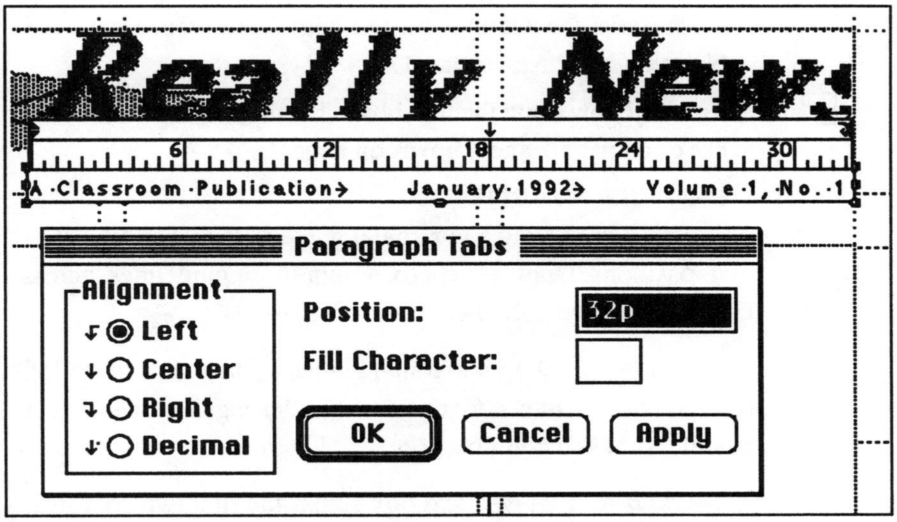

Figure 6.28   *Setting tabs for the folio information.*

PREPARING THE FIRST ISSUE OF THE NEWSLETTER

PLACING TEXT BOXES FOR THE ARTICLES

⌘ S

In this next section of chapter 6, you will place the newsletter text and picture boxes, import text and pictures, format text using the style sheets you created earlier, and print the newsletter.

Before you continue, you will need to create the articles for the newsletter. Although you could accomplish this by entering the text directly in Quark, you will use word processed files for this exercise. Quit XPress, launch your favorite word processor, and type each article as shown in the final newsletter example at the back of this chapter. *Do not format the text:* you will accomplish the formatting in XPress. Save each article as a separate document. When you have finished, quit the word processing application, launch XPress, and open the Newsletter template again.

1. To preserve the template for use with future issues, save the Newsletter as "Newsletter 1."

2. You will now draw the text boxes for the articles and titles: 4 boxes on page 1 and 4 boxes on page 2.

   Page 1 (figure 6.29)
   Text Box 1: Drag a horizontal guide to the 2" and 4.375" positions. Draw a text box within those guidelines, across the first two columns.

   Text Box 2: Drag horizontal guides to the 4.5" and 4.875" positions. Draw a text box within those guidelines, across the first two columns.

   Text Box 3: Draw a text box across the first two columns, from the 4.875" guide to the bottom margin guide (10.5"). Select ITEM/MODIFY and enter 2 into the Columns field. Click OK to return to the page.

   Text Box 4: Draw a text box in the third column from the 2" guide down to the 9.875" guide, just above the page number.

   Page 2 (figure 6.30) — Double-click on the page 2 icon on the Document Layout Palette to move to page 2.

   Text Box 1: Draw a text box in the first column, from the top margin guide down to the 9.875" guide, just above the page number.

   Text Box 2: Draw a text box across the second two columns, from the top margin guide to the 6.666" guide.

NOTES

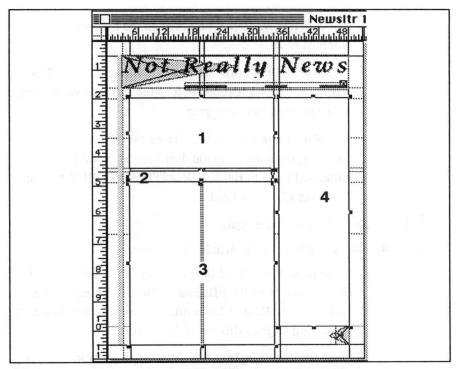

Figure 6.29 *The four text boxes after they have been placed on page 1.*

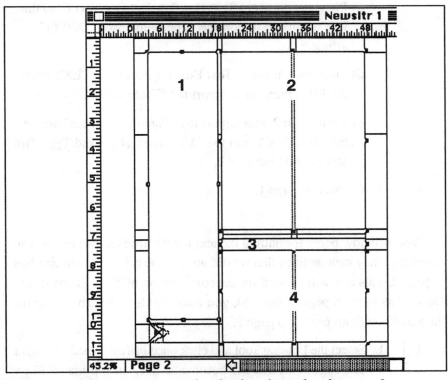

Figure 6.30 *The four text boxes after they have been placed on page 2.*

IMPORTING TEXT FOR THE ARTICLES

Select ITEM/MODIFY and change the number of columns to 2.

Text Box 3: Drag horizontal guides to the 7" and 7.378" positions. Draw a text box across the second two columns, between these two new guides.

Text Box 4: Draw a text box across the second two columns, from the 7" guide down to the bottom margin guide and Send to Back. Select ITEM/MODIFY and enter 2 into the Columns field.

3. Save the newsletter again.

4. Import the text for the articles as follows: *Start Here*

   a) Go to page 1 and place the cursor in Text Box 1. Select GET TEXT from the FILE menu (⌘E) and import the "DTP For the Rest of Us" article (you may have named it something slightly different). See figure 6.31.

   b) Place the cursor in Text Box 2 and type the title
   `The Elements of Design`

   c) Place the cursor in Text Box 3, select Get Text from the File menu and import the "The Elements of Design" article.

   d) Place the Cursor in Text Box 4, select GET TEXT from the FILE menu and import the "Technicalities" article.

   e) Go to page 2, and import the "Personal Profiles" article into Text Box 1, and the "Macintosh Hints and Type Tips" article into Text Box 2.

5. Go back to page 1.

LINKING TEXT BOXES TOGETHER

You will now begin formatting the text for the articles. But before you do so, you may have noticed that we did not pour text into the 4th text box in page 2. This box will be used for the continuation of "The Elements of Design" story from page 1. But first, you must first link these boxes so that the text flows from page 1 to page 2.

1. Select the Linking Tool and click once in Text Box 2 on page 1. The edge of the box will become "active," in appearance like a movie marquee (figure 6.32).

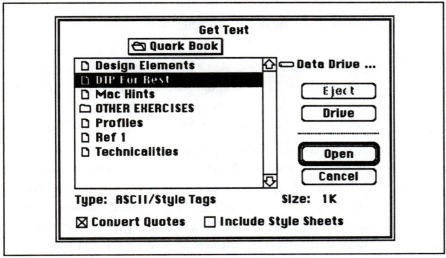

Figure 6.31   Selecting an article from the Get Text dialog box.

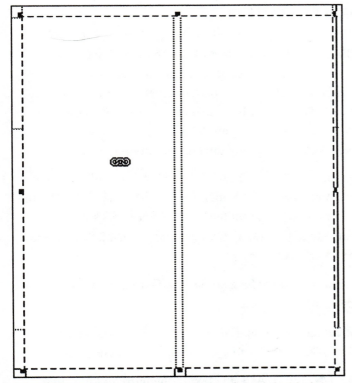

Figure 6.32   When a text box has been activated with the Linking Tool, a rotating dashed line will appear around it.

NOTES

**APPLYING STYLE
SHEETS**

2. Go to page 2 by double-clicking on the page 2 icon in the Document Layout Palette.

3. Click one time in Text Box 4 on page 2. The text from the first article will flow into the box. If the text does not fill the box, or perhaps overflows the box, do not worry. That condition will be remedied when you apply the style sheets.

   If you make a mistake, such as clicking on the wrong text box, you may unlink the boxes and then repeat the linking procedure. To unlink the boxes, select the Unlinking Tool (directly beneath the Linking Tool), select the first text box in the chain (in this case, Text Box 2 on page 1) and then click directly on the "tailfeather" of the linking arrow.

   Figure 6.33 shows a reduced view of the two-page newsletter after the unformatted text has been imported.

4. To apply the style sheets:

   a) Go to page 1 again. Click in the first text box, EDIT/SELECT ALL of the text (⌘A) , press the SHIFT key down and tap the number 2 on the keypad (your previously defined keyboard equivalent for the Copy style sheet). The text will automatically format as defined by the style sheet (see figure 6.34). If the text does format as displayed, try tracking the text slightly (-1 or -2).

   b) Select the title "DTP For The Rest of Us" and, this time, pull down the STYLE menu, select STYLE SHEETS, and select HEADER from the STYLE SHEETS submenu. Note the keyboard equivalent which is displayed next to the style sheet name.

   A style sheet may be applied by either method —menu or keyboard equivalent.

   c) Select the title "The Elements of Design" and press SHIFT-KEYPAD 1 to apply the Header style sheet.

   d) EDIT/SELECT ALL the text in the third text box, and apply the Copy style sheet (SHIFT-KEYPAD 2).

   Then, select the indented bulleted portion of the text (from "balance" down to "contrast," (see figure 6.35) and apply the CopyIndent style sheet (SHIFT-KEYPAD 3).

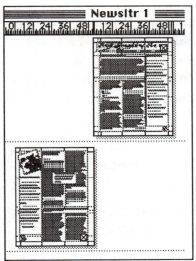

Figure 6.33   *The newsletter after all of the articles have been imported.*

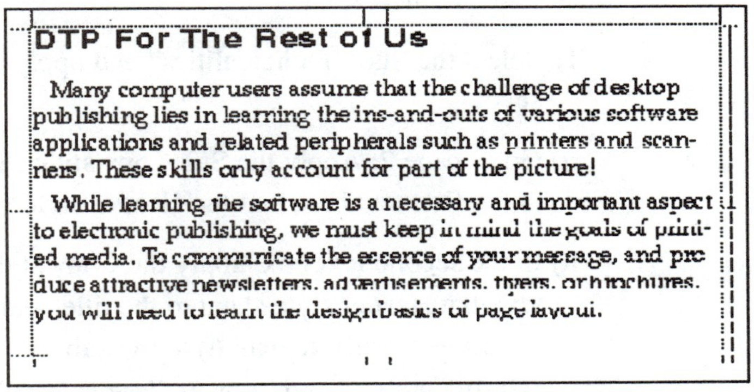

DTP For The Rest of Us

Many computer users assume that the challenge of desktop publishing lies in learning the ins-and-outs of various software applications and related peripherals such as printers and scanners. These skills only account for part of the picture!

While learning the software is a necessary and important aspect to electronic publishing, we must keep in mind the goals of printed media. To communicate the essence of your message, and produce attractive newsletters, advertisements, flyers, or brochures, you will need to learn the design basics of page layout.

Figure 6.34   *Text after a style sheet has been applied.*

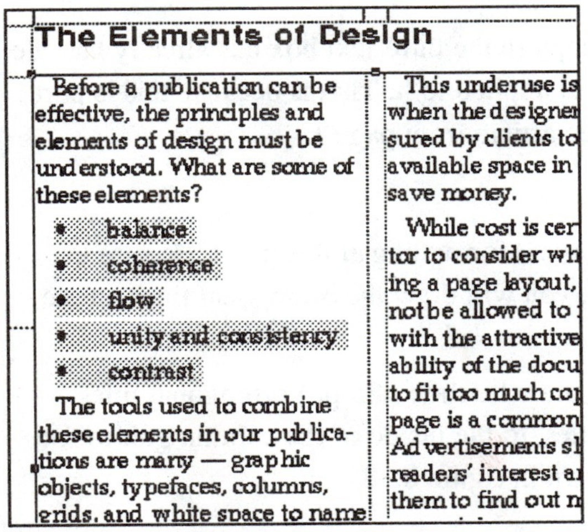

The Elements of Design

Before a publication can be effective, the principles and elements of design must be understood. What are some of these elements?

* balance
* coherence
* flow
* unity and consistency
* contrast

The tools used to combine these elements in our publications are many — graphic objects, typefaces, columns, grids, and white space to name

This underuse is when the designer sured by clients to available space in save money.

While cost is cer tor to consider wh ing a page layout, not be allowed to with the attractive ability of the docu to fit too much co page is a common Advertisements sl readers' interest a them to find out n

Figure 6.35   *Selecting the text for the CopyIndent style sheet.*

*Note: if the text does not indent or reformat properly, it is probably because it was typed without tabs. **The proper way to have entered the text would be to type the bullet, then a tab, followed by the word, then a return, a bullet, a tab, the second word,** etc. You can enter the tabs at this time to reformat the text.*

If you did not type the bullets in, you can do so now by holding down the Option key and typing an "8." This creates a round bullet.

e) EDIT/SELECT ALL the text in Text Box 4 and apply the SideCopy style sheet (SHIFT-KEYPAD 4).

Select the paragraphs from "The addition of..." to "Greater control..." (see figure 6.36) and apply the IndentSideCopy style sheet (SHIFT KEYPAD 5). Type in bullets if necessary.

f) Select the title "Technicalities" and apply the Header style sheet.

g) Go to page 2. Apply the SideCopy style sheet to the text in the first text box, and the Header style to the title.

h) In the second text box, apply the Copy style sheet to the text, the Header style sheet to the title, and the Subhead style sheet (shift-keypad 6) to the subheadings, "Dashes," "Curly Quotes," and "Lower Case is Best." (See figure 6.37.)

 Note that the copy in the third text box has already had the Copy style sheet applied to it. That is because this is part of the formatted article from page 1.

You have finished the major text formatting at this point. Be sure to save the newsletter again. Next, you will draw the orthogonal lines on the newsletter pages.

1. Go to page 1 and draw hairline (.25 pt.) orthogonal lines after the article titles, to the inside of the column guides for that article as shown in figure 6.38.

PLACING RULES BETWEEN COLUMNS

⌘ S

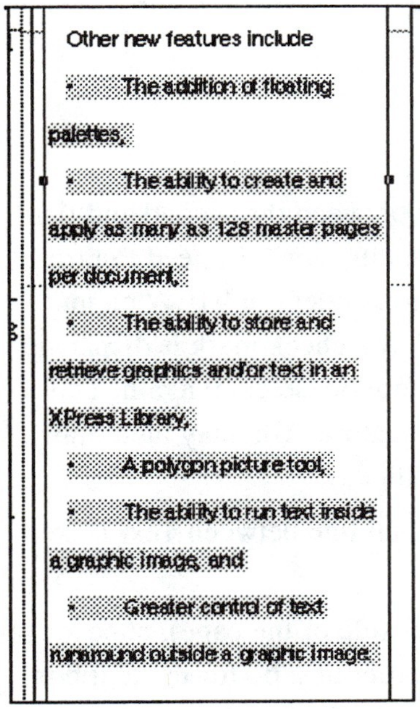

Other new features include

* The addition of floating palettes,

* The ability to create and apply as many as 128 master pages per document,

* The ability to store and retrieve graphics and/or text in an XPress Library,

* A polygon picture tool,

* The ability to run text inside a graphic image, and

* Greater control of text runaround outside a graphic image.

Figure 6.36 *Highlighted paragraphs to which the "IndentSideCopy" style sheet will be applied.*

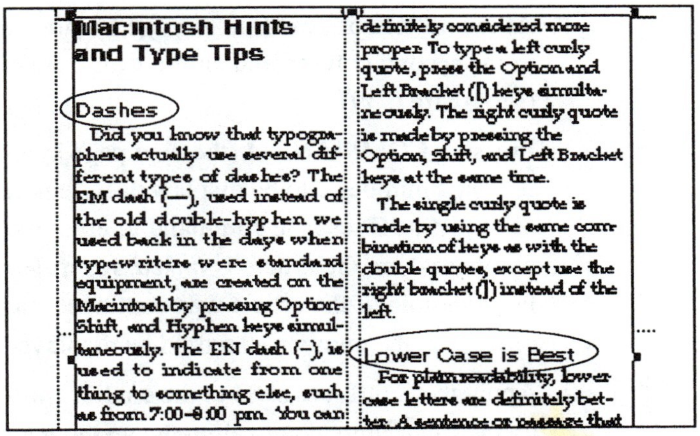

Macintosh Hints and Type Tips

Dashes

Did you know that typographers actually use several different types of dashes? The EM dash (—), used instead of the old double-hyphen we used back in the days when typewriters were standard equipment, are created on the Macintosh by pressing Option, Shift, and Hyphen keys simultaneously. The EN dash (–), is used to indicate from one thing to something else, such as from 7:00–8:00 pm. You can

definitely considered more proper. To type a left curly quote, press the Option and Left Bracket ([) keys simultaneously. The right curly quote is made by pressing the Option, Shift, and Left Bracket keys at the same time.

The single curly quote is made by using the same combination of keys as with the double quotes, except use the right bracket (]) instead of the left.

Lower Case is Best

For plain readability, lower case letters are definitely better. A sentence or passage that

Figure 6.37 *Subheads after a style sheet has been applied.*

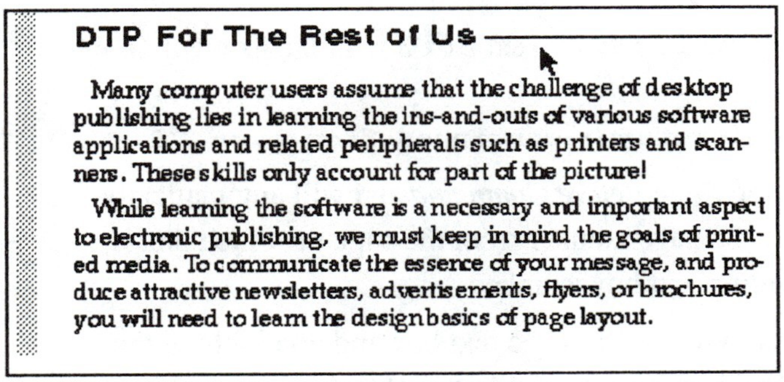

DTP For The Rest of Us

Many computer users assume that the challenge of desktop publishing lies in learning the ins-and-outs of various software applications and related peripherals such as printers and scanners. These skills only account for part of the picture!

While learning the software is a necessary and important aspect to electronic publishing, we must keep in mind the goals of printed media. To communicate the essence of your message, and produce attractive newsletters, advertisements, flyers, or brochures, you will need to learn the design basics of page layout.

Figure 6.38 *Placing a horizontal rule between the title and the column guide.*

NOTES

CONTINUATION LINES

⌘ S

2. Then draw another vertical line between the second and third columns. In order to accomplish this, you will need to turn off the SNAP TO GUIDES option under the VIEW menu. Pull down the VIEW menu and, if a check mark is displayed next to the SNAP TO GUIDES option, select it again. This action will deselect the Snap to feature. You may then draw the line between the columns with ease.

3. Go to page 2 and draw a horizontal line between Text Boxes 2 and 3.

4. Select text box 1 (the box on left side of the page), choose ITEM/FRAME and specify a border of 1 pt. for the text box.

The next step to completing the newsletter is to include *continuation lines* (also called *jump lines*) so that the reader will know that the article on page 1 is continued on page 2.

1. At the bottom of Text Box 2 (page 1), draw a small text box in the second column and enter: `Continued on page ⌘4` (see figure 6.39).

   Pressing COMMAND-4 (the next page symbol) will cause the page number 2 to be displayed. By entering a ⌘4, you have given XPress the command to enter the next page number where the article is *linked*, regardless of that page. For example, if the article was continued on page 10, instead of page 2, the number 10 would be displayed.

2. Apply the ContLines style to the continuation line. Then, click on the right-align icon to align the text to the right side of the box, choose ITEM/MODIFY and select a Bottom alignment. *Note: You may wish to adjust the position of the continuation line and may do so by adjusting the position of its box.*

3. Go to page 2. Activate Text Box 3 with the Content Tool and enter:

   `Design…<return> continued from page ⌘2`

   ⌘2 is the *Page Before Command* and will automatically display the page number from the page on which the proceeding text box is linked.

   The text will overflow the text box and you will see the overflow indicator in the lower right corner of the box.

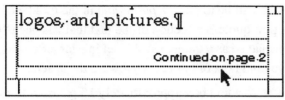

Figure 6.39   *The continuation line.*

4. Resize the text box from the bottom so that you can view all of the text. Apply the Subhead style sheet to the first line, and ContLines style to the second line.

5. Position the text cursor before the "c" of the word "continued" and press the delete (backspace) key. Although the lines are now part of the same paragraph, style formatting will remain the same (see figure 6.40).

PLACING AND FORMATTING A PULL-QUOTE

The next task will be to place a *pull-quote* in the middle of the story in Text Box 2. A pull-quote is a section of the text that has been "pulled" (copied) and displayed as a quote, usually set in a larger typesize to direct the reader's eye (and hopefully interest) toward the article.

1. Create a text box approximately 15 picas wide and 2 inches tall, and place it in the center of Text Box 2, between the two columns. The text will automatically wrap around the box.

2. Select and copy the portion of the last sentence which reads, "A sentence of passage…tiring to read." Paste the quote into the text box you drew in the previous step.

3. Type a left curly quote (OPTION-[) at the front of the pasted text and a right curly quote (SHIFT-OPTION-[) at the end of the quote. Then, place the cursor right after the word "read" and type an ellipsis (OPTION-;).

4. Next, apply the pull-quotes style sheet to the quote by typing a SHIFT-8 (see figure 6.41).

5. Lastly, select ITEM/MODIFY (or double-click on the text box with the Item Tool) and change the vertical alignment of the text box to Center. The pull-quote is finished.

CREATING A DROP-SHADOWED BOX

The last item to place on your newsletter is the rotated picture box with a drop shadow. To accomplish this,

1. Draw a square picture box, approximately 12 picas in width, and center it in the top of Text Box 1 (figure 6.42). Remember that holding the SHIFT key down while drawing constrains the box to a perfect square.

⌘S

NOTES

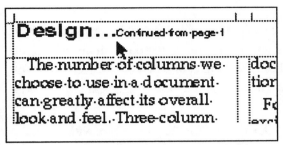

Figure 6.40   *Style formatting remains the same after pressing the delete key to remove the paragraph marker.*

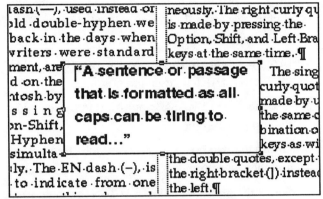

Figure 6.41   *The pull-quote after it has been placed and formatted, but before it has been vertically centered in its text box.*

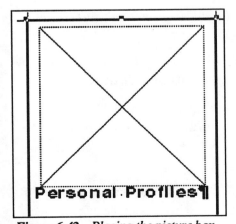

Figure 6.42   *Placing the picture box.*

USING STEP AND
REPEAT TO DUPLICATE
AN ELEMENT

SHADING AND
POSITIONING THE
"SHADOW"

GROUPING THE BOXES

ROTATING THE ELEMENTS

POSITIONING GROUPED
ELEMENTS

2. With the picture box still activated, select ITEM/STEP AND REPEAT. The Step and Repeat dialog box will appear (figure 6.43). Enter a horizontal offset of 6 pt. and a vertical offset of 6 pt. Click OK. The new picture box will appear slightly offset to the original.

3. Select ITEM/MODIFY and fill the picture box with a black background shade of 50%.

4. With the Content Tool, select the original picture box, bring it to front, and then use the FILE/GET PICTURE command to import a picture into the box. In this case, the Handlebars.eps picture was used. It is usually located in the Sample Pictures folder inside the QuarkXPress application folder.

   Size the picture to fit the box by using the COMMAND-OPTION-SHIFT-F keyboard command.

5. Use the ITEM/FRAME command to place a .25 pt. border on the top picture box.

6. Group the two boxes together by selecting both picture boxes and then selecting GROUP from the ITEM menu.

7. Select the group with the Item Tool and then rotate the group 20° by entering that value into the rotation field on the Measurements Palette.

   Check the x and y coordinates of the group and, if necessary, change the x coordinate to 2p3 and the y coordinate to 1". *If the edges of the group are too close to the edge of the page, the laser printer will not be able to print it and parts of the group will be "cut off."*

   The rotated box should now be complete (see figure 6.44). You will next adjust the placement of the article's title and text.

8. Place the text cursor before the word "Personal" and press RETURN until the title sits on one line just beneath the rotated picture box. Figure 6.44 displays the paragraph invisibles.

   Then, select ITEM/MODIFY and change the text inset to 3 pt. This action will cause the text be inset from the edges of the border, giving the type a little more "air."

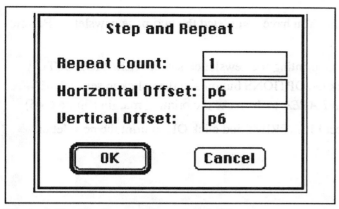

Figure 6.43   *The Step and Repeat dialog box.*

Figure 6.44   *Pressing the RETURN key will help position the title of the article below the rotated picture box.*

Congratulations! You have completed the two-page newsletter. Be sure to SAVE it again.

☐ 1. Before printing the newsletter, select FILE/PAGE SETUP. Click the OPTIONS button and then click to select *LARGER PRINT AREA* to decrease the printing margin (figure 6.45).

Select FILE/PRINT and click OK to print the newsletter.

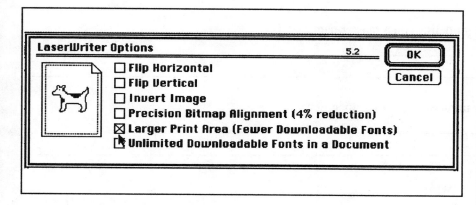

NOTES

Figure 6.45 *The Options dialog box with Larger Print Area selected.*

1. Why is it a good idea to place guidelines on a master page?
    _____
    _____

2. List the steps to automatically number pages of a document.
    _____
    _____

3. How do you rotate a page element?
    _____
    _____

4. List two ways to insert a new page in a document.
    _____
    _____

5. What does *H&J* refer to?
    _____
    _____

6. Define the term *style sheet*. List the steps to create a new style sheet.
    _____
    _____

7. How is a style sheet applied to a paragraph?
    _____
    _____

8. What is the difference between a *soft* return and a *hard* return?
    _____
    _____

9. List the steps to link text boxes. What does linking accomplish?
    _____
    _____

10. List the steps to create a box shadow.
    _____
    _____

Not Really News

A Classroom Publication   January 1992   Volume 1, No. 1

DTP For The Rest of Us

Many computer users assume that the challenge of desktop publishing lies in learning the ins-and-outs of various software applications and related peripherals such as printers and scanners. These skills only account for part of the picture!

While learning the software is a necessary and important aspect to electronic publishing, we must keep in mind the goals of printed media. To communicate the essence of your message, and produce attractive newsletters, advertisements, flyers, or brochures, you will need to learn the design basics of page layout.

Correct on mine

The Elements of Design

Before a publication can be effective, the principles and elements of design must be understood. What are some of these elements?

- balance
- coherence
- flow
- unity and consistency
- contrast

The tools used to combine these elements in our publications are many — graphic objects, typefaces, columns, grids, and white space to name a few.

Spacing

White space is a particularly important page layout element to consider when planning your newsletter, brochure, or advertisement. White space, which includes the space in the margins and between lines of text as well as around pictures and graphic lines, is typically under used.

This under use is exacerbated when the designer is pressured by clients to use every available space in an effort to save money.

While cost is certainly a factor to consider when designing a page layout, it should not be allowed to interfere with the attractiveness or readability of the document. Trying to fit too much copy onto a page is a common mistake. Advertisements should pique readers' interest and motivate them to find out more. If potential customers or members are not drawn to read our ads, how good are the ads?

The use of grids is another important organizational tool. Grids bring consistency to publications. They help us to lay out margins, borders, columns, and place text boxes, logos, and pictures.

Continued on page 2

Technicalities

The new version of QuarkXPress has incorporated a number of features that are new to the program. Previous XPress users are excited about the changes — especially the unrestrained ability to rotate text and graphics.

Other new features include

- The addition of floating palettes,
- The ability to create and apply as many as 128 master pages per document,
- The ability to store and retrieve graphics and/or text in an XPress Library,
- A polygon picture tool,
- The ability to run text inside a graphic image, and
- Greater control of text runaround outside a graphic image.

1

Personal Profiles

In this one-and-only issue of Not Really News, we are featuring Bongo Jones (that's his picture up there), a neophyte desktop designer. This guy really takes the cake for disregarding all design rules and making every mistake in the book!

First of all, he tried to use all available Macintosh fonts on one flyer. Then, he scattered his publications with silly little clip art cartoons. However, Bongo really deserves true notoriety for not checking his spelling!

Well Bongo, cheers!

Macintosh Hints and Type Tips

Dashes

Did you know that typographers actually use several different types of dashes? The EM dash (—), used instead of the old double-hyphen we used back in the days when typewriters were standard equipment, are created on the Macintosh by pressing Option-Shift, and Hyphen keys simultaneously. The EN dash (–), is used to indicate from one thing to something else, such as from 7:00–8:00 pm. You can type an EN dash on the Macintosh by pressing the Option and Hyphen keys.

Curly Quotes

Curly Quotes, also known as "smart quotes" can be created directly on the Macintosh. The quotes we see and use from the standard Macintosh keyboard are the straight inch marks ("). Curly quotes are definitely considered more proper. To type a left curly quote, press the Option and Left Bracket ([) keys simultaneously. The right curly quote is made by pressing the Option, Shift, and Left Bracket keys at the same time.

> **"A sentence or passage that is formatted as all caps can be tiring to read…"**

The single curly quote is made by using the same combination of keys as with the double quotes, except use the right bracket (]) instead of the left.

Lower Case is Best

For plain readability, lower case letters are definitely better. A sentence or passage that is formatted as all caps can be tiring to read and so should only be used for short headings.

Design... Continued from page 1

The number of columns we choose to use in a document can greatly affect its overall look and feel. Three-column designs are used quite frequently for newsletters. It is a good model to use because the columns are narrow enough to be easily read, yet not so narrow that word spacing becomes a problem, or that they become difficult to read. However, 3-column designs can also become too predictable, if enough visual interest is not added to the document through the addition of other graphic elements.

Four-column designs can be exciting, if handled correctly. Four columns on a single letter-sized page can be rather narrow, but tightening the space between columns and using a smaller font can help.

There are many things to take into consideration when planning a publication design, but with practice and the willingness to experiment, we can all become better designers.

Need to add

Chapter Seven

Document Construction and Management

Managing Documents With Menu Commands

The File Menu

The FILE/NEW command is used to create a new QuarkXPress document. Because QuarkXPress allows you to have more than one document open at a time, it is not necessary to close a current document before opening another one.

To create a new document:

✔ Pull down the FILE menu and select NEW. The NEW dialog box will appear (figure 7.1) which allows you to define the first master page (called Master Page A) and the first page of your document. You can specify the following:

Page Size: defines the size of your electronic page. You can choose one of the pre-defined sizes, such as US Letter, or enter custom measurements into the WIDTH and HEIGHT fields.

Margin Guides: positions items on the page. These guides define the margin area around the perimeter of the page.

Facing Pages: determines whether or not the document will be double-sided.

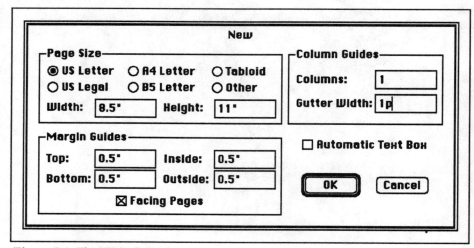

Figure 7.1 *The NEW dialog box.*

Automatic Text Box: creates a text box for every new page. This feature is set on by default, but it can be turned off by deselecting AUTOMATIC TEXT BOX in the New dialog box.

Column Guides: This specification defines the number of columns and gutter width in the automatic text box.

✔ After entering the desired settings, click the OK button to accept and open the new document.

❀ ❀ ❀ ❀ ❀ ❀ ❀ ❀ ❀ ❀ ❀ ❀ ❀ ❀ ❀ ❀ ❀ ❀ ❀ ❀

⌘ O   FILE/OPEN

The FILE/OPEN command opens a document that has already been created and saved in QuarkXPress.

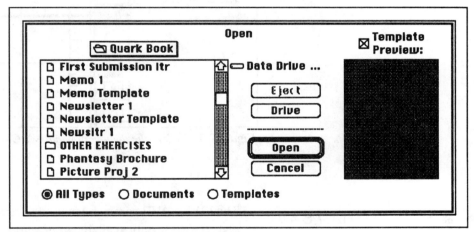

Figure 7.2 The OPEN dialog box.

To open a document:

✔ Pull down the FILE menu and select OPEN. A directory dialog box will appear (figure 7.2).

✔ Using the DRIVE button and the Directory Title pop-up menu, navigate to the desired file's location.

✔ Select a document or template from the list of titles that appear and click OPEN (or double-click on the document title) to bring the document onto your screen. If the selected file is a QuarkXPress template, a miniaturized picture of the template will appear in the template preview window on the right side of the Open dialog box. If you do not wish to preview templates, deselect the Template Preview Box.

◈ ◈ ◈ ◈ ◈ ◈ ◈ ◈ ◈ ◈ ◈ ◈ ◈ ◈ ◈ ◈ ◈ ◈

FILE/CLOSE

The FILE/CLOSE command closes an open file.

To Close an active file:

✔ Pull down the FILE menu and select CLOSE. Or, click in the document window's close box in the upper left-hand corner (figure 7.3). If you have not yet saved your document, or have made changes since the last save, Quark will ask you if you want to save the document before closing it.

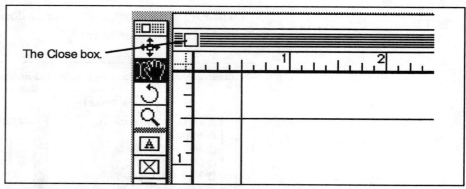

Figure 7.3 Click in the document window's Close box to close a document.

◈ ◈ ◈ ◈ ◈ ◈ ◈ ◈ ◈ ◈ ◈ ◈ ◈ ◈ ◈ ◈ ◈ ◈

⌘S   FILE/SAVE

The FILE/SAVE command is used to save a QuarkXPress document to disk. SAVE is only available after starting a new document or after modifying a document that was previously saved. When using the SAVE command, the new version of the document (including any changes you have made) replaces the previous version. If you are saving a new document for the first time, or if you wish to change the name of the document, refer to the instructions for the SAVE AS command.

◈ ◈ ◈ ◈ ◈ ◈ ◈ ◈ ◈ ◈ ◈ ◈ ◈ ◈ ◈ ◈ ◈ ◈

FILE/SAVE AS

The FILE/SAVE AS command is used when you are first saving a document to disk or if you wish to save a document under a new name: it allows you to assign a name and disk location for the file.

To save a new document:

✔ Pull down the FILE menu and select SAVE AS. The SAVE AS dialog box will appear (figure 7.4). This dialog box will also appear the first time you select SAVE from the FILE menu for a new, untitled document.

✔ If necessary, change the disk drive/folder using the DRIVE button and the Directory pop-up menu to assign a location for the new file.

✔ Type a name for the document in the "Save current document as:" box.

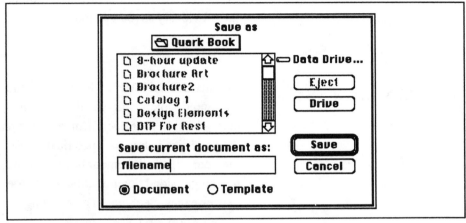

Figure 7.4 The Save As dialog box.

✔ Select Document (preselected by default) or Template.

✔ Click the SAVE Button.

To save with a new name or location:

✔ Pull down the FILE menu and select SAVE AS. The SAVE AS dialog box will appear.

✔ Using the DRIVE button and the Directory pop-up menu, assign a location for the document.

✔ Type the document's new name in the "Save current document as:" box. If you do not enter a new name, and attempt to save this file in the same disk/folder location as before, a dialog box will appear asking you to confirm your wish to replace the existing file. Clicking OK will save the new, changed document over the old one. Clicking CANCEL will return you to the SAVE AS dialog box so you can enter a different name.

✔ Click the SAVE Button.

❈ ❈

FILE/REVERT TO SAVED

The FILE/REVERT TO SAVED command is used to discard changes you have made to a document and returns you to the most recently saved version of the document. If you do not like the results of a recent change and find that the changes are difficult to "undo," select REVERT TO SAVED from the FILE menu. The on-screen document will be replaced by the previously saved version.

❈ ❈

FILE/DOCUMENT SETUP

The FILE/DOCUMENT SETUP command allows you to change the page size and double/single-sided document specifications defined in the New dialog box. If your document contains page elements, you may not reduce the page size below the specifications needed for the pasteboard to contain the items. If the document is a facing-pages document, you may change it to a single-sided document only if it does not contain any facing-pages master pages. See section on creating and manipulating master pages for more information.

To change a document's electronic page size, or to switch a document from a single-sided to a facing pages format:

✔ Select DOCUMENT SETUP from the FILE menu. The Document Setup dialog box will appear (figure 7.5). Select one of the pre-defined page sizes or enter custom dimensions into the Width and Height fields. Check the Facing Pages box to toggle between the facing pages (double-sided) and single-sided options.

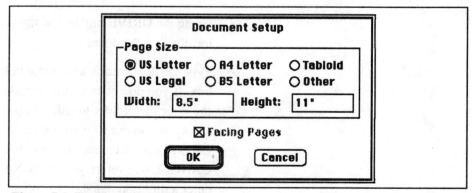

Figure 7.5 Document Setup Window.

FILE/PAGE SETUP

The FILE/PAGE SETUP command is used to specify printing instructions, such as paper size, scale of output, printer effects, paper orientation (portrait or landscape), printer type, halftone screen, and other printing options. To use PAGE SETUP with a postscript laser printer:

Pull down the FILE menu and select PAGE SETUP. The Page Setup dialog box will appear. Options that are available will change, depending upon the printer type that is selected (figures 7.6 and 7.7).

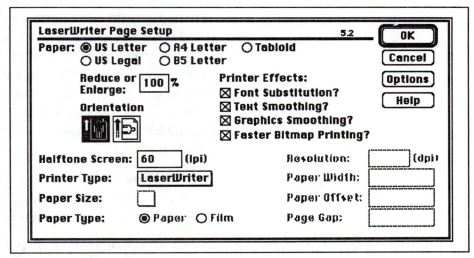

Figure 7.6 LaserWriter Page Setup.

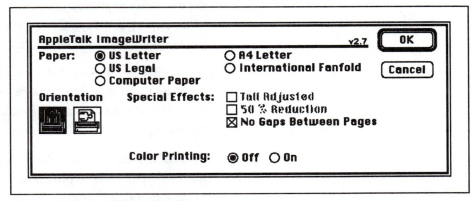

Figure 7.7 ImageWriter Page Setup.

The following specifications are available for the laser printer:

Paper — Select the paper size you will be using in your printer. The paper size options (up to 7) will vary, depending upon the printer driver you have selected in the Chooser desk accessory. Figure 7.6 shows the LaserWriter Page Setup dialog box.

Reduce or Enlarge — You can print your document at any percentage from 25% to 400% of original size. Enter the desired value in the Reduce or Enlarge field.

Orientation — Select the upright figure to choose a portrait orientation. Select the sideways figure to select a landscape orientation.

Halftone Screen — This specification defines the number of lines per inch (lpi) that QuarkXPress will use when printing screens, shaded items, and halftone pictures contained in a document. The default for a LaserWriter is 60 lpi. Since the optimum lpi for a laser printer are from 50–60 lpi, it is not recommended that you change this value if you are printing to a standard laser printer. If your output will be sent to a Linotronic or some other imagesetting device, you should talk to your service bureau about the optimum setting for their devices.

Printer Type — Use printer type to select the type of device for output. Different Page Setup options will be displayed in the dialog box, depending upon which printer type you have selected.

If you select Linotronic, the Paper Type (paper or film), Resolution (from 72 to 5,000 dots per inch), Paper Width, Paper Offset (specifies the distance the printed image will be offset from the upper left edge of the paper), and Page Gap (specifies space to be inserted between pages) fields will become active.

Paper Size — The paper size menu will become available when you select a printer type that supports many different standard paper sizes. It will not be available if you have selected LaserWriter as your printer type.

Printer Effects — Font substitution will substitute postscript fonts for bitmapped fonts to provide a higher-quality output. When Font Substitution is selected, Times will be substituted for New York, Helvetica for Geneva, and Courier will be substituted for Monaco.

Text Smoothing and Graphic Smoothing smooths the edges of bitmapped graphics/text to produce a higher quality print image.

When Faster Bitmap Printing is selected, text and graphics will be printed faster than usual.

Options — Checking the OPTIONS button will bring up another dialog box (figure 7.8) that allows you make changes to the way all pages of the document will be printed. These options include flipping pages horizontally, flipping pages vertically, inverting page image (all blacks become white and vice-versa), reducing bitmap printing by 4%, defining a larger print area, and allowing an unlimited number of downloadable fonts in a document.

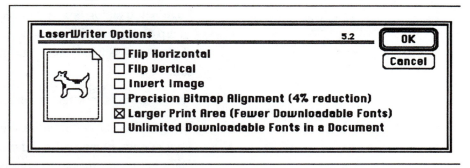

Figure 7.8 The Print Options dialog box with LARGER PRINT AREA selected.

To use Page Setup with a postscript imagesetting device such as a linotronic:

✔   Pull down the FILE menu and select PAGE SETUP. Select output device. The following additional specifications are available for the Linotronic:

Printer Effects — these effects are not normally used by an imagesetter.

Halftone Screen — consult your service bureau to find out the optimum lines per inch for your image setting device, document resolution, etc.

Paper Type — You may choose paper or film.

Resolution — The resolution setting here must match the resolution setting on the output device.

Paper Width — This field is used to define the width measurement of the paper or film in the imagesetting device.

Paper Offset — This setting may be used to move the print location of the document to the right of its usual placement on the paper (or film). Offset may only be used if the electronic page size is smaller than the paper or film size.

Page Gap — This allows you to define how much space you wish between pages when outputing to a Linotronic.

To use Page Setup with an Apple ImageWriter:

✔ Pull down the FILE menu and select PAGE SETUP. The ImageWriter Page Setup dialog box will appear (figure 7.7). The ImageWriter Page Setup dialog box limits you to the following selections: Paper size (US letter, US legal, computer paper, A4 letter, or international fanfold).

Orientation — portrait or landscape.

Special Effects — Tall adjusted (this should be selected, otherwise your document may print out of proportion), 50% reduction, and No Gaps between pages (allowing you to eliminate the printer-default top and bottom margins between pages).

Color Printing — On or Off.

⌘ P   FILE/PRINT

The FILE/PRINT command allows you to output your document to a printer or other output device.

To print on a laser printer:

✔ Pull down the FILE menu and select PRINT. The LaserWriter print dialog box will appear (figure 7.9).

In most cases, to print your document you will merely need to click the OK button at this point. However, the following options are also available to you:

✔ Enter the number of copies you wish to print.

✔ If you want to print only a section or certain pages of your document, enter the page numbers in the From and To boxes.

✔ If you wish to automatically print a cover page that identifies the name of the document, the user, time and date it is printed, select

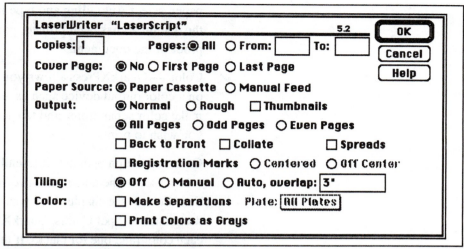

Figure 7.9 *The LaserWriter PRINT dialog box.*

First Page or Last Page to specify the sequence in which it will be printed.

✔ Select whether the paper will be supplied from the paper cassette or will be fed manually to the printer.

✔ Selecting Color/Grayscale will allow you to get color output from a color printer.

✔ Select Output mode — normal is the default setting. Rough will print your document without printing the pictures. Instead, it will print the picture box frame with an "X" through it. Thumbnails will print a miniature representation of your document (8 document pages per printed page).

✔ You may select pages to be output — All Pages, Odd Pages, or Even Pages only.

✔ Selecting Back to Front will print your document starting from the last page through to the first page.

✔ Collate allows you to print collated multiple copies of a document. Normally if you are printing more than one copy of a document (for example, 10) all copies of each page will print at one time.

✔ Selecting Registration Marks will print registration marks in the margin of the document for use when aligning color separations.

✔ Selecting Tiling options (Off, Manual, or Auto) allows you to control the printing of a larger document. For example, if you wish to print a tabloid size document on a laser printer that is limited to letter size paper, select Auto tiling and type in the desired overlap area. After the document has been printed, you may paste it together to obtain a proof of the document.

✔ Color — QuarkXPress allows you to print a color document directly on a color output device such as an inkjet or color laser printer, to make color separations, and to specify which color-separated plates you wish to print.

Color separation operates differently, depending upon whether the colors used in the document have been defined as Process Colors or as Spot Colors (see chapter 11, Managing Colors). If the colors have been designated as Spot Colors, QuarkXPress will print a separate plate for each color (and one for black). If the colors have been designated as Process Colors, XPress will print a plate for each of the four process colors (Cyan, Magenta, Yellow, and Black). If the document uses both types of color definitions, XPress will print the four process color plates *in addition to* a separate plate for each spot color.

✔ Select Print Colors as Grays when you wish to proof a color document on a laser printer. The different colors used in the document will be printed in shades of gray, making them easy to differentiate from the black page elements.

⌘ Q   FILE/QUIT

To close all open documents and exit QuarkXPress, select QUIT from the FILE menu. If you have not saved changes to any open document a dialog box will appear asking if you wish to save those changes before closing. Click OK to save changes and exit XPress. Click CANCEL to cancel quit process and return to the currently active document.

The Edit Menu

EDIT/PREFERENCES

The PREFERENCES commands allow you to change program and/or document defaults for many aspects of QuarkXPress. Defaults are simply preset definitions of certain document parameters. For example, the default ruler measurement unit is the inch; the default setting for automatic page insertion is set to "End of Section." These options, and many others, can be set to accommodate your personal working preferences.

If you invoke a PREFERENCES command and change settings while a document is active (open) those default settings with be saved with the document and will apply *only* to that document.

If you invoke a PREFERENCES command when *no* document is active (you are looking at a blank QuarkXPress desktop), all changes will be saved to the program default. This means that any new documents opened will contain the new default settings.

XPress preferences are divided into three categories: **General, Typographic,** and **Tools.**

⌘Y EDIT/GENERAL
PREFERENCES

Horizontal and Vertical Measure — You may set the default ruler measurement display for both the horizontal and vertical rulers. Possible units of measure include:

Inches — standard ruler-inches divided into eighths.

Inches Decimal — divides inches into tenths.

Picas — picas and points are standard typesetting measurements. A pica is equal to 12 points, and there are 12 picas to the inch. Each mark on the pica ruler is 1/2 pica (6 points).

Points — similar to the pica ruler, except each mark is equal to 12 points.

Millimeters — uses the metric system for ruler display.

Centimeters — uses the metric system for ruler display.

Ciceros — a French typesetting measurement system. Each cicero is equal to approximately 4.552 millimeters.

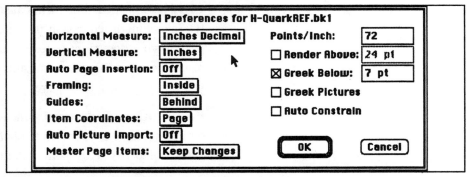

Figure 7.10 The General Preferences Dialog Box.

Auto Page Insertion — This feature allows you to turn the auto page insertion feature off or on, and when on, allows you to control where the pages will be inserted.

On/Off: Auto Page Insertion is normally on. You may turn it off by selecting Off from the pop-up menu.

End of Section: This is the default setting and automatically inserts pages at the end of the currently defined section of the document.

End of Document: Pages will be inserted after the last page of the document.

Framing — Normally, frames for text and graphic boxes are placed inside the perimeters of the box. Select OUTSIDE from the pop-up menu to change this default.

Guides — This option specifies whether the guides appear in *front* of all objects on the page or in *back* of all objects.

Item Coordinates — Normally, when working with a spread or with documents that contain facing pages, the horizontal ruler displays continuous measurement across the pages. If you wish the measurement to repeat from zero across each page, select Page from the pop-up menu.

Auto Picture Import — With this feature turned on, QuarkXPress automatically updates any pictures that have been modified since you last opened your document. The default is normally set to OFF. If you wish to receive a warning before QuarkXPress updates modified pictures, select ON (VERIFY) from the pop-up menu.

Master Page Items — This feature allows you to control how master page items are applied to pages in your document. Selecting KEEP CHANGES (the default) will cause the pages of your document to retain any modified master page items when you apply a new master page to your document page. Selecting DELETE CHANGES will cause those modified master items to be automatically removed when you apply a new master page.

Points/Inch — The normal standard for points per inch is 72 (the default setting). If you wish to change this setting, enter the new value (up to 73) in .01-point increments in this field.

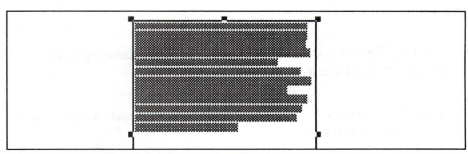

Figure 7.11   Text when it has become "greeked."

Render Above — This feature allows you to control the screen resolution of display fonts while in QuarkXPress. The default value of 24 pts. defines the size above which QuarkXPress will optimize screen font resolution of type 3 fonts (Bitstream, Compugraphic, Casady, The Font Company, and others). It will not optimize Type 1 fonts (Adobe Systems, Inc.).

Greek Below — This feature affects on-screen display, only. When font size falls below a certain point level, screen refresh is optimized by displaying grey bars on screen to indicate areas of text. You may control the point size beneath which you want QuarkXPress to greek the text (see figure 7.11).

Greek Pictures — Selecting this feature will speed screen refresh time and therefore working time. When GREEK PICTURES is selected, imported pictures will be displayed as a grey box on screen. Text runaround is not affected. However, when selected the pictures are displayed.

Auto Constrain — Auto constrain simulates the child-parent effect of earlier QuarkXpress versions. Prior to version 3.0, any items created within other items automatically became "children" of the "parent" items and were constrained by the size and location of the "parent" elements.

When AUTO CONSTRAIN is selected, any element that is created or pasted within another element such as a text box pasted into another text box is automatically constrained and cannot be resized or moved outside the enclosing element. Constrained elements are defined as *constrained groups*. If AUTO CONSTRAIN is unchecked you can move items anywhere on the page.

To unconstrain previously constrained items, select the group, then choose CONSTRAIN/UNCONSTRAIN from the ITEM menu.

✣ ✣ ✣ ✣ ✣ ✣ ✣ ✣ ✣ ✣ ✣ ✣ ✣ ✣ ✣ ✣ ✣ ✣

EDIT/TYPOGRAPHIC
PREFERENCES

See Chapter 9, Managing Text.

✣ ✣ ✣ ✣ ✣ ✣ ✣ ✣ ✣ ✣ ✣ ✣ ✣ ✣ ✣ ✣ ✣ ✣

EDIT/TOOLS
PREFERENCES

See Chapter 8, Creating and Managing Page Elements.

The Page Menu

✣ ✣ ✣ ✣ ✣ ✣ ✣ ✣ ✣ ✣ ✣ ✣ ✣ ✣ ✣ ✣ ✣ ✣

PAGE/INSERT

To add new pages to your document, pull down the PAGE menu and select INSERT. The following dialog box will appear (figure 7.12):

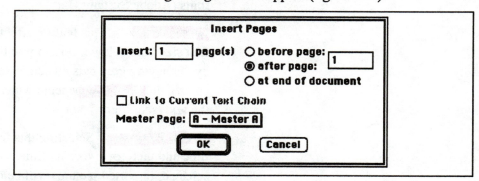

Figure 7.12 The Insert Pages dialog box.

✔ Specify the number of pages to be added in the Insert: field. You may also specify where you wish QuarkXPress to insert the pages — before the current page, after the current page, or at the end of the document — by clicking on the appropriate button. The current page number is shown in the field to the right of the buttons. Type another page number in this field if you want to specify another location for the pages to be inserted.

✔ Selecting the LINK TO CURRENT TEXT CHAIN option will link the automatic text boxes on the new pages with the active text box of the document. Link to Current Text Chain will not be available if the selected master page does not contain an automatic text chain (see Master Page Management) and/or if a text box is not active in the document. To activate a text box, select it with the Content Tool.

✔ The MASTER PAGE pop-up menu allows you to select a master page format from among the master pages currently available in the document. This master page format will be applied to the inserted pages. For more information on how to create and use master pages, see Reference Guide section on Master Page Management.

PAGE/DELETE

The PAGE/DELETE PAGES dialog box (figure 7.13) allows you to specify which page or pages you want to remove from the document. If part of a chain of linked boxes is contained on the deleted pages, text and anchored elements will reflow into the linked text boxes that remain in the document. Elements that are not anchored to the text will be deleted. If, by deleting the specified pages, you delete the entire chain of linked text boxes, the text will also be deleted. Note that you cannot delete all of the pages in a document (you must leave at least one).

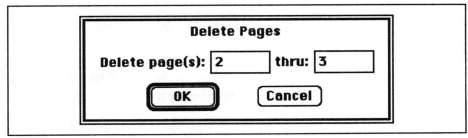

Figure 7.13 The DELETE PAGES dialog box.

PAGE/MOVE

The PAGE/MOVE command lets you rearrange pages in your document. Specify the pages you wish to move and the page number where you wish to insert the moved pages. As with the PAGE/INSERT command, you can specify the page to be moved before the specified page, after the page, or at the end of the document (see figure 7.14).

When pages are moved, QuarkXPress automatically renumbers all document pages to correspond with the new page order. Text boxes remain linked as originally specified.

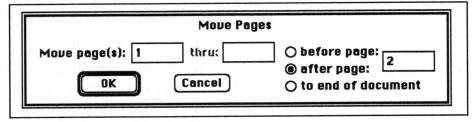

Figure 7.14 The MOVE PAGES dialog box.

PAGE/ MASTER GUIDES

Select the PAGE/MASTER GUIDES command if you want to change the margin and/or column guide positions after the document has been created. The MASTER GUIDES dialog box (see figure 7.15) is similar to the NEW dialog box (figure 7.1).

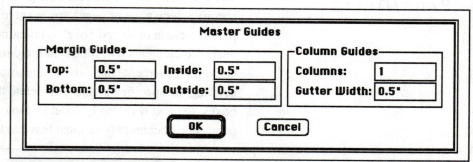

E 10 : Theory

Master Guides

┌─ Margin Guides ──────────────────┐   ┌─ Column Guides ─┐
Top: `0.5"`   Inside: `0.5"`   Columns: `1`
Bottom: `0.5"` Outside: `0.5"`   Gutter Width: `0.5"`

[OK]   (Cancel)

Figure 7.15   The MASTER GUIDES dialog box — only available when a Master Page is displayed.

The PAGE/MASTER GUIDES command is available only if a master page is currently in view on the screen.

Changes made to margin and column guide positions (see instructions for specifying margin and column guides in the FILE/NEW section) apply only to the currently selected master page(s). Automatic text boxes that fit the margin guides will be resized according to the new margin guide specifications. All other page elements will remain the same and may need to be repositioned or resized.

PAGE/SECTION

Through the PAGE/SECTION command, QuarkXPress allows you to divide your document into separately numbered sections.

To create a section within your document, move to the first page of the desired section. (Make sure that the page number appears in the bottom left corner of the screen before continuing.) Select SECTION from the PAGE menu. The dialog box as shown in figure 7.16 will appear.

✔ Select SECTION START.

The PAGE NUMBERING fields allow you to specify the numbering system for the section. If desired, enter a prefix for the section numbers. Enter the starting number for the section in the NUMBER field. This number must be an Arabic numeral such as 1, 2, 3, etc., even if you wish another numbering format, such as Roman numerals, to be applied. The number format is specified by selecting you choice from the FORMAT pop-up menu.

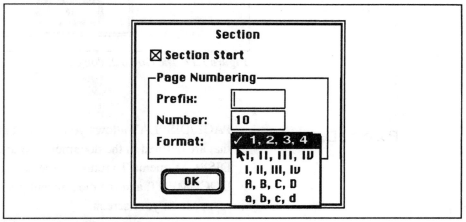

Figure 7.16 *The Section dialog box.*

PAGE/PREVIOUS

This command moves you to the previous page of the document.

PAGE/NEXT

This command moves you to the next page of the document.

PAGE/FIRST

This command moves you to the first page of the document.

PAGE/PAGE/LAST

This command moves you to the last page of the document.

PAGE/GOTO

The GO TO PAGE dialog box (figure 7.17), which allows you to move to a specific page in your document, is accessed by selecting GO TO from the PAGE menu.

✔ To use, simply enter the desired page number and click OK. If the page is part of a section that has been assigned a prefix, the prefix must also be entered because it is an integral part of the page number.

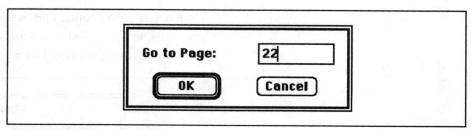

Figure 7.17 The Go To dialog box.

❖❖❖❖❖❖❖❖❖❖❖❖❖❖❖❖❖❖❖❖❖❖

PAGE/DISPLAY

PAGE/DISPLAY allows you to select and view any of the master pages that are defined in the document. Figure 7.18 shows an example of the DISPLAY menu. To return to the document, select PAGE/DISPLAY/ DOCUMENT, and the most recently viewed page of the document will reappear on your screen.

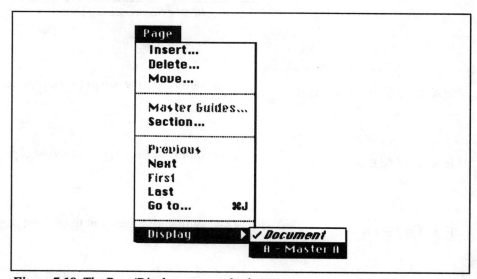

Figure 7.18 The Page/Display menu and submenu.

Screen Management

The View Menu

⌘0 FIT IN WINDOW
50%; 75%;
⌘1 ACTUAL SIZE
200%

These view options allow you to view the document at various percentages. You may also change the viewing percentages by double-clicking on the percentage field in the lower left corner of the document window and changing the percentage value.

VIEW/THUMBNAILS

This command displays a reduced view of the document. In Thumbnails view, you can select, copy, delete, and move (rearrange) document pages. You may also copy pages from one document to another (for more information see pages 216–217). You may not select individual page elements in Thumbnails view.

VIEW/SHOW/HIDE GUIDES

The SHOW GUIDES command will cause XPress to display all non-printing lines (guidelines and box outlines) on a page. When SHOW GUIDES has been selected, the HIDE GUIDES command will be available under the VIEW menu.

The HIDE GUIDES command removes the guideline display from the screen, allowing you to see the document as it will appear when printed. When HIDE GUIDES has been selected, the SHOW GUIDES command will be available under the VIEW menu.

VIEW/SNAP TO GUIDES

The SNAP TO GUIDES command, normally active by default, helps you to align page elements to ruler or page guides. When an element is placed within three points of a guide, the element will automatically snap to the guide. To check whether or not the SNAP TO GUIDES command is activated, pull down the VIEW menu. If the command is active, a checkmark will appear next to it.

To turn off the SNAP TO GUIDES feature, select SNAP TO GUIDES again from the VIEW menu. The checkmark will disappear, indicating that the command is no longer active.

VIEW/SHOW/HIDE RULERS

The SHOW RULERS command displays the QuarkXPress horizontal and vertical rulers according to the measurement units specified in the General Preferences dialog box (see figure 7.10). The SHOW RULERS command is available when the rulers are hidden from view.

The HIDE RULERS command removes the QuarkXPress document rulers from screen view. The HIDE RULERS command is available when the rulers are currently displayed.

VIEW/SHOW/HIDE TOOLS

Normally, when you open or create a QuarkXPress document, the Tool Palette is displayed on the left side of the screen. When the Tool Palette is displayed, the HIDE TOOLS command, which removes the Tool palette from view, will be available under the VIEW menu.

The SHOW TOOLS command will be available if the Tool Palette is hidden.

VIEW/SHOW/HIDE MEASUREMENTS

To display the Measurements Palette, select the SHOW MEASUREMENTS command from the VIEW menu. The SHOW MEASUREMENTS command is available when the Measurements Palette is not currently displayed on screen.

The HIDE MEASUREMENTS command, available when the Measurements Palette is displayed, is used to close or remove the palette from view.

VIEW/SHOW/HIDE DOCUMENT LAYOUT

The SHOW DOCUMENT LAYOUT command is used to display the Document Layout Palette. This command is available when the Document Layout Palette is hidden from view.

The HIDE DOCUMENT LAYOUT command is used to close or remove the Document Layout Palette from screen view.

Creating and Managing Master Pages Using the Document Layout Palette

The Document Layout Palette is used to create, edit, name, rearrange apply and otherwise manipulate master pages. To display the Document Layout Palette, select SHOW DOCUMENT Layout from the VIEW menu. The Document Layout Palette is a floating palette, meaning that its window will always appear on top of the other document windows and may be moved independently of the other windows. The Document Layout Palette will appear initially on the right side of the screen.

CREATING MASTER PAGES

The first master page, Master A, is created automatically from the specifications entered in the New dialog box when a document is created.

To create a new master page:

✔   Click on one of the blank master page icons (see figure 7.19) and drag it to the right, between the existing master page icons and the scroll arrows on the Document Layout Palette. A new, blank master page will be created and will automatically be assigned a letter name (A,B,C, etc.) depending upon the master page placement in relationship to the existing master pages.

Note of Caution: If an existing master page is highlighted (darkened) when you release the mouse button, the existing master page will be replaced by the blank master page.

To copy a master page as a basis for creating a new master page:

✔   Create a new blank master page by following the previous instructions Then, click on the master page you wish to copy and drag its icon onto the blank master page. When the blank master page icon is highlighted, release the mouse button. All of the elements on the source master page will be copied onto the new master page.

NAMING MASTER PAGES

To name a master page, select the master page icon and enter a name from the keyboard. The name will be displayed in the name field (see figure 7.20). The name may contain up to 63 characters.

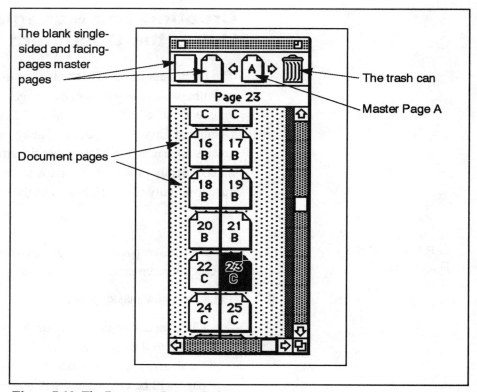

The blank single-sided and facing-pages master pages

The trash can

Master Page A

Document pages

Figure 7.19 The Document Layout Palette.

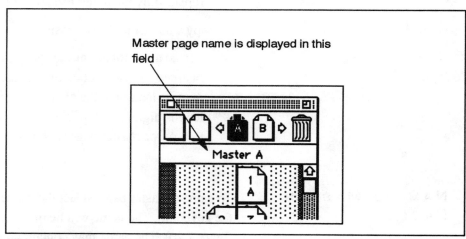

Master page name is displayed in this field

Figure 7.20 Naming a master page.

DELETING MASTER PAGES

To delete a master page, simply drag its icon into the trash can located on the right side of the Document Layout Palette. *Note: You cannot undo a master page deletion. Also, you cannot delete the blank master page icons*

DISPLAYING MASTER PAGES

To display a master page, double-click on the master page icon in the Document Layout Palette, or pull down the Page menu and select Display. Then select the appropriate master page from the Display submenu. The master page will appear on screen.

To return to the document, double-click on a document page on the Document Layout Palette, or pull down the Page menu and select Display. Then select Document from the Display submenu.

EDITING A MASTER PAGE

You may edit (modify) a master page once it is displayed in the document window. Page elements, text, and pictures are placed on the master page just as they would be placed on a document page.

To change the Master Page Guides on a master page, first display the master page. Then select Master Guides from the Page menu (this command cannot be accessed unless a master page is displayed). A dialog box will appear (see figure 7.15) that allows you to change the column guide and margin specifications. The changes you make to a Master Page Guides will apply only to the master page that is currently displayed in the document window.

When a master page is modified, the changes will appear on all pages to which that master page has been applied.

USING MASTER PAGES TO AUTO-NUMBER PAGES

QuarkXPress allows you to automatically number the pages of a document and its sections by placing a text box on the appropriate master page and entering a page number command. To have Quark automatically number the pages of a document:

✔ Display the master page on which you wish the page numbering to apply.

✔ Create a text box and place in its desired position.

✔ Select the text box with the Content Tool and enter the Current Box Page Number Command (⌘3). A <#> will be displayed on the master page, but the current page number will be displayed on the document pages, including any specifications entered in the Section dialog box. (See page 206 for information regarding sectioning a document.)

APPLYING MASTER PAGES

To apply a master page to a document page:

✔ Drag the desired master page icon on top of the document page icon. When the document page is highlighted, release the mouse button and the master page elements will be copied onto the document page (see figure 7.21).

When a master is applied to a document page, QuarkXPress normally deletes unmodified master elements from the document page and places the new master page elements on the document page.

Modified master elements will either be deleted or kept, depending upon the specifications in the General Preferences dialog box for Master Page Items.

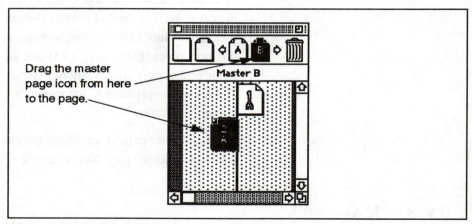

Drag the master page icon from here to the page.

Figure 7.21 Applying a master page to a document page.

Creating and Managing Document Pages using the Document Layout Palette

INSERTING DOCUMENT PAGES

To insert a new page into a document:

✔ Select the master page format you wish to use and drag the master page icon into the document layout area.

If a page icon pointer is displayed, it indicates that the new page will be inserted as a left page ⬜, right page ⬜, or single-sided page ⬜ and will not affect the placement or pagination of the document's existing pages.

If a Force Left pointer ⊢ appears, it indicates that the new page will force existing pages in the spread to the left.

If a Force Right pointer ⊣ appears, it indicates that the new page will force existing pages in the spread to the right.

If a Force Down pointer ⊤ is displayed, it indicates that the new page will force existing pages down to the next page position.

INSERTING MORE THAN ONE PAGE

To insert more than one page at a time:

✔ Hold down the option key when dragging the master page icon into the document layout area. The Insert Pages dialog box will appear.

✔ Specify the number of pages you wish to insert by entering the number in the Insert field. Select where you wish the pages to be inserted, either by clicking on before page or after page and entering a page number, or by clicking at end of document.

✔ If the automatic text box on the page that is before the page to be inserted is active, the Link to Current Text Chain option will be available. Check this box if you wish the automatic text box on the new page to be linked to the previous page.

✔ The name of the Master Page icon you selected in the Document Layout Palette will be displayed in the Master Page pop-up menu. You can choose a different master page from the pop-up menu.

❊❊❊❊❊❊❊❊❊❊❊❊❊❊❊❊❊❊❊❊

Dᴇʟᴇᴛɪɴɢ
DOCUMENT PAGES

To delete one page of a document:

✔ Drag the page icon to the trash at the top of the Document Layout Palette. When the trash can is highlighted, let go of the mouse button and the page will be deleted. *Note: Pages deleted in this manner cannot be UNDONE.*

To delete more than one page at a time:

✔ Hold down the SHIFT key while selecting pages in the document. Then drag the page icons to the trash at the top of the Document Layout Palette in the same manner as the previous step.

❊❊❊❊❊❊❊❊❊❊❊❊❊❊❊❊❊❊❊❊

Rᴇᴀʀʀᴀɴɢɪɴɢ
DOCUMENT PAGES

To move a document page (or pages) from one location to another:

✔ Select the document page and drag to its desired location.

If a Force Left pointer � appears, it indicates that the page will force existing pages in the spread to the left.

If a Force Right pointer ⊣ appears, it indicates that the page will force existing pages in the spread to the right.

If a Force Down pointer ⊤ is displayed, it indicates that the page will force existing pages down to the next page position.

Copying Pages from One Document to Another

You may wish to copy entire pages from one document to another document.

(In QuarkXPress 2.12 or earlier versions, you used the FILE/GET DOCUMENT command to accomplish this task. Again, Quark has made this much easier to do in QuarkXPress 3.0.)

To copy a page from one document to another,

✔ Open the source document and select THUMBNAILS from the VIEW menu. Resize the document window to 1/2 the screen size and move it to one side of the desktop.

✔ Open the target document, change the view to THUMBNAILS, resize the document window and move it to the other side of the desktop (figure 7.22).

✔ Activate the source document by clicking on its window. Select the page to be copied and drag it to its desired position in the target document. If you wish to select more than one page at a time, hold the SHIFT key down while selecting pages. Or, to select noncontiguous pages, hold down the COMMAND key while selecting the pages.

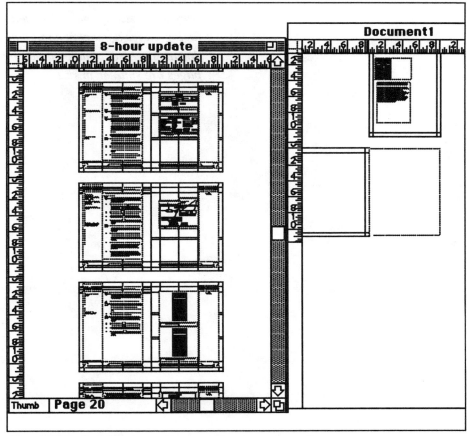

Figure 7.22 Copying a page from one document to another.

When you drag the page(s) to the target document you will see one of several icons.

If a page icon pointer is displayed, it indicates that the copied page(s) will be inserted as a left page ☐, right page ☐, or single-sided page ☐ and will not affect the placement or pagination of the document's existing pages.

If a Force Left pointer ⊢ appears, it indicates that the copied page(s) will force existing pages in the spread to the left.

If a Force Right pointer ⊣ appears, it indicates that the copied page(s) will force existing pages in the spread to the right.

If a Force Down pointer ⟂ is displayed, it indicates that the copied page(s) will force existing pages down to the next page position.

Note: When you copy a page from document to another, you also copy the master page associated with that page. A page from a facing-pages document cannot be copied into a single-sided document. Also, a page cannot be copied into a document whose pages are smaller in size.

Chapter Eight

Creating and Managing Page Elements

Creating Page Elements

Page elements (text and picture boxes and lines) are drawn on the page using element creation tools from the Tool Palette. If the Tool Palette is not displayed on screen, select SHOW TOOLS from the VIEW menu.

BOXES

To create a box (picture or text) select one of the box tools from the Tool Palette. Move the mouse pointer over the document page: the pointer icon will change to a small plus mark $+$.

Press the mouse button, establishing the first corner of the box, and drag the mouse in a diagonal direction. An outline of the box shape will appear on screen. When the outline is the desired size/shape, let go of the mouse button. The Tool will revert to either the Item Tool or the Content Tool, whichever was last used, and the newly created box will be active, as shown by the display of resizing handles (see figure 8.1).

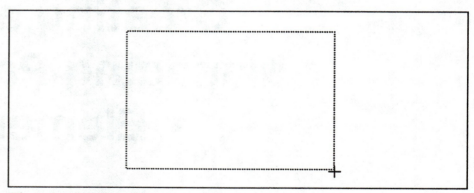

Figure 8.1 Drawing a box.

To create more than one box at a time, without having to reselect the tool, press the Option key while selecting a Box Tool from the Tool Palette.

LINES

To create an Orthogonal (straight horizontal or vertical) line, select the Orthogonal line tool from the Tool Palette, Move the mouse pointer over the document page: the pointer icon will change to a small plus mark $+$. Move the pointer to the desired position for the starting point of the line.

Press the mouse button and drag the mouse in a horizontal or vertical direction. When the line is the right length, let go of the mouse button (figure 8.2). The Tool Palette will revert to either the Item Tool or the Content Tool, whichever was last used, and the newly created line will be active, as shown by the display of handles on both ends of the line.

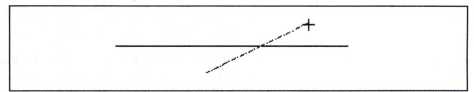

Figure 8.2 An orthogonal line has been drawn, and a diagonal line is being drawn.

To create more than one line at a time, without having to reselect the Line Tool, press the Option key while selecting the Line Tool on the Tool Palette.

To create a diagonal line, select the Line Tool from the Tool Palette. Move the mouse pointer over the document page: the pointer icon will change to a small plus mark ＋ . Move the pointer to the desired position for the starting point of the line.

Press the mouse button and drag the mouse in any direction. When the line is the desired length and angle, let go of the mouse button. The Tool Palette will revert to either the Item Tool or the Content Tool, whichever was last used, and the newly created line will be active, as shown by the display of handles on both ends of the line.

To create more than one line at a time, without having to reselect the Line Tool, press the OPTION key while selecting the Line Tool on the Tool Palette.

POLYGONS

To create a polygon, select the Polygon Tool from the Tool Palette and move the mouse cursor over the document page: the cursor will change to the shape of a small plus mark ＋ . Click to establish the first point of the polygon. Without holding the mouse button down, move the mouse to the desired position of the second point. Click the mouse button to establish the second point. Continue the clicking action for each point you wish the polygon to have (figure 8.3).

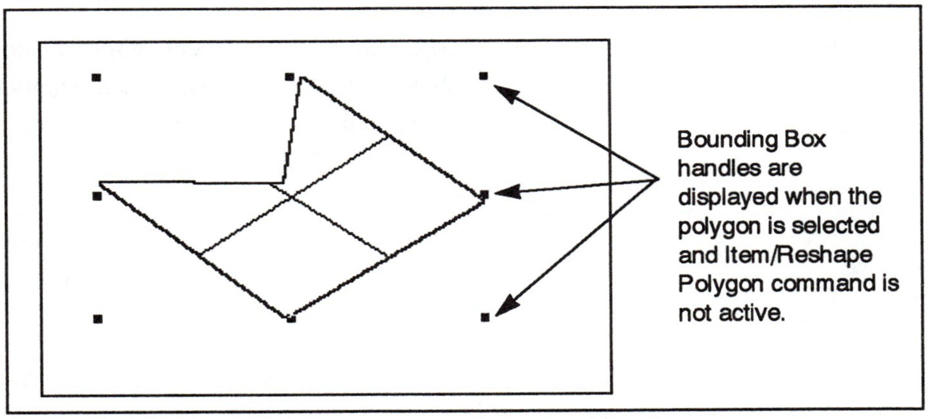

Bounding Box handles are displayed when the polygon is selected and Item/Reshape Polygon command is not active.

Figure 8.3 Click the mouse button to establish each point of the polygon.

To close the polygon, double-click on the last point of the polygon or click once on the first point of the polygon.

To create more than one polygon at a time, without having to reselect the Polygon Tool, press the OPTION key when selecting the tool.

Selecting Page Elements

To select a page element:

✔ Click on the element with either the Item or Content Tool.

When you select an element with the Content Tool, you may then edit the *contents* of that box, or the style of the line. But you may not move, cut, or copy that element. However, you may resize or duplicate the element.

When you select an element with the Item Tool, you may then manipulate the element by resizing, duplicating, copying (including the contents), moving, pasting, and deleting it.

Cutting/Clearing/Deleting Page Elements

To cut a box or line,

✔ Select it with the Item Tool — *the Content Tool will not allow you to cut or delete a page element.* Then pull down the EDIT menu and select CUT. The object will be removed from the page, but a copy of it will be placed on the clipboard.

To Clear/Delete an object, while not storing it on the clipboard, select the object with the Item Tool. Then simply press the Delete (backspace) key on the keyboard.

Resizing Page Elements

B O X E S

To resize a box, first activate the box by clicking on it with either the Item or Content Tool. Move the pointer over one of the handles: the pointer will change to the resizing icon ☞. When the resizing pointer appears, press the mouse button and then drag the handle to its new location.

The corner handles will allow you to drag in a diagonal direction and simultaneously resize the box in both horizontal and vertical directions. The side, bottom, and top handles constrain the resizing direction to a left-right or up-down direction.

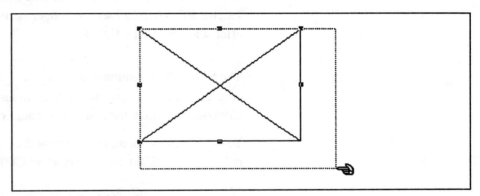

Figure 8.4 Resizing a box.

L I N E S

To resize a line, select it with either the Item or Content Tool. Move the pointer over one of the endpoint handles: the pointer will change to the resizing icon ☞. When the resizing pointer appears, press the mouse button and then drag the handle to its new location. The angle of a diagonal line may be changed at the same time. However, the angle of an orthogonal line may only be changed by rotating.

Using the Menu Commands to Work with Page Elements

The Edit Menu

⌘ Z   Eᴅɪᴛ/ Uɴᴅᴏ/Rᴇᴅᴏ

The EDIT UNDO command allows you to undo the previous action, whether moving, resizing, deleting, or otherwise modifying a page element. EDIT/UNDO is only available *immediately* following the action you wish to Undo. If you perform any other action such as clicking to activate an element on screen, or changing tool selection on the Tool Palette, EDIT/UNDO will no longer be available. EDIT/REDO is accessed after selecting EDIT/UNDO.

⌘ X   Eᴅɪᴛ/Cᴜᴛ

The EDIT/CUT command allows you to cut (remove) a page element from your document. A copy of the element and its contents is placed on the Clipboard and may then be pasted back into a document.

To cut a page element, first activate the element with the Item Tool. Then, pull down the EDIT menu and select CUT.

⌘ C   Eᴅɪᴛ/Cᴏᴘʏ

EDIT/COPY is similar to the EDIT/CUT command, in that a copy of the page element and its contents is placed on the Clipboard. But, when you select the COPY command the original element is not removed from the page.

To copy an element into the Clipboard, activate the element with the Item Tool, pull down the EDIT menu and select COPY.

⌘ V   Eᴅɪᴛ/Pᴀsᴛᴇ

The PASTE command allows you to paste a copy of whatever is on the Clipboard into an active document.

To paste a page element into a document, select the Item Tool, then pull down the EDIT menu and select PASTE. If you do not first select the Item Tool, the page element will not be pasted onto the page.

Eᴅɪᴛ/Cʟᴇᴀʀ

EDIT/CLEAR is used to clear page elements from the document without saving a copy of the element(s) on the Clipboard.

To clear a page element, activate it with the Item Tool, then pull down the EDIT menu and select CLEAR.

To clear more than one element at a time, press the SHIFT key while selecting the desired elements with the Item Tool. Pull down the EDIT menu and select CLEAR. A dialog box will appear warning you that several page elements, once cleared in this manner, cannot be restored through the EDIT/UNDO command. If you are certain you wish to clear these elements from the page, click on OK. Otherwise click CANCEL to return to the document without clearing the elements.

⌘ S   SELECT ALL

The EDIT/SELECT ALL command allows you to quickly select all of the elements on a page. With the Item Tool selected, pull down the EDIT menu and choose SELECT ALL.

PREFERENCES
TOOLS

The dialog box that appears after selecting the TOOLS PREFERENCES command allows you to change default settings for QuarkXPress tools (see figure 8.5). In addition to selecting from the menu, you can access this dialog box by double-clicking on any tool icon on the XPress tool menu.

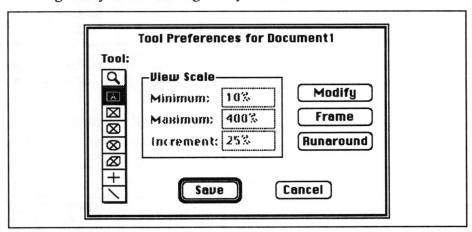

Figure 8.5 The Tool Preferences dialog box with the Text Box tool selected.

View Scale — This section is active when the Zoom Tool is selected in the Tools Preferences dialog box, and allows you to control the minimum and maximum sizes, and incremental steps (by percentage) of page views obtainable through use of the Zoom Tool. The default settings are Minimum of 10%, Maximum of 400%, increments of 25%.

Modify — The MODIFY button is active only when one of the element creation tools, such as the Text Box Tool or the Line Tool, is selected. Clicking the modify button will bring up the specifications dialog box for that tool (figure 8.6) and will allow you to define defaults for such attributes as scaling, background shading/color, etc. (For more information regarding item modification specifications, see the reference section for the ITEM/MODIFY command.)

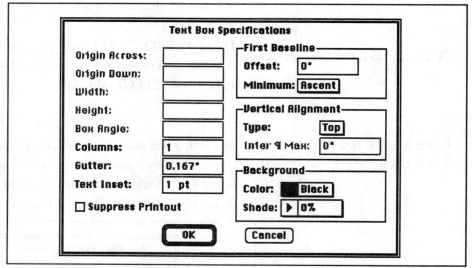

Figure 8.6 *The Text Box Specifications dialog box appears after clicking the Modify button when the Text Box Tool is selected.*

Frame — The FRAME button is active when one of the box tools is selected, and allows you to set defaults for frame type, size, color, and shade (figure 8.7).

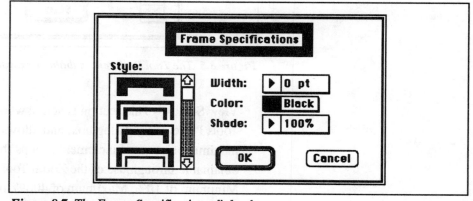

Figure 8.7 *The Frame Specifications dialog box.*

Runaround — RUNAROUND is active when any of the element creation tools are selected, and allows you to set the default runaround for the selected tool. For example, if you wish newly created text boxes to have runaround disabled, set the runaround to None. (See the section on the ITEM/ RUNAROUND command for more information.)

The Item Menu

⌘ M   ITEM/MODIFY

The ITEM/MODIFY command brings a dialog box on screen that allows you to change attributes of the active page elements. The MODIFY command is available when one or more elements are selected with *either* the Item or Content Tool. A different Item Specification dialog box will be displayed for each type of page element as follows: Text Box Specifications, Picture Box Specification, Line Specifications, or Group Specifications.

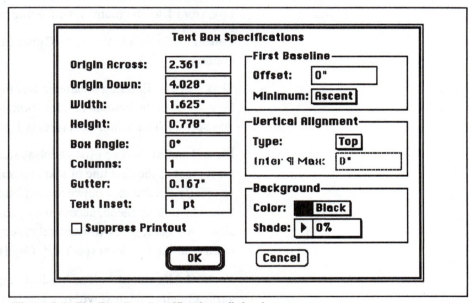

Figure 8.8 The Text Box Specifications dialog box.

Text Box Specifications (figure 8.8):

Origin Across — This field displays the current position of the box origin (the upper left corner of the text box) in relationship to the zero point on the horizontal ruler at the top of the page. To change the horizontal position of the origin point, select this field and enter a new value.

Origin Down— This field displays the current position of the box origin (the upper left corner of the text box) in relationship to the zero point on the vertical ruler displayed on the left side of the page. To change the vertical position of the origin point, select this field and enter a new value.

Width — The Width field displays the current width of the text box and may be modified by entering a new width value into the field.

Height — The Height field displays the current height of the text box and may be modified by entering a new width value into the field.

Box Angle — Entering a value in this field will allow you to rotate an active text box around its center. You may rotate a text box in increments of .001°, from -360° to 360°. Rotating a text box will also rotate the contents of the box, but will not affect the contents' editability and will not change the other text box attributes.

Columns — This field allows you to specify columns for the active text box, from 1 to 30 columns, with a minimum column width of 10 points.

Gutter — Enter a value in the Gutter field to specify the width between columns.

Text Inset — Entering a value in this field allows you to cause the text to be inset from the borders of a text box by the amount of the measurement you specify. The default text inset is 1 pt.

First Baseline — The First Baseline fields allow you to control the placement of the first line of text in a text box. The offset field allows you to specify the distance between the first baseline and the top of the text box. The pop-up menu, accessed by pressing on the Minimum drop-shadowed field, gives you several choices for placing the first baseline, relative to the text inset specified: Cap Height, Cap+Accent, and Ascent.

Vertical Alignment — The Vertical Alignment pop-up menu allows you to vertically align the text within a text box. You can justify, center, align the text to the bottom, or align it to the top of the text box. Top is the default alignment.

When Justify is selected, Quark adds equal space between the lines of text, automatically overriding the leading that was specified for the paragraphs. You can control the maximum amount of space that Quark will add between paragraphs by entering a value in the Inter Max ¶ field.

Background — The Background fields allow you to select a color and shade (or tint) to fill the background of a text box. Select the color from the pop-up color menu. Selecting None will make the text box transparent (see through). A Shade value may either be selected from the pop-up menu or may be entered directly into the field from the keyboard in increments as small as .1%.

Suppress Printout — Clicking to select Suppress Printout will prevent the box contents, background, and frame from printing.

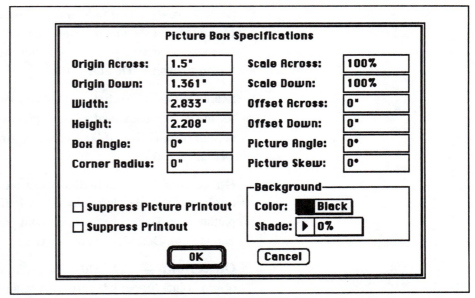

Figure 8.9 The PICTURE BOX SPECIFICATIONS dialog box.

Origin Across — This field displays the current position of the box origin (the upper left corner of the text box) in relationship to the zero point on the horizontal ruler at the top of the page. To change the horizontal position of the origin box's point, enter a new value into the field.

Origin Down — This field reports the current position of the box origin (the upper left corner of the text box) in relationship to the zero point on the vertical ruler displayed on the left side of the page. To change the vertical position of the origin box's point, enter a new value into the field.

Width — The Width field displays the current width of the picture box and may be modified by entering a new width value into the field.

Height — The Height field displays the current height of the picture box and can be modified by entering a new width value into the field.

Box Angle — Entering a value in this field will allow you to rotate an active picture box around its center. You may rotate a picture box in increments of .001°, from -360° to 360°. Default is 0°.

Corner Radius — The Corner Radius field is available when a rectangle or rounded-rectangle picture box is active, and is used to change the radius of the circles that make up the corners of a rectangle. The corner radius may be specified from 0 to 72 pts (2") in any measurement system, in increments of .001 points or equivalent. Default is .25".

Scale Across — This field is used to specify a horizontal scaling percentage for the picture contained within a picture box. You may horizontally scale a picture in increments of .1% from 10% to 1000% of the original size. Default is 100%.

Scale Down — This field is used to specify a vertical scaling percentage for the picture contained within a picture box. You may vertically scale a picture from 10% to 1000% of the original size in increments of .1%. Default is 100%.

Offset Across — This field displays the horizontal position of the picture's origin points (upper left corner) in relationship to the left edge of the picture box. To change the horizontal position of the picture, enter a value in this field. Default is no offset (0°).

Offset Down — This field displays the vertical position of the picture's origin points (upper left corner) in relationship to the top edge of the picture box. To change the vertical position of the picture, enter a value in this field. Default is no offset (0°).

Picture Angle — Using this field, you may specify a rotation angle for a picture within a picture box (without rotating the box itself). A picture can be rotated in increments of .001° from 360° to -360°. Default is 0°.

Picture Skew — Picture Skew allows you to specify a slant angle for a picture within a picture box. A picture can be skewed in increments of .001°, from -75° to 75°. Default is 0°.

Background — The Background fields allow you to select a color and shade (or tint) to fill the background of a picture box. Select the color from the pop-up color menu. Selecting None will make the box transparent (see through). A Shade value may either be selected from the pop-up menu or may be entered directly into the field from the keyboard in increments as small as .1%. Default is black at 0%.

Suppress Picture Printout — Clicking to select Suppress Picture Printout will prevent the picture from printing, but will allow the background and frame (if any) to print.

Suppress Printout — Clicking to select Suppress Printout prevents the picture, background, and frame of a picture box from printing.

Style — The Style pop-up menu allows you to change the style of the active line.

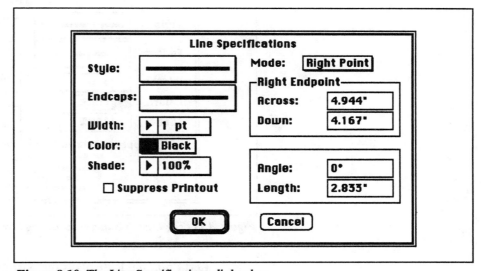

Figure 8.10 The Line Specifications dialog box.

Endcaps — The Endcaps pop-up menu allows you to select an endcap from several options.

Width — The width field displays the current line width and allows you to specify another width by selecting from the pop-up menu or by entering a line width directly into the field from the keyboard. Line widths may be specified in increments as small as .001 unit of any measurement system you choose.

Color — The Color pop-up menu allows you to select a color and shade (or tint) of a line. A Shade value may either be selected from the pop-up menu or entered directly into the field from the keyboard in increments as small as .1%.

Suppress Printout — Clicking to select Suppress Printout prevents the active line from printing.

Mode — The Mode options allow you to specify how you want QuarkXPress to display and describe the measurement attributes of a line, and the fields that are displayed below this pop-up menu are determined by the mode you specify.

Endpoints mode displays the position of both endpoints of a line (see figure 8.11) in relationship to the horizontal and vertical rulers.

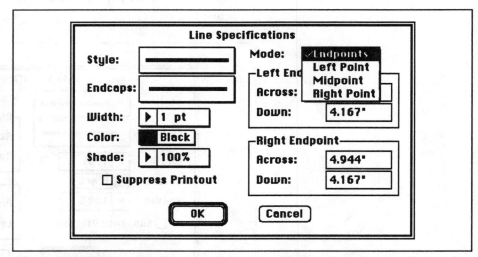

Figure 8.11 The Line Specifications dialog box with Mode Pop-up menu displayed.

Left Point mode displays the position of the left endpoint, the length, and angle of a line.

Midpoint mode displays the position of the center of the line, its length and angle.

Right Point mode displays the position of the right endpoint, the length and angle of a line.

Group Specifications: (Note: Item/Modify is not available for groups that contain other groups).

Text Boxes —The Text Box specifications dialog box for a group containing only text boxes is essentially the same as for ungrouped boxes, except that Width and Height specifications are not available. All other controls are available and any modifications made, such as vertical alignment, will affect all of the boxes within the group.

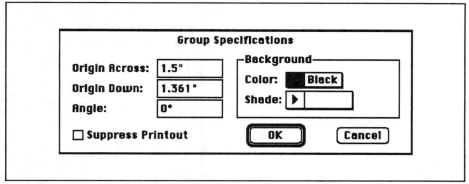

Figure 8.12 *The Group Specifications dialog box appears when a group consists of mixed element types.*

Picture Boxes — The Picture Box specifications dialog box for a group containing only picture boxes is essentially the same as for ungrouped boxes, except that Width and Height specifications are not available. All other controls are available and any modifications made to the specifications will affect all of the boxes within the group.

Lines — The Line specifications dialog box for a group containing only lines is the same as for ungrouped boxes. All controls are available and any modifications made will affect all of the lines within the group.

Mixed Groups — The Group Specifications dialog box will appear for a groups consisting of mixed element types — boxes and lines, for example. You may change origin across, origin down, rotation angle (rotating around the center of the groups bounding box), background color and shade, and specify whether or not you wish to suppress printing the group.

Anchored Element Specifications:

Choosing ITEM/MODIFY when an anchored box is active displays the Anchored Element specification dialog box. A box is anchored to text when it has been pasted into the text box as a text character (see page 248 for how-to instructions on anchoring elements). You may modify specifications for anchored elements, as well as regular and grouped page elements. Note that anchored lines, called rules, are handles as part of the text paragraph formatting and are therefore not manipulated as separate elements and are not accessed through the Item/Modify command.

Text Boxes — The Anchored Text Box specifications dialog box (figure 8.13) gives you the following new or different options:

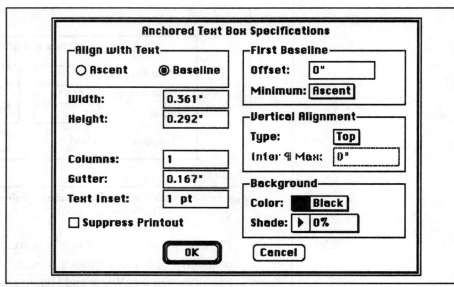

Figure 8.13 The Anchored Text Box Specifications dialog box.

Align with Text: Instead of the Origin Across and Down fields, you can specify whether you want to align the text box to the top of the text's ascenders or to the bottom of the baseline by clicking on the button next to the desired choice.

In addition, the following controls are available for anchored text boxes (see option descriptions under Text Box Specifications): Width/Height, Columns, Gutter, Text Inset, First Baseline, Vertical Alignment, Background, and Suppress Printout.

Picture Boxes —The Anchored Picture Box specifications dialog box (figure 8.14) gives you the following new or different options:

Align with Text: Instead of the Origin Across and Down fields, you can specify whether you want to align the picture box to the top of the text's ascenders or to the bottom of the baseline by clicking on the button next to the desired choice.

In addition, the following controls are available for anchored picture boxes (see option descriptions under Picture Box Specifications): Width/Height, Scale Across/Down, Offset Across/Down, Picture Angle, Picture Skew, Background, Suppress Picture Printout, and Suppress Printout.

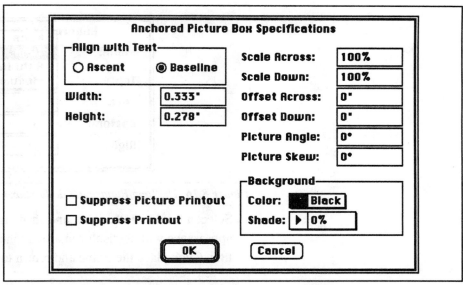

Figure 8.14 *The Anchored Picture Box Specifications dialog box.*

⌘ B   F R A M E

Frames (decorative borders) may be placed around boxes through the ITEM/FRAME command.

To place a frame around a box:

Activate the box with either the Item or Content Tool. Select ITEM/ FRAME and the Frame Specifications dialog box will appear (figure 8.15).

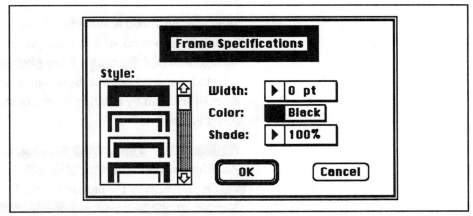

Figure 8.15 *Placing a printable frame around a text or picture box.*

Select a frame style from the scrolling selection window. *Bitmapped frames, created with Quark's Frame Editor program are available only for rectangular boxes.*

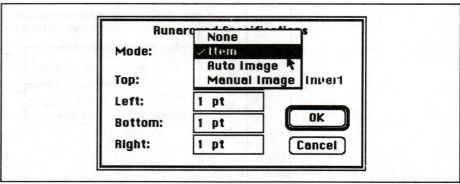

Figure 8.16 The Item/Runaround dialog box with Item selected.

Select a frame width, color, and shade from the pop-up menus. The frame's appearance will be displayed around the frame specifications dialog box title. Click place the frame and return to the document.

⌘T   ITEM/
               RUNAROUND

The ITEM/RUNAROUND command allows you to specify how you want text to wrap around page elements, and is available when any page element is selected. QuarkXPress offers the following runaround modes, which may be selected from the Mode pop-up menu:

None — This mode is available for all page elements and is the default setting for newly created lines. When None is selected, the text will flow behind the element.

Item — This mode is available for all page elements and is the default setting for newly created text and picture boxes. Selecting Item will cause the text to wrap around the outside borders of the box or line. When Item is selected, you may control the distance from the top, left, bottom, and right sides of the item by entering values in the respective fields. The default text offset is 0 pt.

Auto Image — This mode is available only for picture boxes. Selecting Auto Image causes the text to flow around the outlines of the actual picture, rather than the picture frame. When Auto Image is selected, you may change the uniform distance that text stays from the image by entering a value in the text outset field.

Manual Image — Manual Image, also available only for picture boxes, causes a runaround polygon to appear around a picture. A runaround polygon is a dotted-line polygon with handles that allow you to manually control text runaround an image.

Lines and handles may be moved by dragging to new locations with the mouse. To keep the text from reflowing every time you modify the polygon, and therefore increase time efficiency, hold down the space bar while dragging the points or lines to their new locations. When you let go of the space bar, the text will reflow to the new shape of the polygon.

Handles may be added to the polygon by pressing the Command key and then clicking on the dotted line of the polygon.

Handles may be deleted by pressing the Command key and clicking on an existing handle.

Invert — The Invert option is only available when Manual Image has been selected as the runaround mode for a picture box. Invert allows you to flow text inside a graphic image instead of around the outside of the image.

To flow text within a runaround polygon, first make sure that the picture box is layered on *top* of the text box. The picture box should be the same size (or larger) than the text box. Select Manual Image from the Mode pop-up menu, Then click Invert to activate it. Click OK to return to the document. Select the picture with the Content Tool and delete or cut the picture from the box. The runaround polygon will remain in the picture box and the text will flow inside the box.

To delete a runaround polygon, hold down the Shift and Command keys, and click on the polygon.

⌘ D   ITEM/DUPLICATE

The ITEM/DUPLICATE command automatically makes one copy of an active element and positions it according to the offsets specified in the Step and Repeat dialog box. The default setting is .25" horizontal and vertical offsets.

To duplicate an item, including its contents, select it with either the Item or Content Tool, pull down the ITEM menu and select DUPLICATE. You may duplicate individual grouped elements if they are first selected with the Content Tool. You may not duplicate text boxes that are linked to other text boxes.

ITEM/
STEP AND REPEAT

The STEP AND REPEAT command allows you to specify how many copies you want of the page element and also the offset positions of these copies.

To duplicate and element, including its contents, with the STEP AND

REPEAT command, first activate the element(s), pull down the ITEM menu and select STEP AND REPEAT. The Step and Repeat dialog box (figure 8.17) will appear. Enter the desired number of copies in the Repeat Count field, and the Horizontal and Vertical offset positions in the respective fields.

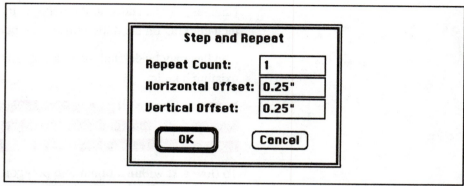

Figure 8.17 The Step and Repeat dialog box.

Positive horizontal values will place the copies to the right of the original, and negative horizontal values will place the copies to the left. Positive vertical values will place the copies below the original and negative vertical offset values will place the copies above the original.

You may Step and Repeat individual grouped elements if they are first selected with the Content Tool. You may not Step and Repeat text boxes that are linked to other text boxes.

⌘ G   GROUP
⌘ U   UNGROUP

Page elements may be grouped with the EDIT/GROUP command in order to manipulate them as a unit. To select and group several elements, press the SHIFT key and then click on the individual elements with the Item Tool. When the desired elements are selected, pull down the ITEM menu and select GROUP (⌘G). A dashed line will appear surrounding the group perimeter.

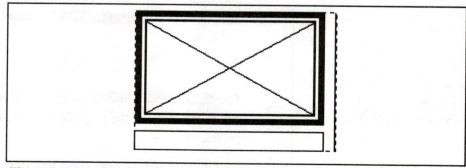

Figure 8.18 Appearance of grouped objects when selected with Item Tool.

Working with Grouped Elements

To select and activate a group, click on any element of the group with the Item Tool.

Moving, cutting, copying, and pasting a group is handled in the same manner as working with individual elements. However, when cutting or deleting a group, a dialog box will appear warning you that you may not Undo the deletion using the EDIT/UNDO command. If you use the EDIT/CUT command, a copy of the group will be placed on the Clipboard and may then be pasted back into the document. If you use the DELETE or CLEAR commands, you will not be able to retrieve the group again.

To ungroup the elements, activate the group with the Item Tool, then pull down the ITEM menu and select UNGROUP or press ⌘U.

MODIFYING GROUPED ELEMENTS

Grouped elements may be modified and their contents edited.

To resize a grouped element, activate it with the Content Tool and then resize as usual (see resizing an element).

To move an element, activate it with the Content Tool. Then, press the Command key — the pointer will temporarily transform to the Item Tool — then, drag the element to its new position. It will remain a part of the group.

To delete an element from a group, activate the element with the Content Tool and then press ⌘K. You cannot UNDO a deletion from a group.

To cut, copy, or paste elements using the EDIT menu commands, you must first ungroup the elements.

To duplicate a grouped element, activate it with the Content Tool and then select duplicate or STEP AND REPEAT from the ITEM menu.

EDIT/CONSTRAIN/ UNCONSTRAIN

The EDIT/CONSTRAIN command causes grouped elements to be constrained to the inner confines of their constraining box. Constrained elements cannot be moved outside the constraining box or resized beyond the boundaries of the constraining box. A constraining box is a text or picture box, placed behind the grouped elements and must be large enough to contain the group (see figure 8.19).

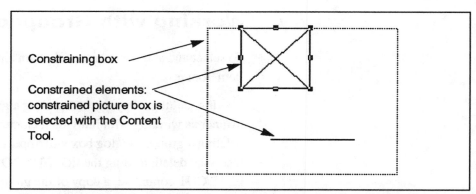

Constraining box

Constrained elements:
constrained picture box is
selected with the Content
Tool.

Figure 8.19 A picture box and line constrained within a larger text box.

The EDIT/CONSTRAIN command is only available if a constraining box
is placed behind the group.

Individual elements within a constrained group are edited and manipulated
in the same manner as grouped items.

The UNCONSTRAIN command is available when a constrained group is
selected with the Item Tool. UNCONSTRAIN releases the constrained
group from the constraining box. The group remains grouped.

⌘ L   I T E M /
L O C K / U N L O C K

Selecting EDIT/LOCK "locks" the active element in place so that you
cannot delete, resize, or move the elements with the mouse. You may,
however, move and resize locked elements using the Measurements Palette
or ITEM/MODIFY specifications. EDIT/LOCK is a good way to protect
your page layout from being accidentally altered.

When an element is locked, a 🔒 icon will appear over the box when
selected with the Item Tool, or over the handles when selected with the
Content Tool.

The contents of a locked text box may be edited as usual. The contents of a
locked picture box may be edited/scaled through the menu commands or
through the Measurements Palette. A locked picture may not be
repositioned within its box using the mouse.

EDIT/UNLOCK is available when locked elements are selected.

ITEM/SEND TO BACK/BRING TO FRONT

In QuarkXPress all page elements are created in layers, with the most recently created or pasted element in front.

ITEM/SEND TO BACK is used to send an active element behind all of the other elements on the page. SEND TO BACK is available when the active element is in front of another element on the page.

ITEM/BRING TO FRONT is used to bring an active element in front of all the other elements on the page. BRING TO FRONT is available when the active element is in back of another element on the page.

ITEM/SPACE/ALIGN

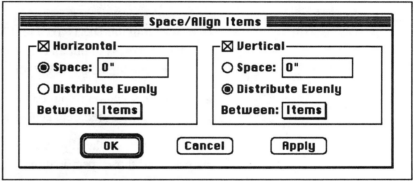

Figure 8.20 *The SPACE/ALIGN dialog box with horizontal and vertical specifications selected.*

The ITEM/SPACE/ALIGN command allows you to align page elements vertically and horizontally and to specify distances between elements.

When spacing items horizontally, Quark uses the left edge of the leftmost active element as the alignment "anchor point." All active items will be spaced relative to that element, which does not move. When spacing items vertically, Quark uses the top edge of the uppermost active element as the alignment "anchor point." All active items will be spaced relative to that element, which does not move.

Select the elements with the Item Tool, then pull down the ITEM menu and choose SPACE/ALIGN. The Space/Align Items dialog box will appear (figure 8.20). Click the Horizontal option. If you wish the elements to be aligned, without space, leave the space setting on the default of zero. Otherwise, you may enter a value in the Space field in increments of .001 measurement unit, from 0" to 10". Or, you may enter a percentage of their current spacing value relative to each other.

✔ Selecting the DISTRIBUTE EVENLY option will cause QuarkXpress to put an equal amount of horizontal space between selected elements and will dim the SPACE field.

✔ The Between pop-up menu allows you to choose whether the space will be measured between items, left edges, centers, or right edges.

Select the elements with the Item Tool, then pull down the ITEM menu and choose SPACE/ALIGN. The Space/Align Items dialog box will appear. Click the VERTICAL option. If you wish the elements to be aligned without space between them, leave the space setting on the default of zero. Otherwise, you may enter a value in the SPACE field in increments of .001 measurement unit, from 0" to 10". Or, you may enter a selected elements and will dim the SPACE field. percentage of their current spacing value relative to each other.

✔ Selecting the DISTRIBUTE EVENLY option will cause QuarkXpress to put an equal amount of vertical space between selected elements and will dim the SPACE field.

✔ The Between pop-up menu allows you to choose whether the space will be measured between items, left edges, centers, or right edges.

After you have set the alignment specifications click APPLY to preview the results of those specifications. Clicking OK will accept the specifications and return you to the document. Clicking CANCEL will cancel the alignment command and return you to the document page.

ITEM/PICTURE BOX SHAPE

The ITEM/PICTURE BOX SHAPE command is available when a picture box is selected with either the Item or Content Tool. You may change the shape of a picture box to any other picture box shape whenever you wish.

To change the shape of a picture box, activate the box, pull down the ITEM menu, select PICTURE BOX SHAPE, and choose the desired shape from the SHAPE submenu (figure 8.21). The following shapes are available: rectangle, rounded-rectangle, inverted rounded-rectangle, oval, and polygon.

ITEM/RESHAPE POLYGON

The RESHAPE POLYGON command is available when a polygon picture box is active. Selecting RESHAPE POLYGON allows you to change the position of individual line segments or handles of a polygon, and also to add or delete handles and segments.

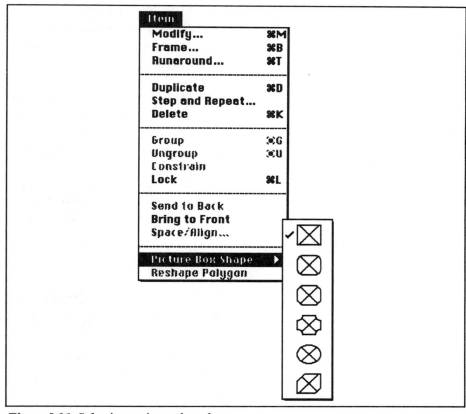

Figure 8.21 *Selecting a picture box shape.*

When you select RESHAPE POLYGON for an active polygon, the polygon's bounding box will be replaced by handles that are placed at the vertices of the polygon (see figure 8.22). To reposition a line segment or handle, move the mouse pointed to the segment or handle. When you see the resizing pointer appear ✋ , press the mouse button down and drag the segment/handle to its new location.

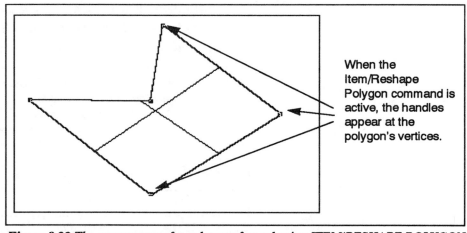

When the Item/Reshape Polygon command is active, the handles appear at the polygon's vertices.

Figure 8.22 *The appearance of a polygon after selecting ITEM/RESHAPE POLYGON.*

To add handles to a polygon, press the COMMAND key and move the mouse pointer over a line segment. When the ☐ pointer appears, click the mouse button once. A new handle will appear and may then be repositioned.

To delete handles from a polygon, press the COMMAND key and move the mouse pointer over an existing handle. When the delete handles ⊠ pointer appears, click the mouse button once. The handle will be deleted and one new segment will replace the two segments on either side of the deleted handle.

To turn off RESHAPE POLYGON and display a polygon's bounding box, select RESHAPE POLYGON from the ITEM menu again.

Using the Measurements Palette for Managing Page Elements

The Measurements Palette displays different fields and options depending upon the type of element that is currently active.

The fields in the Measurements Palette may be accessed by clicking the mouse pointer over the desire field. Double-clicking on a field will select and highlight current information displayed in the field. You may move from field to field in the Measurements Palette by using the TAB key. To accept a value and return to the document, click on the document window or press either of the RETURN or ENTER keys.

TEXT BOXES

The following fields (figure 8.23), similar to the fields in the Text Box Specifications dialog box, are available on the Measurements Palette when a text box is selected with the Item Tool. The other fields on the Measurements Palette are used to edit text and are covered in the Using Text section.

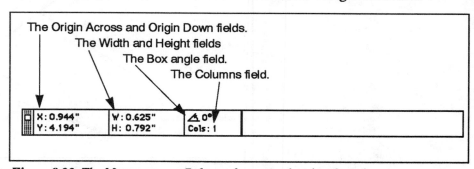

Figure 8.23 The Measurements Palette when a text box is selected.

Origin Across — The X-coordinate displayed on the Measurements Palette is the same as the Origin Across field in the Text Box Specifications dialog box. You may change the Origin across by double-clicking on the X-coordinate field and typing in a new value.

Origin Down — The Y-coordinate displayed on the Measurements Palette is the same as the Origin Down field in the Text Box Specifications dialog box. You may change the Origin Down by double-clicking on the Y-coordinate field and typing in a new value.

Width — To change the width of a text box double-click or tab to the Width field and enter a new value. Press Enter or Return to accept changes and return to the document.

Height — To change the height of a text box double-click or tab to the Height field and enter a new value. Press Enter or Return to accept changes and return to the document.

Box Angle — To change the angle of rotation applied to a text box double-click or tab to the rotation field and enter a new value, from -360° to 360° in .001° increments.

Columns — To change the number of columns defined within a text box, double-click or tab to the columns field and enter the number of columns you wish the text box to have.

PICTURE BOXES

The following fields, similar to the fields in the Picture Box Specifications dialog box, are available on the Measurements Palette when a picture box is active. The other fields on the Measurements Palette are used to edit/modify pictures and are covered in the Using Pictures section.

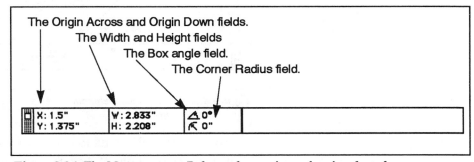

Figure 8.24 The Measurements Palette when a picture box is selected.

Origin Across — The X-coordinate displayed on the Measurements Palette is the same as the Origin Across field in the Picture Box Specifications dialog box. You may change the Origin Across by double-clicking on the X-coordinate field and typing in a new value.

Origin Down — The Y-coordinate displayed on the Measurements Palette is the same as the Origin Down field in the Picture Box Specifications dialog box. You may change the Origin Down by double-clicking on the Y-coordinate field and typing in a new value.

Width — To change the width of a picture box double-click or tab to the Width field and enter a new value. Press Enter or Return to accept changes and return to the document.

Height — To change the height of a picture box double-click or tab to the Height field and enter a new value. Press Enter or Return to accept changes and return to the document.

Box Angle — To change the angle of rotation applied to a picture box double-click or tab to the Rotation field and enter a new value, from -360° to 360° in .001° increments.

Corner Radius — To change the corner radius of a picture box, double-click or tab to the Corner Radius field and enter a new value/measurement in the field. Press Enter or Return to accept changes and return to the document.

LINES

The following fields, similar to the fields in the Line Specifications dialog box, are available on the Measurements Palette for when a line is active. In addition, the coordinates display is different, depending upon which line display mode is selected.

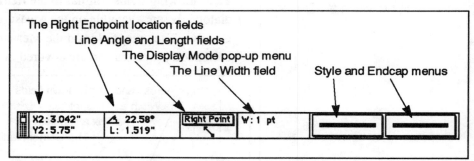

Figure 8.25   *The Measurements Palette — a line is selected, in Right Point display mode.*

Endpoints — When Endpoints is selected, the Measurements Palette will display the positions of the left endpoint (X1 and Y1), the positions of the right endpoint (X2 and Y2), and the line width. In addition, two pop-up menus allow you to choose from among the different line Style and Endcaps available.

Left Point — When Left Point is selected, the Measurements Palette will display the position of the left endpoint (X1 and Y1), the length of the line, the line angle from the left endpoint, and the width of the line. In addition, two pop-up menus allow you to choose from among the different line Style and Endcaps available.

Midpoint — When Midpoint is selected, the Measurements Palette will display the position of the line's center (XC and YC), the length of the line, the line angle, and the width of the line. In addition, two pop-up menus allow you to choose from among the different line Style and Endcaps available.

Right Point — When Right Point is selected, the Measurements Palette will display the position of the right endpoint (X2 and Y2), the length of the line, the line angle from the right endpoint, and the width of the line. In addition, two pop-up menus allow you to choose from among the different line Style and Endcaps available.

ANCHORED TEXT/PICTURE BOXES

The Measurements Palette for anchored text boxes (figure 8.26) displays the alignment with text icons. Clicking on the ▦ icon selects Align with Baseline, and clicking on the ▦ icon selects the Align with Ascent option. In addition, the Width, Height, and Column fields are also available.

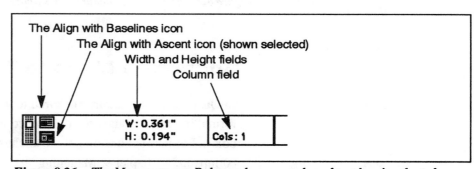

Figure 8.26   The Measurements Palette when an anchored text box is selected.

GROUPED ELEMENTS

The Measurements Palette for grouped elements displays only the following modification options: Origin Across, Origin Down, and Rotation Angle of group. (See ITEM/MODIFY for grouped elements for more detailed description of these fields.)

Anchoring Picture and Text Boxes to Text

To anchor a text or picture box within a text box, so that the anchored element flows with the text when text reformats, select the element with the Item Tool.

✔ EDIT/CUT the element into the clipboard.

✔ Select the Content Tool and place the text cursor in the position where you wish the anchored box to appear.

✔ Select EDIT/PASTE. The box will be pasted into the text box and may then be selected and manipulated as if it were a text character (see figure 8.27). Normally, the bottom of the anchored box will align with the baseline of text. If you wish the top of the box to align with the top of the text ascenders, click on the Ascent icon on the Measurements Palette or select Ascent text alignment in the ANCHORED TEXT BOX SPECIFICATIONS dialog box, accessed through the ITEM/MODIFY command.

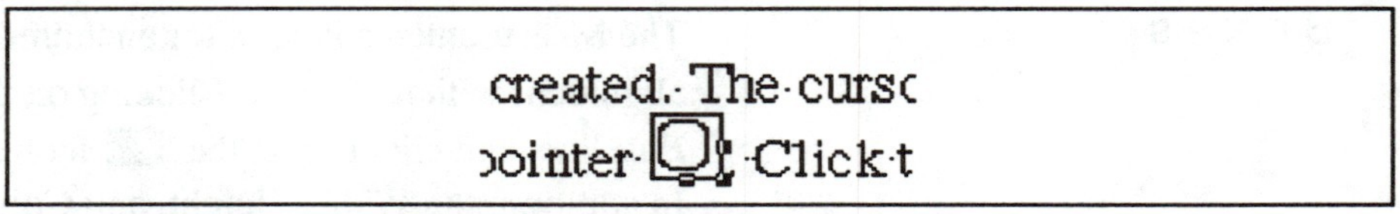

created. The curso
pointer [Q] Click t

Figure 8.27 An anchored picture box's appearance when selected.

Anchoring Lines to Text

In QuarkXPress, lines are anchored to text as part of the paragraph formatting process and are not handled in the same manner as text picture boxes. For instructions on how to anchor rules to text, see the Style/Rules command in Chapter 9, Managing Text.

Copying Page Elements From One Document to Another

You may occasionally find it necessary or convenient to copy elements from one document to another. Fortunately, XPress's interface has made this task easy, because the material can be dragged from one open document to the other.

✔ To copy an element from one document to another, open the *source document* and change the screen view/size so that you can view the elements to be copied. Resize the window to 1/2 the screen size and move it to one side of the desktop.

✔ Open the *target document*, change the screen view/size, move to the destination page, resize the window and move it to the other 1/2 of the screen (see figure 8.28).

✔ Select the element with the Item Tool and quickly drag the item from the source document onto the target document. (If you drag the element too slowly, you will simply move its position within the source document and the window will scroll.) An outline of the element will appear, as shown in figure 8.28. Release the mouse button after you have placed the copied item in the desired position.

You can also cut and paste elements from one document to another using the EDIT/CUT and EDIT/PASTE commands.

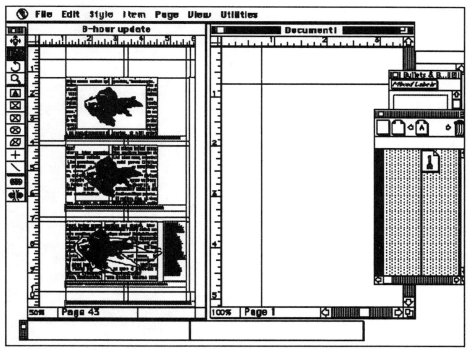

Figure 8.28 Two document windows displayed on screen.

Chapter Nine

Managing Text

Introduction to Working with Text

In QuarkXPress a text area must be defined before placing text in the document. To define an area of text, a text box is drawn using the Text Box Tool from the Tool Palette. For more detailed information about creating and working with text boxes, see the section titled Creating and Managing Page Elements. Once a text box has been created, text may be placed into the text box through several means: entering text directly from the keyboard, pasting text from the Clipboard, or importing text from a word processor file stored on disk.

Entering Text

To enter text directly into a QuarkXPress text box, select the box with the Content Tool. A blinking cursor will appear in the upper left corner of the box. Text may then be entered directly from the keyboard.

Selecting Text

To select a character or any amount of text, place the mouse cursor in front of the text, press and drag the mouse to the end of the desired text selection. This action highlights the text in order to show that it is selected.

✔ To quickly select a word, double-click anywhere on the word.

✔ To quickly select a line of text, triple-click anywhere on the line.

✔ To quickly select a paragraph of text, quadruple-click anywhere in the paragraph.

✔ To select all of the text in a text box or a linked set of boxes, either choose SELECT ALL from the EDIT menu, type or quickly click the mouse button five times anywhere within the text box.

Menu Commands for Working with Text

The File Menu

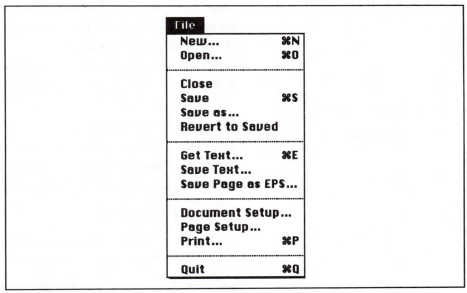

Figure 9.1 *The FILE menu when a text box is selected with the Content Tool.*

⌘ E   FILE/GET TEXT

The GET TEXT command, under the FILE menu (figure 9.1), allows you to retrieve text from a word processor or ASCII text file and flow that text into QuarkXPress text boxes. GET TEXT is available only when a text box has been made active by selecting it with the Content Tool.

To import text into a QuarkXPress Document:

✔ With the Content Tool, select the text box into which you want to "pour" the text.

✔ Pull down the FILE menu and select GET TEXT. A directory dialog box, similar to the OPEN dialog box, will appear. Using the Drive button and Directory Title bar, move to the desired location until the file is listed in the dialog box.

✔ Select the desired file and click the OPEN button. The text will automatically flow into the text box and reformat according to the specifications you have defined for the text box(es) in your QuarkXPress document.

Text formats that can be imported by QuarkXPress: from word processor files created in MacWrite®, MacWrite II, Microsoft® Word, Microsoft® Works, Word Perfect®, WriteNow®, and any ASCII text files.

Note: To import text files created with any of the above-named word processing applications, the necessary import filters must be installed in the same folder as the QuarkXPress application on your hard disk. These filters are included on your original QuarkXPress disks and are transferred to the hard disk during the installation process.

FILE/SAVE TEXT

The SAVE TEXT command is used to export text for use in other programs or in other QuarkXPress documents. For example, you may wish to export text from a QuarkXPress document so that you can edit it in a word processing program such as Microsoft® Word.

To export and save text:

✔ With the Content Tool select *either* the desired text or simply select the text box that contains the text.

✔ Pull down the FILE menu and select SAVE TEXT. A dialog box, similar to the SAVE AS dialog box will appear.

✔ Enter a name for your text file.

✔ If you wish to export all of the text that is in a text box or linked set of boxes, select ENTIRE STORY. If you wish to export only a selected portion of text within a text box, choose SELECTED TEXT.

✔ Select the text format from the FORMAT pop-up menu. To access the different choices available to you, place the mouse pointer on the format menu and hold down the mouse button.

A list of available formats, corresponding to the import/export filters installed in your QuarkXPress application folder, will be presented. If you are not sure which program will be reading the file, or if you need to use the text on another type of computer system, then choose ASCII text. However, you should be aware that when saving text in ASCII format, any character styling, formatting and paragraph formatting will not be saved.

Selecting the Style Tags format will create an ASCII text file that includes text formatting code. Some applications are able to translate this code and then reformat the text as originally formatted in your QuarkXPress document.

✔ Click SAVE to complete the export process and save the new file to disk.

The Edit Menu

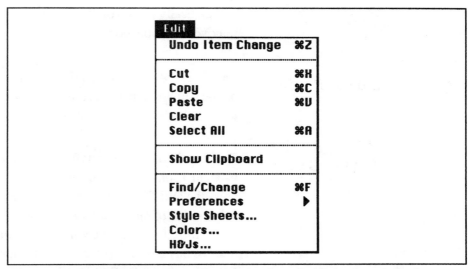

Figure 9.2 The EDIT menu when a text box is selected with the Content Tool.

⌘ Z   EDIT/
         UNDO/REDO

The EDIT UNDO command allows you to undo the previous action, whether cutting, deleting, copying, typing, replacing, or otherwise editing the text in a text box. EDIT/UNDO is only available *immediately* following the action you wish to UNDO. If you perform any other action such as clicking to activate an element on screen, or changing tool selection on the Tool Palette, EDIT/UNDO will no longer be available.

EDIT/REDO is available after the EDIT/UNDO command has been used.

⌘ X   EDIT/CUT

To remove text, first select the text you wish to remove with the Content Tool. Then pull down the EDIT menu and select CUT. The text will be removed from the document, but a copy of the text will remain on the Clipboard.

To move text to a new location CUT the text, place the cursor in the desired text placement location, pull down the EDIT menu and select PASTE.

⌘ C   E D I T / C O P Y

To copy text and then place in another location on your document, first select the text you wish to duplicate with the Content Tool.

Pull down the EDIT menu and select COPY. A copy of the text will be automatically placed on the Clipboard, but the text itself will not be removed from the document.

⌘ V   E D I T / P A S T E

The EDIT/PASTE command allows you to place a copy of the text stored on the Clipboard in a text box. Place the cursor in the desired location for the text. Pull down the EDIT menu and select PASTE.

E D I T / C L E A R

To CLEAR/DELETE text, first select the text you wish to remove with the Content Tool. Then *either* pull down the EDIT menu and select CLEAR, or press the DELETE (backspace) key on the keyboard. *If you delete text using either of these methods, a copy of the text will not be stored on the Clipboard.* If you change your mind about deleting it, the only way to retrieve this text is to select UNDO from the EDIT menu *immediately* following the CLEAR or DELETE command.

⌘ A   E D I T /
S E L E C T A L L

Choosing the SELECT ALL command with the cursor in text allows you to select all of the text in a story at once whether it lies in one box or many. To do so, activate the text box with the Content Tool, pull down the EDIT menu and choose SELECT ALL.

E D I T /
S H O W C L I P B O A R D

The SHOW CLIPBOARD command allows you to view whatever has been stored on the Clipboard. If you cut or copy text and want to be sure that you have done so correctly, select SHOW CLIPBOARD from the EDIT menu to display the Clipboard's contents. To close the Clipboard window, click in the close box in the upper lefthand corner, or select HIDE CLIPBOARD from the EDIT menu (it replaces SHOW CLIPBOARD when the Clipboard window is open).

⌘ F   E D I T /
F I N D / C H A N G E

The EDIT/FIND/CHANGE displays a dialog box that allows you to find and change characters in a story or even in an entire document. You can look for specific words or characters and you can look for characters that have specific attributes: for example, the word "Theater" in 12 pt. Helvetica.

The FIND/CHANGE command is always available. If settings are changed in the FIND/CHANGE dialog box when no document is open, those settings become the default settings for all new documents created after that change.

To find and change a word or characters:

✔ Activate the text box with the Content Tool and place the cursor at the top of the story. The FIND command searches a story from the cursor to the end of the story: if the cursor is not at the top of the story, the search will not be complete.

✔ If you wish to search for all instances of a word or characters within a whole document, then make sure that no text boxes are active before you begin the search.

✔ Select FIND/CHANGE from the EDIT menu (see figure 9.3). In the *FIND WHAT:* text field type the word you wish to find. Then in the *CHANGE TO:* text field enter the correction. You may use the FIND/CHANGE dialog box to find text that you do not wish to change by leaving the *Change to:* field blank.

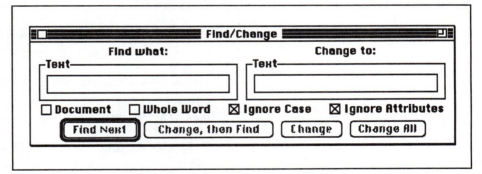

Figure 9.3 The FIND/CHANGE dialog box with IGNORE ATTRIBUTES checked.

✔ Unless you wish to search the entire document, make sure that the DOCUMENT option is unchecked. If an "x" appears next to the DOCUMENT option then click on the box to uncheck it.

✔ Click WHOLE WORD if you only want to find instances of the text as whole words — that is, with a space or punctuation on either side of it. If you wish to find characters that may be part of a larger word, then make sure that the WHOLE WORD option is unchecked.

✔ In most cases, IGNORE CASE should be checked. But, if you wish to find characters that match in upper or lower case, check this option.

✔ IGNORE ATTRIBUTES should also be checked if it does not matter what font, style, size, or other text attributes the text is that you trying to find and or change. To find or change words whose text attributes are significant, see the following section on searching for attributes.

✔ When the settings are as desired, click the FIND NEXT button. The first instance of the word or characters will be highlighted and the other three buttons will be available. At this point, you may choose to change the highlighted word and then find the next instance, to simply change the currently highlighted word and not search for the next instance, or to change all instances where those characters appear.

Be careful when choosing the CHANGE ALL option — you may find that words or characters you had no intention of changing are also changed! For example, you may wish to find all instances of the word "hi" and change to "hello." But if you forget to check the WHOLE WORD option, then "hit" would be changed to "hellot," and "him" would be changed to "hellom."

Using the FIND/CHANGE dialog box with attributes:

To use the expanded FIND/CHANGE dialog box with attributes:

✔ Deselect the IGNORE ATTRIBUTES option. The dialog box will then appear as shown in figure 9.4.

✔ To specify the text you wish to find, click the FIND WHAT text option and enter the text you wish to find. Repeat this procedure on the CHANGE TO: side of the dialog box.

✔ To specify the font you wish to find, click to select the FONT option and then select the desired font from the pop-up menu, or enter the font name directly into the field from the keyboard.

✔ To specify a particular font size to be found, click to activate the SIZE option, then either select the font size from the pop-up menu or enter the desired size directly into the field.

✔ To specify a particular style to be found, click to active the STYLE option. Clicking one time next to any style will cause the selection box to be filled with gray. This means that QuarkXPress will not consider that style as essential to the search. Clicking two times next to any style will place an "x" in the box and will cause that style to be considered criteria for the search. An unchecked box means that

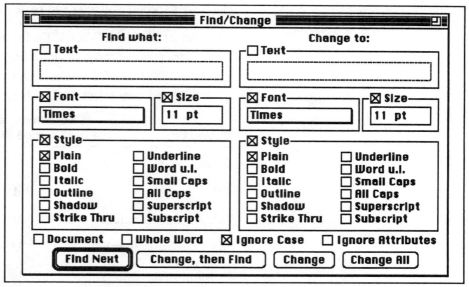

Figure 9.4 *The FIND/CHANGE dialog box when text attributes are used as search or replace criteria.*

the text must not be formatted in that style in order to be found or changed.

✔ To specify Font, Size, or Style to change the text to something else, repeat the above procedures in the *Change to:* field of the Find/Change dialog box.

✔ Clicking the zoom box in the upper right side of the Find/Change window will shrink the dialog box to its smallest functional size and make it easier for you to view the find/change process as it occurs.

✔ Click on FIND NEXT to begin the search, then select one of the other options, as described in the previous section, to complete the search.

Searching for Special Characters

QuarkXPress allows you to search for special characters such as paragraph returns, spaces, and tabs, as well as for alphabet characters. The procedure is the same. Either type in the code for the special character (see the following table of characters) or if you can't remember the code for a special character, QuarkXPress allows you to copy and paste the character from the document into a Find or Change field.

To copy a special character and paste to the Find/Change dialog box,

✔ Select SHOW INVISIBLES from the VIEW menu. Select the special character(s), choose COPY from the EDIT menu, choose FIND/CHANGE from the EDIT menu, click in the *FIND WHAT:* field and then select PASTE from the EDIT menu.

Character	Character to enter in Find/Change dialog box	Keystrokes
Space		Space bar
Tab	\t	⌘-Tab
Paragraph (hard return)	\p	⌘-Return
New line (soft return)	\n	⌘-Shift-Return
New Column	\c	⌘-Enter
New Box	\b	⌘-Shift-Enter
Wild Card	\?	⌘-?
Previous Box Page #	\2	⌘-2
Current Box Page #	\3	⌘-3
Next Box Page #	\4	⌘-4

PREFERENCES/ TYPOGRAPHIC

The TYPOGRAPHIC PREFERENCES dialog box (see figure 9.5) is used to specify or change default settings for many typographical features offered by QuarkXPress.

Superscript — The fields in this section allow you to control the placement and size of superscript characters. Offset (the distance a character is moved up from the baseline) is defined as a percentage of the font size in use. The default for offset is 30%. VScale and HScale are percentage values for vertical and horizontal scaling of the superscript characters. Normally, 100% scaling is retained for the superscript characters. However you may change scaling values from 0% to 100% in .1% increments.

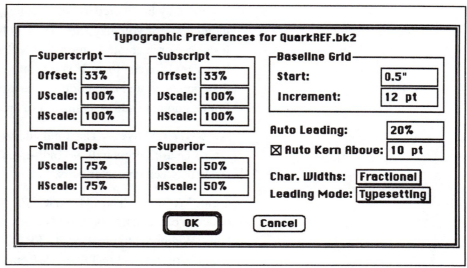

Figure 9.5 *The TYPOGRAPHIC PREFERENCES dialog box.*

Subscript — The fields in this section are identical to those of the superscript section, except that they control the placement and size of subscript characters. Values are entered in the same manner as for superscript.

Small Caps — This section allows you to control the vertical and horizontal scaling of electronically created small caps. The default setting is 75%, but you may enter values from 0% to 100% in .1% increments.

Superior — This section allows you to control the vertical and horizontal scaling of superior characters. The default setting is 50% for both fields. Values may be entered in the same manner as for other VScale and HScale fields in this dialog box.

Baseline Grid — QuarkXPress allows you to define and use a baseline grid (an invisible underlying text grid). When selected paragraphs are locked to the baseline grid, the text will automatically line up across columns. The baseline grid, as defined in the Typographic Preferences dialog box, applies to an entire document.

To change where the grid starts (measured from the top of the page) and the gridline increments, enter values in the Start and Increment fields. Increment values may be entered in .001-point increments, from 5 to 144 points.

Auto Leading — The amount of leading (vertical space between lines of text, measured from baseline to baseline) that is automatically placed between lines when entering text is defined in this section. Normally, auto leading is set to 20%. For example, 10 point type would then have 12 point leading, 12 point type would have 14.4 point leading. Values for auto leading may be entered as percentages, from 0% to 100% in 1% increments, or you may enter an "absolute" number for incremental auto leading. For example, entering +2 will add 2 points of space (in addition to font size) between lines. If you want to use any measurement system other than points, you must enter the measurement unit, as well as the amount. For example, to add 1 centimeter of space, enter +1 cm.

Auto Kern Above — This field allows you to define the point size above which QuarkXPress will use built-in automatic kerning tables to control space between character pairs.

Char. Widths — The CHARACTER WIDTHS menu controls spacing between characters. For output on any postscript device, you should leave Char. Widths set to the default - FRACTIONAL. For output to an ImageWriter, select INTEGRAL from the pop-up menu.

Leading Mode — QuarkXPress allows you to choose from either of two modes of leading. Typesetting, the default mode, measures leading from the baseline of one line of text to the baseline of the line *above* it. Word processing mode, on the other hand, measures leading from the top of the ascender on one line to the top of the ascender on the line *beneath* it.

STYLE SHEETS

Style sheets are an important and powerful part of any page layout application. To create, edit, append, or duplicate style sheets, select the EDIT/STYLE SHEETS command.

Style sheets that are created or modified when no document is active become part of the default style sheet menu and are available in any new document created subsequently.

Style sheets that are created or modified when a document is active are saved with that document and only found on the style menu of that document.

There are basically two major ways to create a new style sheet: 1) format text first, create a style sheet based upon already formatted text, and then apply the style sheet to the text; or 2) define the style sheet text attributes first, then apply to text.

To create a new style sheet:

✔ Pull down the EDIT menu and select STYLE SHEETS. The Style Sheets dialog box will appear (figure 9.6).

✔ Click the NEW button. The EDIT STYLE SHEET dialog box will appear (figure 9.7).

TEXT

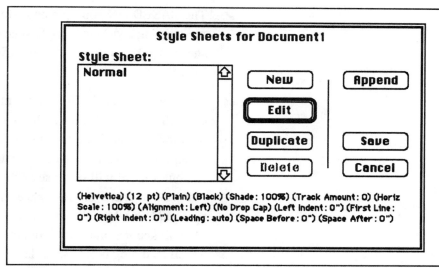

Figure 9.6 The Style Sheets dialog box.

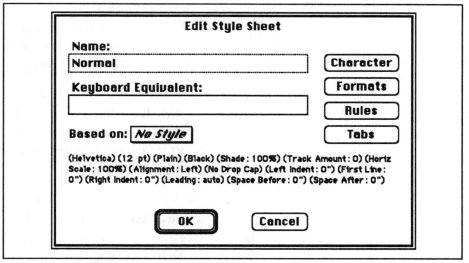

Figure 9.7 The Edit Style Sheet dialog box.

✔ Enter a name for the style sheet in the NAME field.

✔ If you wish, enter a keyboard command for the style sheet in the KEYBOARD EQUIVALENT field so that you can apply the style to text without using the mouse. Keyboard commands can be any combination of numbers from the keypad (not the numbers at the top of the keyboard), the function keys (F-1 to F-14 on the extended keyboard), and the COMMAND, OPTION, CONTROL, and SHIFT keys.

✔ The BASED ON pop-up menu allows you to base a style sheet on a pre-existing style sheet. Style sheets that are based on other style sheets will be automatically modified when the base style sheet is modified.

✔ Beneath the BASED ON pop-up menu is a list of text attributes currently selected for the style. If a text box is currently activated with the Content Tool, the attributes displayed will be those of the paragraph where the cursor is located. If no text box is active, the attributes listed will be those of the Normal (default) style sheet. If you wish to create the style sheet from settings already within the paragraph in which the cursor is currently located, click OK to accept these linked text attributes, and then click SAVE in the STYLE SHEETS dialog box to save the new style sheet. If you wish to change text attributes, go to the following step.

✔ Click the CHARACTER button to display the Character dialog box. Select the desired character attributes and then click OK (see description under STYLE/CHARACTER for more detailed description of Character dialog box).

✔ Click the FORMATS button to display the PARAGRAPH FORMATS dialog box. Select the desired paragraph formatting attributes and then click OK (see description under STYLE/FORMATS for more detailed description of Paragraph Formats dialog box).

✔ Click the RULES button to display the Rules dialog box. Select line above and/or line below and desired line attributes and then click OK (see description under STYLE/RULES for more detailed description of the Rules dialog box).

✔ Click the TABS button to display the TABS dialog box. Place tabs where desired and then click OK (see description under STYLE/TABS for more detailed description of how to set Tabs).

✔ Click OK. Then click SAVE in the STYLE SHEETS dialog box to save the new style sheet and return to the document.

To edit an existing style sheet:

✔ Select STYLE SHEETS from the EDIT menu. Click on the name of the style sheet you wish to edit, then click the EDIT button. Click the CHARACTER, FORMATS, RULES, or TABS buttons to change character attributes or edit the NAME or KEYBOARD

EQUIVALENT. Click OK and then SAVE to save the modified style sheet. If you click CANCEL, all changes you have made to the style sheet will be cancelled and the style sheet will remain unmodified.

To duplicate an existing style sheet:

✔ Select STYLE SHEETS from the EDIT menu. Click on the name of the style sheet you wish to duplicate, then click the DUPLICATE button. Quark will give the style sheet a name, "Copy of..." style sheet name. The style sheet can then be edited in the manner described above.

To delete a style sheet:

✔ Select STYLE SHEETS from the EDIT menu. Click on the name of the style sheet you wish to delete, then click the DELETE button. If the style sheet has been applied to text in the active document, a dialog box will appear that allows you to confirm or cancel the style sheet deletion. If you wish to delete the style sheet, click OK. The text to which a deleted style sheet has been applied will remain unmodified, but NO STYLE will be applied to it.

To append (import) style sheets from another document:

✔ Select STYLE SHEETS from the EDIT menu. Click the APPEND button. A directory dialog box, similar to the FILE/OPEN dialog box will appear. Select the QuarkXPress or Microsoft Word (versions 3.0 or 4.0) documents from which you desire to copy style sheets. All of the style sheets in the selected document will be imported, except those style sheets with names exactly like those listed in the current STYLE SHEET dialog box. Style sheets with duplicate names will not be imported.

H & J s

H&Js stands for Hyphenation and Justification Settings. To create new hyphenation and justifications settings or to edit pre-existing settings, select the EDIT/H&Js command. The H&JS dialog box will appear (figure 9.8).

H&J settings that are created or modified when no document is active become part of the paragraph formats H&J pop-up menu and will be available in any new document created subsequently.

H&J settings that are created or modified when a document is active are saved with that document and apply only to that document.

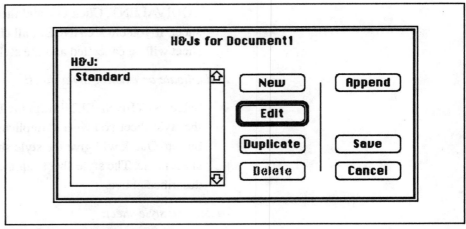

Figure 9.8 The H&Js dialog box.

To create a new H&J setting:

✔ Select H&Js from the EDIT menu. Click on the NEW button in the H&J dialog box. The EDIT HYPHENATION AND JUSTIFICATION dialog box will appear (figure 9.9).

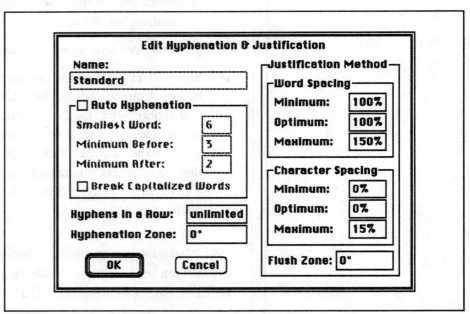

Figure 9.9 The Edit Hyphenation & Justification dialog box.

✔ Enter a name for the H&J setting in the NAME field.

✔ If you wish automatic hyphenation to be activated, click the square next to the Auto Hyphenation option. You can then specify the following:

Smallest Word: enter the number of characters in the smallest word you wish QuarkXPress to hyphenate.

Minimum Before: enter the minimum number of characters before which QuarkXPress will allow along the right edge of the text box before it hyphenates a word.

Minimum After: enter the minimum number of characters after a hyphen which QuarkXPress must allow.

Break Capitalized Words: click this option to activate it. By default, it is set to Off because capitalized words are usually left unhyphenated.

Hyphens in a Row: To limit the number of hyphens QuarkXPress will allow to occur in a row down the right edge of the text box, enter a number into this field. The default setting in this field is unlimited hyphens.

Hyphenation Zone: This field allows you to control the area within which XPress will allow hyphenation to occur, as measured from the right indent. Hyphenation zone does not apply to justified text. Set to the default of 0, there is no hyphenation zone. If you specify a hyphenation zone, QuarkXPress will hyphenate a word only if the previous word ends before the hyphenation zone begins and if a normal hyphenation (as defined by the H&J setting) falls within the hyphenation zone.

The Justification Method fields allow you to control how XPress places space between letters and words to achieve justification. You can specify the minimum, optimum, and maximum word spacing and the minimum, optimum, and maximum character spacing. Additionally, you can specify a Flush Zone to define where the last line of a paragraph will be justified.

Word Spacing: These fields specify Minimum, Optimum and Maximum percentage of normal word spacing that Quark will use in justifying the text. XPress will exceed the maximum percentage value when justifying text if there is no alternate way to justify the line.

Character Spacing: These fields specify Minimum, Optimum, and Maximum percentages of an En space (the width of a zero in that particular font). Again, XPress may space letters further apart than the Maximum percentage specified, if there is no other way to achieve line justification.

Flush Zone: enter a value in this field to justify a last line of a paragraph.

To edit an H&J setting:

✔ Select H&Js from the EDIT menu. Click on the EDIT button in the H&J dialog box. The Edit Hyphenation and Justification dialog box will appear (figure 9.9). Enter values for the different options as described in the previous section.

To duplicate an H&J setting:

✔ Select H&Js from the EDIT menu. Select the H&J setting you wish to copy and click on the DUPLICATE button in the H&J dialog box. A copy of the H&J will appear in the name list. You may then edit the H&J in the normal way.

To delete an H&J setting:

✔ Select H&Js from the EDIT menu. Select the H&J setting you wish to delete and click on the DELETE button in the H&J dialog box. If you have applied that H&J setting to paragraphs within the document, a dialog box will appear with a warning and allow you to confirm or cancel the deletion. Text to which a deleted H&J setting has been applied will reformat according to the Standard (default) H&J setting.

To append H&J settings:

✔ Select H&Js from the EDIT menu. Click on the APPEND button in the H&J dialog box. A dialog box, similar to the FILE/OPEN dialog box will appear. Select the XPress file from which to import the H&J settings. All H&Js *except* those with duplicate names will be imported into the active document.

The Style Menu

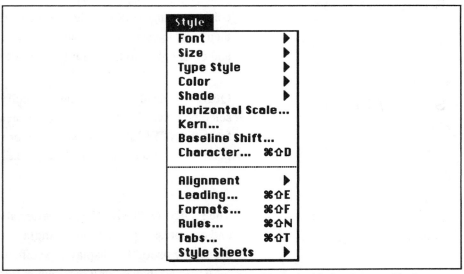

Figure 9.10 *The Style menu when a text box is selected with the Content Tool.*

S T Y L E / F O N T

Use the STYLE/FONT command to select a font for a range of text. Either, select the font from the STYLE/FONT submenu and then enter the text or enter the text, select the range of text you wish to change, and then select the font from the STYLE/FONT submenu.

S T Y L E / S I Z E

Use the STYLE/SIZE command to select a font size for a range of text. Either, select the size from the STYLE/SIZE submenu and then enter the text or enter the text, select the range of text you wish to change, and then select the font from the STYLE/SIZE submenu. ⌘-Shift-< decreases the font size in one point increments. ⌘-Shift-> increases the font size in one point increments. Pressing ⌘-Shift-\ brings up the Font Size dialog box, where you can directly enter a new font size.

S T Y L E / T Y P E   S T Y L E

Use the STYLE/TYPE STYLE command to change the style attributes, such as plain, bold, or italic, for a range of text. You may select a style from the STYLE/TYPE STYLE submenu and then enter the text, or enter the text, select the range of text you wish to change, and then select the desired style.

STYLE/COLOR

When editing text, you may use the STYLE/COLOR command to apply a color to a range of text. Select the color from the STYLE/COLOR palette and then enter the text or enter the text, select the text and then select the color. To add other colors to the Color Palette, see Chapter 11, Managing Color.

STYLE/SHADE

QuarkXPress also allows you to specify a percentage (shade) of the selected text color. Select a a predefined percentage, in 10% increments, from the STYLE/SHADE submenu or select Other and enter the desired percentage in the resulting dialog box.

STYLE/ HORIZONTAL SCALE

The HORIZONTAL SCALE feature allows you to electronically expand and compress type, without changing the vertical point size of the type. It is especially useful for display type effects. Select STYLE/HORIZONTAL SCALE and then enter a percentage into the Scale dialog box, where 100% is normal. For example, an entry of 75% will compress the type; an entry of 110% will expand the type.

Press ⌘-[to compress type and ⌘-] to expand type in 5% increments.

STYLE/KERN/TRACK

QuarkXPress's kerning and tracking commands (increasing or decreasing the space between characters) are based upon a relative measurement, called an EM. QuarkXPress defines an EM as the width of two zeros (00) of the particular font/size with which you are currently working. The EM is then divided into 200 parts. Entering a negative value, from -1 to -100 in increments as small as .01, decreases the space between characters and a positive number, from 1 to 100 in increments as small as .01, increases the space between characters.

The STYLE/KERN command is used to increase or decrease space between a *pair* of characters, and will be available if the cursor is placed between a pair of characters (but no characters are actually selected). To kern the space between a pair of characters, click between the desired characters, select the STYLE/KERN command and enter a value of from -100 to +100.

The STYLE/TRACK command is used to increase or decrease space between a *range* of characters (more than two), and is available when one or more characters have been selected. To track the space in a range of text, select the text, select the STYLE/TRACK command and enter a value of from -100 to +100 in the Track Amount field.

Press ⌘-Shift-{ to decrease or ⌘-Shift-} to increase kerning or tracking values in increments of 10/200. Additionally pressing the Option key (⌘-Shift-Option-{ or ⌘-Shift-Option-}) decreases or increases the kerning or tracking values in increments of 1/200.

STYLE/ BASELINE SHIFT

Use the STYLE/BASELINE command to shift a range of text above or below its normal baseline (the imaginary line upon which the characters "sit"). To shift a range of text upwards, enter a positive number in the Baseline Shift field, up to 3 times the font size. To shift a range of text below the baseline, enter a negative number in the Baseline Shift field, up to 3 times the font size.

Pressing ⌘-Shift-Option+ (plus) shifts the text above the baseline in 1 pt. increments. Pressing ⌘-Shift-Option- (minus) shifts the text below the baseline in 1 pt. increments.

⌘-SHIFT-D STYLE/CHARACTER

The Character Attributes dialog box that is displayed after you choose the STYLE/CHARACTER command allows you to change many character attributes at one time: font, size, color, shade, type style, horizontal scale amount, kern (or track) amount, and baseline shift amount. (See discussion of each of these choices under the Style menu.)

STYLE/ALIGNMENT

The STYLE/ALIGNMENT command allows you to align a paragraph of text within a paragraph's indents: left aligned (right ragged) ⌘L, right aligned (left ragged) ⌘R, centered ⌘C, and justified (simultaneously left and right aligned) ⌘J.

STYLE/LEADING

Leading is the vertical space between lines of text, which, in Typesetting mode, is measured from the baseline of a line of text to the baseline of the line above it. In Word Processing mode, leading is measured from the ascent of a line of text to the ascent of the next line. The default leading mode is Typesetting and is defined in the Typographic Preferences dialog box.

QuarkXPress's STYLE/LEADING command allows you to specify leading in three different ways: auto, absolute, and incremental.

The default Auto leading is defined in the Typographic Preferences dialog box as 20% — that is, it calculates leading by adding 20% of the largest font size on a line of text to the font. For example, if the largest letter on a line of text is 24 pts., the leading will be 28.8 pts. (20% of 24 = 4.8 + 24 = 28.8). The definition for automatic leading may be changed by entering another percentage in the Typographic Preferences dialog box.

✔ To specify auto leading in the STYLE/LEADING dialog box, enter "auto" or a 0 (zero) in the Leading field.

✔ To specify an absolute leading value, enter a number (in any measurement system) in the leading field. Absolute leading is not affected by different font sizes. Because leading is usually measured in points, values entered in other measurement systems will be displayed in point the next time you display the leading dialog box.

✔ To specify incremental leading, enter a value (in any measurement system) with a + or – mark in front of it. XPress will add (or subtract) that value from the font size. For example, an incremental value of +3 pt. will add three points to a line of 12 pt. helvetica, giving a final leading value of 15 pts.

Pressing ⌘-Shift-: decreases and ⌘-Shift-" increases paragraph leading in 1 pt. increments. Adding the Option key (⌘-Shift-Option-: or ⌘-Shift-Option-") decreases or increases the paragraph leading in .1 pt. increments.

⌘-Shift-F FORMATS

The STYLE/FORMATS command displays the Paragraph Formats dialog box (figure 9.11) allowing you to control several paragraph formatting specifications at one time: left indent, first line indent, right indent, leading, the space before a paragraph, the space after a paragraph, lock to baseline grid, drop caps, keep with next ¶, keep lines together, alignment, and H&J setting. After entering specifications in the Paragraph Formats dialog box, click Apply to see the results of the settings without closing the dialog box. Clicking OK accepts the specifications and closes the dialog box.

Left Indent —Left Indent is the space from the left edge of the text box (or column within a text box) to the left edge of a paragraph. Left Indent specifications may be entered in any measurement system, but will be displayed in the current ruler measurement system when the Format dialog box is redisplayed.

First line indent —First Line Indent is the distance of the first line of a paragraph from the left indent of the paragraph. For example, to create a hanging indent, a negative value must be entered for the First Line Indent

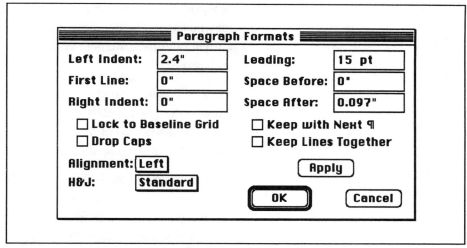

Figure 9.11 *The Paragraph Formats dialog box.*

and a positive value for the Left Indent First Line Indent specifications may be entered in any measurement system, but will be displayed in the current ruler measurement system when the Format dialog box is redisplayed.

Right indent —Right Indent is the space from the right edge of the text box (or column within a text box) to the right edge of a paragraph. Right Indent specifications may be entered in any measurement system, but will be displayed in the current ruler measurement system when the Format dialog box is redisplayed.

Leading —Leading is the vertical line space measured from the baseline of one line to the baseline of the line above it when in typesetting mode, and from the ascent of one line to the ascent of the next line when in word processing mode, as defined in the Typographic Preferences dialog box.

Leading is normally measured in points, but any measurement system may be used when entering a leading value into the leading field. When the Formats dialog box is redisplayed, the leading value will be displayed in points.

Space Before —The Space Before field is used to add space before the first line of a paragraph. If the paragraph is positioned at the top of a text box, however, the Space Before will not be applied. Space Before specifications may be entered in any measurement system, but will be displayed in the current ruler measurement system when the Format dialog box is redisplayed.

Space After —The Space After field is used to add space after the last line of a paragraph. If the paragraph is positioned at the bottom of a text box, however, the Space After will not be applied. Space After specifications may be entered in any measurement system, but will be displayed in the current ruler measurement system when the Format dialog box is redisplayed.

Lock to Baseline Grid — The Lock to Baseline Grid feature, activated by clicking the Lock to Baseline Grid box, is useful for aligning the baselines of adjacent columns of text to the document's invisible baseline grid as specified in the Typographic Preferences dialog box.

Since leading and the lock to baseline grid feature work interactively, the leading value of the paragraph must also be taken into account when locking paragraphs to baseline grid. For example, if the baseline grid is set to 15 points, and the leading of the paragraph is set to 15 pts. or *less*, the text will align with each line of the grid, with a line spacing of 15 pts. If the leading is set to *more* than 15 pts., the text will align with the next gridline — a line spacing of 30 pts.

Drop Caps —

✔ To create a drop cap, place the cursor in the paragraph to be formatted. (If you do not already have text in your document, enter a 4- or 5-line paragraph for this exercise.) Pull down the Style menu and select Formats.

✔ Click to select Drop Caps. The dialog box will enlarge to include the Drop Caps options (see figure 9.12)

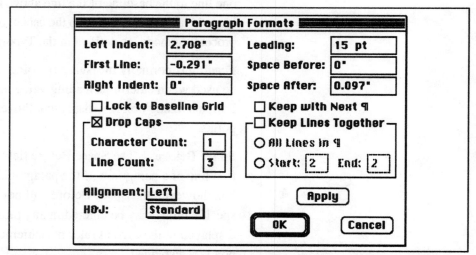

Figure 9.12 The expanded Paragraph Formats dialog box with Drop Caps selected.

✔ Specify the number of lines (from 2 to 8) you want the drop cap to fill.

✔ Specify the number of characters to be included with the drop cap.

✔ Click APPLY to see the results of the specifications you entered. If satisfied, click OK.

Keep With Next ¶ —The Keep With Next ¶ command is activated by clicking the selection box. and will keep two paragraphs together. If the paragraphs fall at the bottom of a text box, both paragraphs will be forced to the next text box or column in the chain.

Keep Lines Together —Selecting Keep Lines Together allows you to control how QuarkXPress breaks a paragraph that falls at the bottom of a text box or column. When you select this command, the Paragraph Formats dialog box will expand (figure 9.13) and give you the following options:

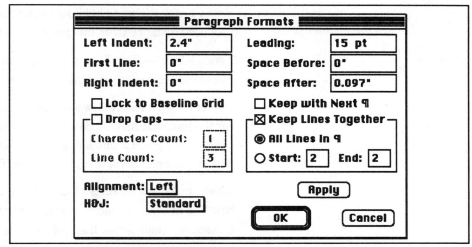

Figure 9.13   The expanded Paragraph Formats dialog box with Keep Lines Together selected.

All Lines in ¶ — check this option if you wish the paragraph to remain as a unit, and not be broken at all.

Start — specifies how many lines must be left at the bottom of a column or text box when breaking the paragraph.

End — specifies how many lines must be left at the top of a column or text box when breaking the paragraph.

Alignment —the Alignment pop-up menu allows you to specify an alignment for the paragraph: Left aligned, Centered, Right aligned, or Justified.

H&J — the H&J pop-up menu allows you to specify an H&J setting to be applied to the paragraph. See the Edit H&Js section for a discussion of H&J settings.

❖ ❖ ❖ ❖ ❖ ❖ ❖ ❖ ❖ ❖ ❖ ❖ ❖ ❖ ❖ ❖ ❖ ❖

⌘-SHIFT-N
STYLE/RULES

The STYLE/RULES command allows you to specify horizontal rules that fall above or below a paragraph and are locked to the text — that is the lines will automatically move with the paragraphs as the text is reformatted. To apply a rule above or below a paragraph, select Style/Rules and click on Rule Above and/or Rule Below. The dialog box will expand to give you the following options:

Length — the Length pop-up menu allows you to define the length of the line, either between paragraph indents, or the length of the text only.

From Left — This field allows you to specify a starting point for the line a specified distance from the paragraph's left indent.

From Right — This field allows you to specify an ending point for the line a specified distance from the paragraph's right indent.

Offset — This field allows you to specify the distance from the paragraph for the line, and may be entered as a percentage or as an absolute value. For example, to place a rule halfway between the paragraph and the following paragraph, enter a value of 50% in this field.

Absolute values for rules placed above a paragraph are measured from the baseline of the first line of text to the bottom of the rule above it, and may be used to create a rule that overlaps the text of the line beneath.

Absolute values for rules placed below a paragraph are measured from the baseline of the last line of text to the top of the rule beneath it.

Style — The style pop-up menu is used to specify a line style.

Width — Choose a preset line width from the Width pop-up menu, or enter a value in the field.

Color — Select a line color from this pop-up menu.

Shade — Choose a color percentage from this pop-up menu or enter a percentage directly into the Shade field.

Click Apply to see the results of the specifications you have entered, without closing the Rules dialog box. Clicking OK accepts the specifications and closes the box. Clicking Cancel will close the dialog box and will cancel any changes to the paragraph rule specifications.

⌘-Sʜɪꜰᴛ-T Sᴛʏʟᴇ/Tᴀʙs

Selecting the STYLE/TABS command allows you to specify tab settings for a paragraph of text. QuarkXPress's default tabs are set at .5" intervals from the left edge of a text box. Specifying tab settings in the Tabs dialog box overrules the default tab settings.

The tabs dialog box (figure 9.14) allows you to set left aligned, centered, right aligned, or decimal tabs. You may specify a leader (repeating character) for the tab. When you choose this command, the Tabs dialog box will appear and a Tabs ruler will also be displayed at the top of the text box or column. To set tabs in the tabs dialog box:

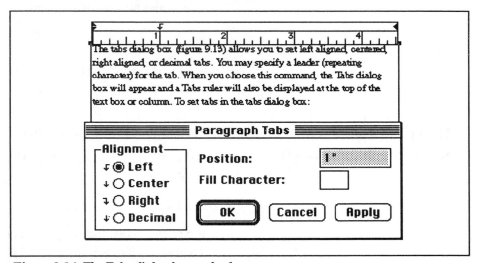

Figure 9.14 The Tabs dialog box and ruler.

✔ Select the type of tab you wish to place (Left, Center, Right, or Decimal).

✔ Either enter a value in the Position field or click the mouse pointer directly on the Tabs ruler in the desired position.

✔ If desired, enter a fill character in the Fill field.

✔ Click Apply to preview the results of the tab specifications.

✔ Click OK to accept the tab settings and return to the document, or click Cancel to cancel the tab specification changes.

✔ To move a tab, click on the tab (on the ruler), press the mouse button and drag to the desired location.

✔ To delete a tab, drag the tab off the ruler and let go of the mouse button.

✔ To clear all tabs from the ruler, press the Option key and then click the Tabs ruler.

STYLE SHEETS

The STYLE SHEETS submenu displays the document's style sheets that may be applied to the selected paragraphs. To apply a style sheet, either select the desired style sheet from this submenu or type the keyboard equivalent for the style sheet, which is displayed to the right of the style sheet name. See the EDIT/STYLE SHEETS section for a full discussion of style sheets and how to create them.

The Utilities Menu

UTILITIES
CHECK SPELLING

To check spelling for an individual word:

✔ Select WORD from the CHECK SPELLING submenu (or press ⌘W).

To check the spelling for a story:

✔ First be sure that the story's text box is selected with the Content Tool. Then select STORY from the CHECK SPELLING submenu. QuarkXPress will display a dialog box (figure 9.15) giving you the total word count for the story, number of unique words, and number of suspect words. Click OK to display the Check Story dialog box. The first suspect word and number of instances will be displayed at the top of the dialog box (figure 9.16).

To look up the correct spelling for the word, click the LOOKUP button.

✔ Select the desired word from the list of possible replacements, or enter the correct spelling directly into the Replace With field and then click Replace to correct the suspect word.

Figure 9.15 The Word Count dialog box.

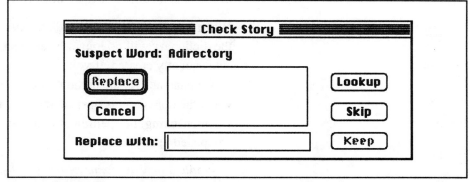

Figure 9.16 The Check Story dialog box with misspelled word displayed.

✔ Pressing the SKIP button will display the next suspect word without initiating any changes to the current suspect word.

✔ Clicking KEEP will add the suspect word to the open user-defined auxiliary dictionary. Keep will not be available if an auxiliary dictionary is not opened.

✔ Clicking CANCEL will end the Spelling Check, close the dialog box and return you to the document.

To check the spelling for an entire document, from first to last page:

✔ Select DOCUMENT from the CHECK SPELLING submenu.

To check the spelling of text boxes on the master pages:

✔ First display a master page. The DOCUMENT option will be replaced by MASTERS on the CHECK SPELLING submenu.

UTILITIES/AUXILIARY DICTIONARIES

QuarkXPress allows you to create user-dictionaries through the Auxiliary Dictionaries command in order to add specialized or new words to the list when checking spelling. Only one auxiliary dictionary may be opened at a time.

The UTILITIES/AUXILIARY DICTIONARY command is always available. When you create an auxiliary dictionary and when no documents are open, that dictionary will be available to all new documents subsequently created. If you create an auxiliary dictionary when a document is open and active, that dictionary will automatically be available to that document.

When you close an auxiliary dictionary and when no documents are open, the dictionary will no longer be automatically available to new documents subsequently created. If you close an auxiliary dictionary when a document is open and active, the dictionary will no longer be automatically available when the document is opened and only the XPress dictionary will be used when checking the spelling of that document. Auxiliary dictionaries may be opened at any time.

To create a new dictionary:

✔ Select AUXILIARY DICTIONARIES from the UTILITIES menu. The Auxiliary Dictionary dialog box will appear (figure 9.17).

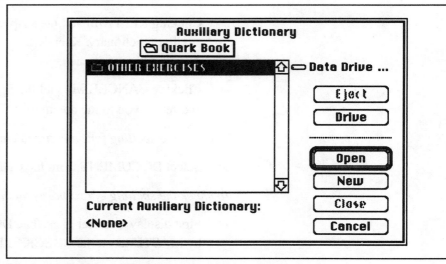

Figure 9.17 *The Auxiliary Dictionary dialog box.*

✔ Click the NEW button. A directory dialog box will be displayed.

✔ Enter a name for the dictionary in the name field and click the CREATE button. A new, empty dictionary will be created and will be available to the currently open document. If no documents are open, the dictionary will become available to all new documents created subsequently.

✔ Words are added to the dictionary through the Utilities/Edit Auxiliary command or by clicking Keep when checking the spelling of a document, story, or word.

To open a previously created dictionary:

✔ Select AUXILIARY DICTIONARIES from the UTILITIES menu. The Auxiliary Dictionary dialog box will appear.

✔ Use the DRIVE button and/or the directory pop-up menu to display the location of the desired dictionary.

✔ Select the dictionary you wish to open and click the OPEN button.

✔ The dictionary will become available to all new documents created subsequently.

To close an open dictionary:

✔ Select AUXILIARY DICTIONARIES from the UTILITIES menu. The Auxiliary Dictionary dialog box will appear.

✔ Click the CLOSE button. The dictionary will close and will no longer be available to the current document. If no documents are open, no auxiliary dictionary will be available to new documents created subsequently.

UTILITIES/
EDIT AUXILIARY

The EDIT AUXILIARY command allows you to add or delete words from an auxiliary dictionary, and is available when an auxiliary dictionary is open.

To add words to an auxiliary dictionary:

✔ Choose EDIT AUXILIARY from the UTILITIES menu.

✔ Enter the new word into the New Word field in the Edit Auxiliary Dictionary dialog box (figure 9.18).

✔ Click the ADD button.

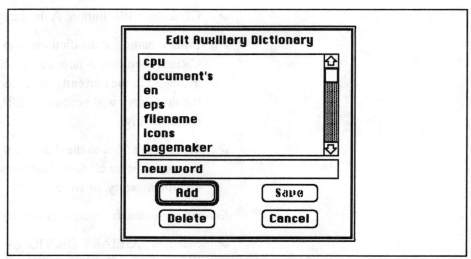

Edit Auxiliary Dictionary

cpu
document's
en
eps
filename
icons
pagemaker

new word

| Add | Save |
| Delete | Cancel |

Figure 9.18 The Edit Auxiliary Dictionary dialog box.

Repeat this process until all desired words are added.

✔ Click SAVE to save the changes to the auxiliary dictionary, or click CANCEL to cancel the changes and return to the document.

To delete words from an auxiliary dictionary:

✔ Choose EDIT AUXILIARY from the UTILITIES menu.

✔ Select the word(s) you wish to delete from the scroll list displayed in the Edit Auxiliary Dictionary dialog box.

✔ Click the DELETE button.

Repeat this process until all desired words are deleted.

✔ Click SAVE to save the changes to the auxiliary dictionary, or click CANCEL to cancel the changes and return to the document.

✳ ✳ ✳ ✳ ✳ ✳ ✳ ✳ ✳ ✳ ✳ ✳ ✳ ✳ ✳ ✳ ✳ ✳ ✳ ✳

⌘H   UTILITIES/
SUGGESTED HYPHENATION

The UTILITIES/SUGGESTED HYPHENATION command, available when a text box is selected with the Content tool, displays the suggested hyphenation for the word positioned to the left of the text cursor or a range of selected words. To use SUGGESTED HYPHENATION, the XPress Hyphenation file must be placed in the same folder with the QuarkXPress application or in the System folder.

UTILITIES/HYPHENATION EXCEPTIONS

Because XPress uses an algorithm (formula) for hyphenating words (see discussion of H&J settings in the EDIT/H&Js section) words may be hyphenated incorrectly. The UTILITIES/HYPHENATION EXCEPTIONS command, which is always available, is used to control how XPress hyphenates certain words.

Hyphenation exceptions are stored in the XPress Data file, so it is important that the data file be placed in the folder with the XPress application. If you transport your document to another location to be printed, be sure to take a copy of your XPress Data file, as well, so that the text will hyphenate as before. Hyphenation exceptions are applied to all documents.

To add words to the hyphenations exception list:

✔ Select the HYPHENATION EXCEPTIONS command from the UTILITIES menu.

✔ Enter the word into the word field in the Hyphenation Exceptions dialog box (figure 9.19), entering hyphens at desired hyphenation points. If you do not wish a word to be hyphenated, enter the word without hyphens.

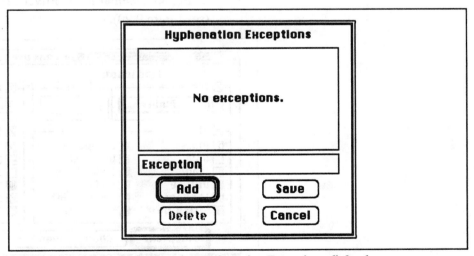

Figure 9.19 *Adding a word to the Hyphenation Exceptions dialog box.*

✔ Click ADD to add the word to the list. If you enter a word that is already contained in the exceptions list, the ADD button will change to REPLACE. Click REPLACE if you desire to replace the old hyphenation specification with the new one.

✔ Click SAVE to save changes to the exceptions list and close the dialog box. Click CANCEL if you wish to cancel changes and return to the document.

To delete words from the hyphenations exception list:

✔ Select the HYPHENATION EXCEPTIONS command from the UTILITIES menu.

✔ Select the word from the Hyphenation Exceptions list in the resulting dialog box.

✔ Click DELETE to remove the word from the list.

✔ Click SAVE to save changes to the exceptions list and close the dialog box. Click CANCEL if you wish to cancel changes and return to the document.

UTILITIES/
FONT USAGE

The UTILITIES/FONT USAGE command displays a list of all fonts used in a document and allows you to globally change those fonts.

To find and change a font:

✔ Select FONT USAGE from the UTILITIES menu. The Font Usage dialog box, similar to the FIND/CHANGE dialog box, will appear (see figure 9.20).

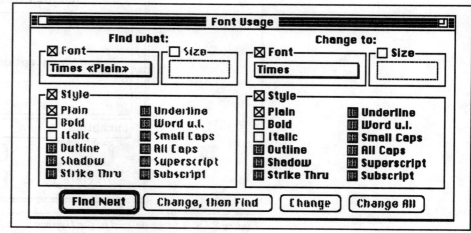

Figure 9.20 The Font Usage dialog box.

✔ Select the font you wish to change from the Find what Font pop-up menu.

✔ Select the font you wish to change to from the Change to Font pop-up menu.

✔ If desired, specify the type style(s) you wish to change from and to.

✔ Click the FIND NEXT button to start the search.

✔ Click the CHANGE THEN FIND button if you wish to progress through a document, instance by instance and control the change process.

✔ Click the CHANGE button if you wish to change the first selection without moving to the next instance.

✔ Click the CHANGE ALL button if you wish to change all instances of that font within the document.

❈ ❈ ❈ ❈ ❈ ❈ ❈ ❈ ❈ ❈ ❈ ❈ ❈ ❈ ❈ ❈ ❈ ❈ ❈

UTILITIES/
TRACKING EDIT

The TRACKING EDIT command allows you to customize how QuarkXPress spaces characters within particular fonts used in XPress documents. The tracking information is then stored in the XPress Data file and changes made to these specifications are used in all XPress documents. The text in documents created before changes are made to the Tracking or Kerning tables will be reflowed according to the new information when they are next opened. TRACKING EDIT will only be available if the Kern/Track Editor extension is placed in the same folder with the QuarkXPress application before launching the program.

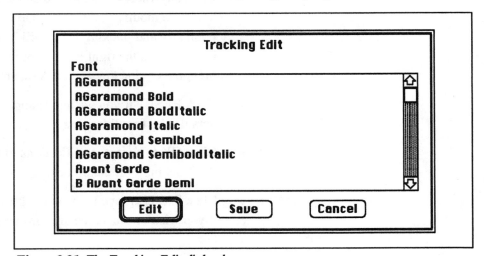

Figure 9.21 The Tracking Edit dialog box.

TEXT

To edit the character spacing for a font:

✔ Select TRACKING EDIT from the UTILITIES menu.

✔ Select the font you wish to edit from the font list in the Tracking Edit dialog box (figure 9.21).

✔ Click the EDIT button. The Tracking Values dialog box (figure 9.22) will appear which allows you to change the tracking values from -100/200 to 100/200 EM space in the selected font, from a point size of 2 pts. up to a size of 250 pts.

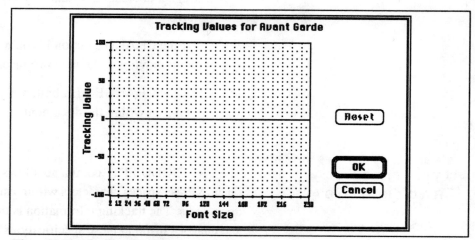

Figure 9.22 The Tracking Values dialog box.

The default value is represented by a straight horizontal line at 0 on the tracking table.

✔ Click anywhere on the line to create a handle and then drag the handle to modify the tracking curve. As you move the handle, the point size and tracking value will be displayed in the Size/Track indicators on the right top side of the dialog box. To delete a handle, press the Option key and click on an existing handle.

✔ Click RESET if you wish to change the tracking values back to the default of 0 for all font sizes.

✔ Click OK to accept modifications to the Tracking table and return to the Tracking Edit dialog box.

✔ Click SAVE to save the new tracking specifications. Click CANCEL if you wish to cancel the changes you have made and close the dialog box.

UTILITIES/
KERNING TABLE EDIT

The KERNING TABLE EDIT command allows you to customize how XPress kerns specific character pairs within particular fonts used in XPress documents. The kerning information is then stored in the XPress Data file and changes made to the Kerning table are then used in all XPress documents. The text in documents created before changes were made to the Kerning table will be reflowed according to the new information when they are next opened. KERNING TABLE EDIT will only be available if the Kern/Track Editor extension is placed in the same folder with the QuarkXPress application before launching the program.

To edit the kerning specification:

✔ Select KERNING TABLE EDIT command from the UTILITIES menu.

✔ Select the font you wish to edit from the font list in the **Kerning Table Edit** dialog box (figure 9.23).

✔ Click the EDIT button. The Kerning Values dialog box (figure 9.24) will appear.

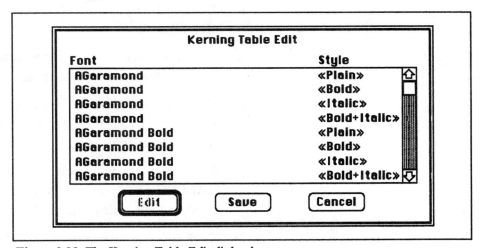

Kerning Table Edit

Font	Style
AGaramond	«Plain»
AGaramond	«Bold»
AGaramond	«Italic»
AGaramond	«Bold+Italic»
AGaramond Bold	«Plain»
AGaramond Bold	«Bold»
AGaramond Bold	«Italic»
AGaramond Bold	«Bold+Italic»

Edit   Save   Cancel

Figure 9.23 The Kerning Table Edit dialog box.

✔ Either select a pair from the Kerning Values pair list, or enter a new pair in the Pair field.

✔ The Value field will display the current kerning value for the selected pair. Enter a new value in this field, from -100/200 to 100/200 of an em.

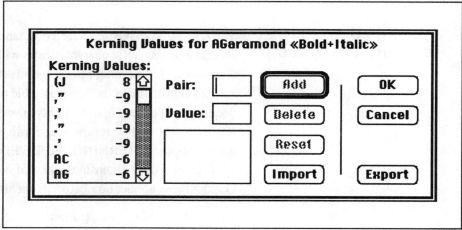

Figure 9.24 *The Kerning Values Edit dialog box.*

✔ Click ADD if you wish to add the new specifications to the list, or REPLACE if you wish to accept new kerning values for an existing pair.

✔ Click RESET if you wish to change the tracking values back to the default for all font pairs in the dialog box.

✔ Click DELETE if you wish to delete a character pair from the Kerning table.

✔ Click EXPORT to create an ASCII text file with all the currently values of the font's Kerning table.

✔ Click IMPORT if you want to replace the kerning values in the current font's table with the values of an ASCII file created previously using the Export command or with a word processor.

✔ Click OK to accept the new kerning value specifications, or click CANCEL if you wish to cancel the changes you have made and return to the Kerning Table Edit dialog box.

✔ Click SAVE to save changes to the Kerning table, or click CANCEL to cancel changes and close the Kerning Table Edit dialog box.

Using the Measurements Palette to Work with Text

The QuarkXPress Measurements Palette allows you to make many character and paragraph formatting changes without pulling down a menu or opening a dialog box. When a text box is activated with the Content Tool, the character and paragraph specifications will be displayed on the right side of the palette. See pages 12 and 13 for a full discussion of how to change specifications in the Measurements Palette when working with text.

Controlling Text Runaround

See the section on the ITEM/RUNAROUND command for discussion and instructions on controlling text runaround of elements and/or pictures.

Chapter Ten

Managing Pictures

Introduction to Working with Pictures

One of the powerful features of QuarkXPress is the ability to import a variety of picture formats and types. The following list outlines the picture file formats that may be imported into QuarkXPress:

Paint — Macpaint®, FullPaint™, SuperPaint, and scanned images saved as bitmapped.

PICT — MacDraw, MacDraft, Cricket Draw, Cricket Graph, SuperPaint, FreeHand, Canvas, Mac3d, MiniCAD, Pro3D, and scanned images saved as PICT.

EPS — Adobe Illustrator, Aldus Freehand, Cricket Draw, LaserFX, EPS pictures created on an IBM-compatible, and scanned images that have been saved as EPS.

TIFF and RIFF — scanned and RIFF edited pictures may also be imported into QuarkXPress.

Selecting Pictures

Once a picture has been placed in a picture box (see FILE/GET PICTURE and EDIT/PASTE commands in this section), the picture is selected by activating the picture box with the Content Tool. If the picture box is selected with the Item Tool, the box itself may be manipulated, but the picture may not.

Positioning Pictures

Once the picture has been selected with the Content Tool, there are several ways to position a picture within a picture box:

1. Position the mouse pointer over the picture; the hand icon will appear. Press the mouse button and drag the picture within the picture box, or

2. Use the x+ and y+ fields in the Measurements Palette to position the left/top offsets of the image, or

3. Enter the picture offset specifications in the Picture Box Specifications dialog box (ITEM/MODIFY), or

4. Use keyboard commands:

⌘-Shift-M centers the image in the middle of the box.

⌘-Shift-F scales the picture to fit the box and centers it.

⌘-Option-Shift-F scales the picture proportionately for the picture box and also centers it within the box.

Scaling Pictures

Once the picture has been selected with the Content Tool, there are also several ways to scale a picture within a picture box:

1. Use the x% and y% fields in the Measurements Palette to specify a scaling percentage, where 100% = the normal size of the picture. If equal values are entered in each field, the picture will be scaled proportionately. To stretch or shrink the picture disproportionately, enter unequal values in the percentage fields.

3. Enter horizontal and vertical scaling percentages specifications in the Picture Box Specifications dialog box (ITEM/MODIFY).

4. Use keyboard commands:

⌘-Option-Shift-< reduces the picture in 5% increments.

⌘-Option-Shift-> enlarges the picture in 5% increments.

⌘-Shift-F scales the picture to fit the box disproportionately and also centers it within the picture box.

⌘-Option-Shift-F scales the picture proportionately for the picture box and also centers it within the box.

Rotating Pictures

To rotate a picture within a picture box without rotating the box, either enter the degree of rotation in the picture angle field on the Measurements Palette or in the Picture Box Specifications dialog box. You may enter a value of -360° to 360° in increments as small as .01°.

Skewing Pictures

To skew a picture, that is to cause the picture to "lean," within a picture box, either enter the degree of lean in the picture skew field ( ) on the Measurements Palette or in the Picture Box Specifications dialog box. You may enter a values from -75° to 75° in increments as small as .01°.

Using Menu Commands to Work with Pictures

The File Menu

⌘ E GET PICTURE

The GET PICTURE command allows you to retrieve a previously created or scanned picture from disk and place it into a picture box in your Quark document. GET PICTURE is active only when you have selected a picture box with the Content Tool.

To Import a Picture into a QuarkXPress Document:

✔ With the Content Tool, select the picture box into which you want to place the picture.

✔ Pull down the FILE menu and select GET PICTURE. A dialog box, similar to the Get Text dialog box, will appear (figure 10.1). Using the Drive and Directory Title bar, navigate to the desired location until the picture or graphic file is listed in the dialog box.

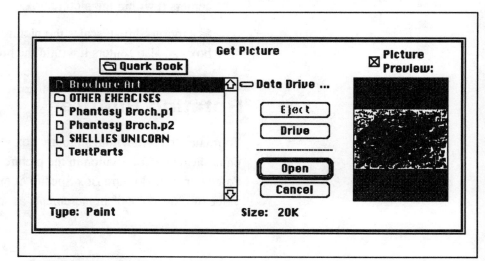

Figure 10.1 *The Get Picture dialog box.*

✔ Select the desired picture. The picture type and size will be displayed at the bottom of the box. Additionally, a thumbnail view of the picture will be displayed in the Picture Preview window on the right side of the Get Picture dialog box. (To deselect this feature, click on the Picture Preview box.)

✔ Click the OPEN button. The picture will automatically be placed into the selected picture box.

SAVE PAGE AS EPS

The SAVE PAGE AS EPS command allows you to save to disk an entire page as an encapsulated postscript image. The page may then be imported as a picture into any other QuarkXPress document or any page layout program that will import EPS files.

If the page to be saved as an EPS document contains pictures in EPS, TIFF, or RIFF formats, the EPS file will contain high resolution printing instructions for the pictures contained on the original page. This means that the EPS file, when printed from any program that supports EPS documents, will print high quality, high resolution images, whether or not the original files are present on disk.

To save a page as an encapsulated postscript image:

✔ Select the SAVE PAGE AS EPS command from the FILE menu. The dialog box, as shown in figure 10.2 will appear.

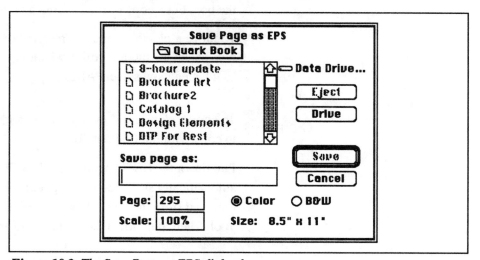

Figure 10.2 The Save Page as EPS dialog box.

✔ Type a name for the file. For clarity and easier identification of files, it is suggested that you name the file with an extension of ".EPS."

✔ Specify the page number you wish to save as an EPS document.

✔ Specify the scale percentage you wish to save it in. The value you enter in the Scale field defines the size of the on-screen (PICT) image that will be used to represent the EPS document. You can save a page at any percentage from 10% to 100% in .1% increments. The actual size of the PICT image will be displayed in the lower right portion of the dialog box.

✔ Select whether you wish the EPS file to be saved in color or B&W.

The Edit Menu

⌘ Z   UNDO/REDO

The EDIT UNDO command allows you to undo the previous action, whether cutting, deleting, copying, typing, replacing, or otherwise editing a picture in a picture box. EDIT/UNDO is only available *immediately* following the action you wish to UNDO. If you perform any other action such as clicking to activate an element on screen, or changing tool selection on the Tool Palette, EDIT/UNDO will no longer be available.

EDIT/REDO is available after the EDIT/UNDO command has been used.

⌘ X   CUT

To cut a picture, first select the picture with the Content Tool. Then pull down the EDIT menu and select CUT. The picture will be removed from the box, but a copy of it will remain on the Clipboard.

To move a picture to another picture box, CUT the picture from the first box, select the picture box in which you want to place it, pull down the EDIT menu and select PASTE.

⌘ C   COPY

To copy a picture and then paste in another box, select the picture you wish to copy with the Content Tool.

Pull down the EDIT menu and select COPY. A copy of the picture will be automatically stored on the Clipboard, but the picture itself will not be removed from the box. Click on the desired picture box with the Content Tool. Then, pull down the EDIT menu and select PASTE.

⌘ V   PASTE

The EDIT/PASTE command allows you to place a copy of the picture stored on the Clipboard in a picture box. Activate the box with the Content Tool. Pull down the EDIT menu and select PASTE.

CLEAR

To CLEAR or DELETE a picture from a picture box, first select the picture you wish to remove with the Content Tool. Then *either* pull down the EDIT menu and select CLEAR, or press the DELETE (backspace) key on the keyboard. If you delete a picture using either of these methods, a copy *will not* be stored on the clipboard. If you change your mind about deleting it, the only way to retrieve this picture is to select UNDO from the EDIT menu *immediately* following the clear or delete command.

SELECT ALL

The SELECT ALL command is not available for picture box contents.

SHOW CLIPBOARD

The SHOW CLIPBOARD command allows you to view whatever has been stored on the Clipboard. If you cut or copy a picture and want to be sure that you have done so correctly, select SHOW CLIPBOARD from the EDIT menu to display the Clipboard's contents. To close the Clipboard window, click in the close box in the upper left-hand corner, or select HIDE CLIPBOARD from the EDIT menu (it replaces SHOW CLIPBOARD when the Clipboard window is open).

The Style Menu

COLOR

The STYLE/COLOR command is available for certain picture formats when the picture is selected with the Content Tool. Color editing is available for Paint, TIFF, RIFF, black-and-white bitmap PICT, and Grayscale Bitmap PICT images. It is not available for EPS pictures. Color for Color TIFF and color bitmap images are adjustable through the Picture Contrast specifications dialog box (STYLE/OTHER CONTRAST).

Selecting a color from the color submenu will replace all shades of black in the picture with the same percentages of the selected color. To add colors to the Color Palette see the EDIT/COLOR command in the section on Working with Color.

SHADE

The STYLE/SHADE command is available for certain picture formats when the picture is selected with the Content Tool. The SHADE command may only be used with Paint and black-and-white bitmap PICT images. Shade is not available for EPS pictures. Adjustments to shading for TIFF, RIFF, Grayscale bitmap PICT, and Color bitmap PICT images are available through the Picture Contrast specifications dialog box (STYLE/OTHER CONTRAST).

To adjust the shade of a picture, select a percentage from the pop-up menu or select Other… and enter the desired percentage in increments as small as .1%.

NEGATIVE

The STYLE/NEGATIVE command produces a negative image of the picture and is available for certain picture formats when the picture is selected with the Content Tool. The NEGATIVE command may be used with TIFF and RIFF line art, TIFF and RIFF grayscale, TIFF color, grayscale bitmap PICT, and color bitmap PICT images. It is not available for Paint, EPS or black-and-white bitmap PICT images.

CONTRAST

The STYLE/CONTRAST commands are available for certain picture formats when the picture is selected with the Content Tool. The CONTRAST commands may be used with TIFF and RIFF grayscale, TIFF color, black-and-white bitmap PICT, and grayscale bitmap PICT images. It is not available for Paint, TIFF or RIFF line art, EPS, black-and-white bitmap PICT or Object PICT picture formats.

✔ NORMAL CONTRAST will leave a picture's contrast specifications unchanged (figure 10.3)

Figure 10.3 A TIFF picture at Normal Contrast.

✔ Selecting the HIGH CONTRAST command will print and display the areas of the picture with less than 30% of black or a color as white, and areas of the picture with more than 30% of black or a color with a 100% saturation (see figure 10.4).

Figure 10.4 The same TIFF picture with High Contrast selected.

✔ Selecting the POSTERIZED command will print and display a "step-graduated" color or black saturation in increments of 20%, up to 80%.

Figure 10.5 The TIFF picture with a Posterized contrast setting.

✔ Selecting OTHER CONTRAST will display the Picture Contrast Specifications dialog box which allows you to customize the pictures' contrast specifications. A different dialog box will appear for color (figure 10.7) or grayscale (figure 10.6) images.

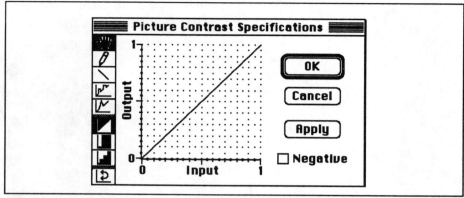

Figure 10.6 Picture Contrast Specifications dialog box for grayscale pictures.

Contrast Specifications dialog box for grayscale pictures:

Hand Tool — use this tool to drag the contrast curve around on the graph. To increase overall output values, drag the curve upwards. To decrease overall input values, drag the curve downwards.

Pencil Tool — this tool enables you to draw a new curve.

Line Tool — use this tool to make adjustments to the curve in straight lines. Press the shift key while using the Line Tool to constrain the lines to 0°, 45°, or 90° angles.

Posterizer Tool — clicking this tool will place handles in 10% increments on the horizontal axis of the graph. Dragging the handles up and/or down will increase or decrease the input-to-output contrast for the range represented by the graph.

Spike Tool — clicking the Spike Tool places handles in 10% increments on the horizontal axis of the graph. Dragging the handles up and/or down will increase or decrease the input-to-output contrast in sharp increments, called spikes.

Normal Contrast Tool — clicking this tool will reset the contrast to Normal specifications.

High Contrast Tool — clicking the High Contrast Tool will set the contrast to High, as described in the previous section (STYLE/HIGH CONTRAST).

Posterized Tool — clicking the Posterized Tool will set the contrast to Posterized, as described in the previous section (STYLE/POSTERIZED).

Inversion Tool — clicking this tool inverts the current contrast curve so that 0% input will result in 100% black output and vice-versa.

Negative — click the Negative box to specify a true negative of the original picture, which is created from the picture's normal contrast instead of a custom contrast.

Apply — click APPLY to preview the results of changes you have made to the picture's contrast without closing the Contrast Specifications dialog box.

OK — clicking OK accepts the contrast modifications and closes the dialog box.

Cancel — clicking CANCEL closes the dialog box without applying any modifications you have made to the contrast specifications.

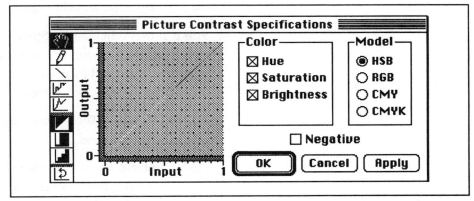

Figure 10.7 Picture Contrast Specifications dialog box for color pictures.

Contrast Specifications dialog box for color pictures:

Color Model — select a color model that you will use when adjusting contrast specifications for a color picture. The models are HSB (Hue, Saturation, and Brightness), RGB (Red, Green, and Blue), CMY (Cyan, Magenta, and Yellow), or CMYK (Cyan, Magenta, Yellow, and Black). See the section on Managing Color for the EDIT/COLORS command for a more complete description of these four models.

Color — you may select which parts of the model you would like to work with. For example if you have selected a CMYK model, you may choose to work with the contrast for only the Cyan values, or the Cyan and Yellows. A contrast curve line will appear on the graph for each one of the color parts you have selected. In addition, a color spectrum indicator will appear on the graph's axes when only one part of a color model is selected and when you are working on a color computer.

Hand Tool — use this tool to drag the contrast curve around on the graph. To increase overall output values, drag the curve upwards. To decrease overall input values, drag the curve downwards.

Pencil Tool — this tool enables you to draw a new curve.

Line Tool — use this tool to make adjustments to the curve in straight lines. Press the shift key while using the Line Tool to constrain the lines to 0°, 45°, or 90° angles.

Posterizer Tool — clicking this tool will place handles in 10% increments on the horizontal axis of the graph. Dragging the handles up and/or down will increase or decrease the input-to-output contrast for the range represented by the graph.

Spike Tool — clicking the Spike Tool places handles in 10% increments on the horizontal axis of the graph. Dragging the handles up and/or down will increase or decrease the input-to-output contrast in sharp increments, called spikes.

Normal Contrast Tool — clicking this tool will reset the contrast to Normal specifications.

High Contrast Tool — clicking the High Contrast Tool will set the contrast to High, as described in the previous section (Style/High Contrast).

Posterized Tool — clicking the Posterized Tool will set the contrast to Posterized, as described in the previous section (Style/Posterized).

Inversion Tool — clicking this tool inverts the current contrast curve so that 0% input will result in 100% color saturation output and vice-versa.

Negative — click the Negative box to specify a true negative of the original picture, which is created from the picture's normal contrast instead of a custom contrast.

Apply — click APPLY to preview the results of changes you have made to the picture's contrast without closing the Contrast Specifications dialog box.

OK — clicking OK accepts the contrast modifications and closes the dialog box.

Cancel — clicking CANCEL closes the dialog box without applying any modifications you have made to the contrast specifications.

SCREEN

The STYLE/SCREEN commands are available for certain picture formats when the picture is selected with the Content Tool. The Screen commands may be used with Paint, TIFF and RIFF line art, TIFF and RIFF grayscale, grayscale bitmap PICT, and color bitmap PICT images. It is not available for TIFF color, EPS, color bitmap PICT, or Object PICT picture formats.

✔ NORMAL SCREEN uses a dot pattern placed at a 45° angle to print a picture, and uses the lines per inch (lpi) specified in the page setup dialog box. Figure 10.3 shows a picture printed with a normal screen and normal contrast.

✔ The 60-LINE LINE SCREEN, 0° command will print a picture with 60 lines per inch, with the lines running horizontally (figure 10.8).

Figure 10.8 TIFF picture with normal contrast and 60-line screen.

✔ The 30-LINE LINE SCREEN, 45° command will print a picture with 30 lines per inch, with the lines running at a 45° angle (figure 10.9).

Figure 10.9 The TIFF picture with a normal contrast and 30-line screen.

✔ The 20-LINE DOT SCREEN, 45° command will print a picture with 20 dots per inch, with the dots running at a 45° angle.

Figure 10.10 The TIFF picture with a normal contrast and 20-line dot screen.

✔ The OTHER SCREEN command allows you to define custom screening values for a selected picture. When selected, the Picture Screening Specifications dialog box (figure 10.11) will be displayed, with the following halftone options:

Screen — the screen field allows you to specify the number of lines per inch, from 15 to 400, in which you wish the picture to be printed. The default specification for lpi is determined by the value entered in the lpi field in the Page Setup dialog box.

Angle — specify the line angle in degrees in this field, from -360° to 360° in 1° increments.

Pattern — select from several halftone patterns in this field: dot, line, ellipse, square, or ordered dither. The *ordered dither* pattern is recommended when you are printing to a 300 dpi laser printer and when you will be making additional copies of the document with a photocopier rather than by commercial printing.

DISPLAY HALFTONING— to view predefined screening specifications on-screen, as limited by your monitor's resolution.

OK — click OK to accept the specifications and return to the document.

CANCEL — click CANCEL to close the dialog box without accepting any modifications to the screen specifications.

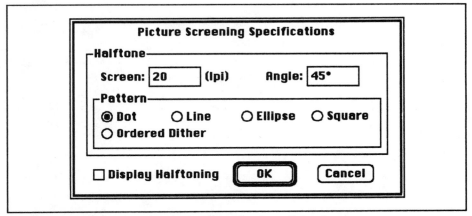

Figure 10.11 The Picture Screening Specifications dialog box.

The Utilities Menu

PICTURE USAGE

The UTILITIES/PICTURE USAGE command displays a dialog box that lists the names of all of the pictures used in a document, their disk locations, their page placement in the document, the picture format type, and current status of the pictures (OK, missing, or modified).

The UPDATE button is used to locate and re-import missing pictures, or to automatically re-import modified pictures.

The SHOW ME button is used to view a picture in a document. Clicking SHOW ME takes you to the page where the picture is located. The command is useful if you cannot recall what the picture looks like.

Using the Measurements Palette to Work with Pictures

The QuarkXPress Measurements Palette allows you to make many modifications to a picture without pulling down a menu or opening a dialog box. When a picture box is activated with the Content Tool, the current scaling, offset, picture angle, and picture skew values will be displayed on the right side of the palette. See page 14 for a description of how to change specifications in the Measurements Palette when working with pictures.

Chapter Eleven

Managing Color

Using the Menu Commands to Work with Color

The EDIT/COLORS command allows you to define, add, delete, and edit colors on the Color Palette that is available for QuarkXPress documents. In addition, the EDIT/COLORS command is used to control how Quark traps colors when color-separating the printed output.

The EDIT/COLORS command is always available and colors that are added to the palette when no document is open will be available for all new documents subsequently created. Colors that are added to the palette when a document is open will be available to that document only, unless appended to another document.

To add a color to the Color Palette:

✔ Select COLORS from the EDIT menu. The Colors dialog box will be displayed (figure 11.1).

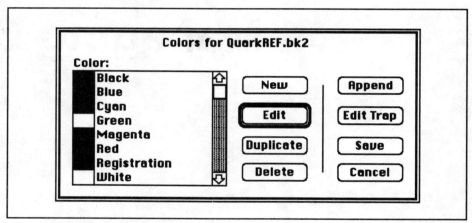

Figure 11.1 The Colors dialog box.

✔ Click the NEW button. The Edit Color dialog box will appear (figure 11.2).

✔ Enter a name for the color in the Name field.

✔ Select a color model in which to work when specifying/editing colors.

✔ Select whether color separation is Off or On. If you select Off, then the color will be treated as a spot color when printing color plates and will not be separated into the four process colors (CMYK). If you

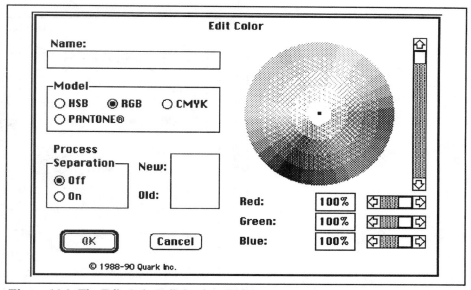

Figure 11.2 The Edit Colors dialog box with RGB color mode selected.

select On, then Quark will print the color on four separate plates, according to the four-color process model when color separation is selected in the Print dialog box.

✔ Select a color using one or a combination of the following methods:

If you are using the HSB, RGB, or CMYK models, you may select a color by clicking on the desired portion of the color wheel, or you can enter the percentages of each component of a color in the color percentage fields, or you can use the scroll bars to the right of the color wheel and/or the color percentage fields to scroll to the desired percentage of each color component.

If you are using the Pantone® color model, scroll to the desired color in the Pantone color chart and then click on the desired color to select it (see figure 11.3).

The selected color will be displayed in the New color field to the right of the Process Separation option.

✔ Click OK to accept the color and return to the Colors dialog box.

✔ Click SAVE to keep the new color in the Color Palette and close the dialog box.

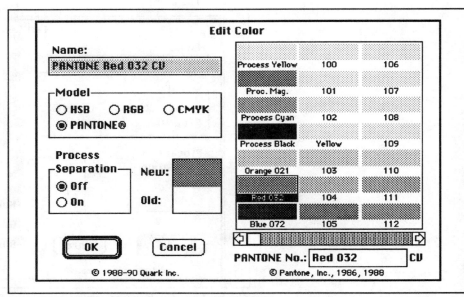

Figure 11.3 *The Edit Colors dialog box with Pantone color mode selected.*

To edit an existing color:

✔ Select COLORS from the EDIT menu. The Colors dialog box will be displayed.

✔ Select the color you desire to edit from the list of color names displayed in the Colors dialog box.

✔ Click the EDIT button. The Edit Color dialog box will appear.

✔ If you wish, enter a new name for the color in the Name field.

✔ Select a color model in which to work when specifying/editing colors.

✔ Select whether color separation is Off or On. If you select Off, then the color will be treated as a spot color when printing color plates and will not be separated into the four process colors (CMYK). If you select On, then Quark will print the color on four separate plates, according to the four-color process model when color separation is selected in the Print dialog box.

✔ Select a new color using one or a combination of the following methods:

If you are using the HSB, RGB, or CMYK models, you may select a color by clicking on the desired portion of the color wheel, or you can enter the percentages of each component of a color in the color percentage fields, or you can use the scroll bars to the right of the color wheel and/or the color percentage fields to scroll to the desired percentage of each color component.

If you are using the Pantone® color model, scroll to the desired color in the Pantone color chart and then click on the desired color to select it.

The selected color will be displayed in the New color field to the right of the Process Separation option and above the previous color, displayed in the Old color field.

✔ Click OK to accept the color and return to the Colors dialog box.

✔ Click SAVE to keep the color changes in the Color Palette and to close the dialog box.

To duplicate a color:

✔ Select COLORS from the EDIT menu. The Colors dialog box will be displayed.

✔ Select the color you desire to duplicate from the list of color names displayed in the Colors dialog box.

✔ Click the DUPLICATE button. The duplicated color will appear in the color names list with a name such as "copy of *(current color name)."* The color may then be edited in the usual manner.

✔ Click OK to accept the color and return to the Colors dialog box.

✔ Click SAVE to keep the color changes in the Color Palette and to close the dialog box.

To delete a color:

✔ Select COLORS from the EDIT menu. The Colors dialog box will be displayed.

✔ Select the color you desire to remove from the list of color names displayed in the Colors dialog box.

✔ Click the DELETE button. The color will be removed from the Color Palette. If the color has been applied to text, pictures, or page elements, QuarkXPress will display a dialog box allowing you to confirm whether or not you really wish to delete the color. If an applied color is deleted, all items to which that color has been applied will revert to Black. You may not remove the following default colors: Cyan, Magenta, Yellow, Black, White, and Registration.

✔ Click OK to accept the color and return to the Colors dialog box.

✔ Click SAVE to keep the color changes in the Color Palette and to close the dialog box.

To append colors from another QuarkXPress document:

✔ Select COLORS from the EDIT menu. The Colors dialog box will be displayed.

✔ Click the APPEND button. A directory dialog box will appear.

✔ Select the document from which you want to append colors and click OPEN. All of the colors contained in the selected document will be imported into the current document (or the list of default colors, if no document is open) except those colors with duplicate names.

✔ Click OK to accept the color and return to the Colors dialog box.

✔ Click SAVE to keep the color changes in the Color Palette and to close the dialog box.

To Edit color trapping:

✔ Select COLORS from the EDIT menu. The Colors dialog box will be displayed.

✔ Click the EDIT TRAP button. The Trap Specifications dialog box will appear (figure 11.4) with the following options:

Background Color — Select the background color(s) for which you want to specify new trapping values. The color called "Indeterminate" is used when a foreground color is placed against a background of more than one color or in a case where QuarkXPress cannot identify the background color.

Value — This field displays the current trapping value applied to the background color.

Automatic — Clicking the AUTOMATIC button applies automatic color trapping. Automatic indicates that QuarkXPress will trap the colors according to Quark's built-in algorithm: If the background color is darker than the object color, it chokes the background color by the difference in shade between the two colors; if the background color is lighter than the object color, it spreads the object color by the difference between the two colors; and if the object color is black with a shade value of 95% or more, it will overprint the background color.

Overprint — Clicking OVERPRINT specifies that the object color will be printed over the background color.

Trap — Enter a trapping value in this field, from -5 pts. to +5 pts., in increments of .001 (in any measurement unit you choose). If you enter a negative value, it will choke the knockout area of the background color. If you enter a positive value, it will spread the object size in relationship to the background color. If you enter a value of 0 (zero), the background color and object color will align with, or "butt against" each other.

OK — click OK to accept modifications to the trapping values and return to the Colors dialog box.

CANCEL — click CANCEL to return to the Colors dialog box without keeping modifications to the trapping specifications.

Click SAVE to keep the color changes in the Color Palette and to close the dialog box.

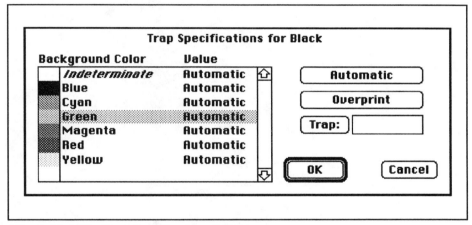

Figure 11.4 The Trap Specifications dialog box.

❖ ❖ ❖ ❖ ❖ ❖ ❖ ❖ ❖ ❖ ❖ ❖ ❖ ❖ ❖ ❖ ❖ ❖ ❖

Sᴛʏʟᴇ/Cᴏʟᴏʀ

The STYLE/COLOR command is available to apply colors from the Color Palette to text, certain types of pictures, and page elements. For complete descriptions of how to apply colors to QuarkXPress elements and contents, see the STYLE/COLOR command in the appropriate sections of this reference.

Also see the section on ITEM/MODIFY in the Managing Page Elements section for a description of how to fill boxes with a color and/or shade.

Chapter Twelve

Using the Libraries Feature

Creating a Library

To create a new library, pull down the UTILITIES menu and select LIBRARY. A directory dialog box will appear (figure 12.1), that allows you to locate a pre-existing library on disk or to establish a new library.

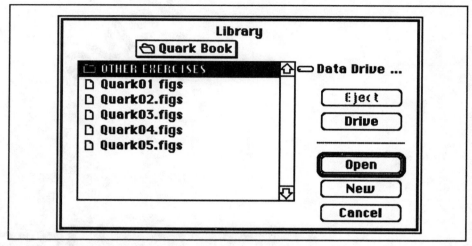

Figure 12.1 *The Library directory dialog box.*

Click on NEW. Then, enter a name for the library in the New Library field. Click on the CREATE button to save the library to disk. An empty Library Palette will appear on the right side of your screen (see figure 12.2).

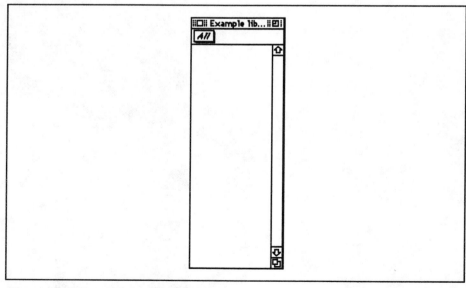

Figure 12.2 *A newly created, empty library.*

Opening a Previously Created Library

To open a library, pull down the UTILITIES menu and select LIBRARY. A directory dialog box will appear (figure 12.1), that allows you to locate a pre-existing library on disk or to establish a new library.

Select the library you wish to open. Click OPEN.

Storing Items in a Library

To store items in the newly created library, click on the items you wish to store (text or picture boxes, lines, or grouped elements) with the Item Tool to select them. Then drag the items into the Library Palette window. As you drag the items into the palette, the cursor changes from the Item Tool icon to a pair of eyeglasses. When the library pointer (two small triangles, one on each side of the palette) appears, you can release the mouse button. A copy of the items will now be stored in the library (see figure 12.3).

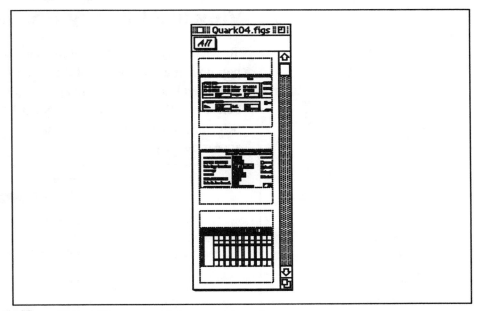

Figure 12.3 A library containing several entries.

Naming Library Entries

To name an item that has been stored in a library, double-click on the library item. The Library Entry dialog box will appear. Enter the name of the item and then click OK.

Deleting Library Entries

To delete an item from a library, select the entry, then select CLEAR from the EDIT menu or press the DELETE key. Then press OK in the dialog box which warns you that you will not be able to UNDO the library entry deletion.

Placing Library Entries in a Document

To use a library entry, click on the entry and drag its icon onto the document page. An outline of the element(s) will appear on the page. With the mouse button still depressed, drag the item to its desired position and let go of the mouse button. The element(s) may then be positioned and/or modified in the usual manner.

Viewing Library Entries by Name

To selectively view certain library entries, press the mouse button on the pop-up menu near the top of the Library Palette (see figure 12.4). A list of all named library entries will appear. Select those you wish to view. Selecting All will cause all library entries to appear on the Library Palette. Selecting Unlabeled will cause only those entries that are unnamed to appear on the palette.

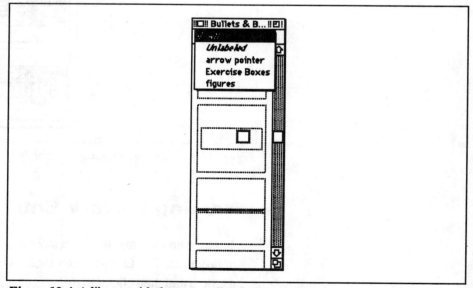

Figure 12.4 A library with the pop-up list displayed. All is selected.

Appendix A

Macintosh Basics

MAC Basics

SYSTEM COMPONENTS

Monitor —The display screen.

Central Processing Unit (CPU) — The "brains" of the computer. It is the central processing unit that processes each instruction that is sent to the computer. For example, when you press the letter "A" on the keyboard, the CPU processes the digital instructions sent from the keyboard, stores the information, and sends instructions to display the letter A on the monitor.

Keyboard — The keyboard is an input device and is similar to a typewriter keyboard.

Mouse — The mouse is also an input device, used to give instructions to the computer through pointing and clicking actions. We use it to select items and/or commands from the Macintosh menus.

Peripherals — Printer or scanner for example.

THE MACINTOSH DESKTOP ENVIRONMENT

The Macintosh graphic interface emulates our business office, and the screen it presents to you when you turn it on is called the "desktop." It even has a trash can so you can throw things away that you don't want.

Icons — Icons are pictures that represent things, and are used by the Macintosh system to communicate to the computer user. Frequently, on the Macintosh, you will select things by pointing to them with the mouse and clicking the mouse buttons.

Hard Disks — A hard drive is usually indicated by a small rounded-rectangle icon. A hard disk, named so because it is made from hard, magnetically encoded aluminum, is usually installed inside your Macintosh and is capable of storing a lot of information. If you can turn on and start up your Macintosh without inserting a floppy disk (see below), then your computer has a hard disk installed in it.

Floppy Disks — Floppy disks are made of thin, "floppy" plastic that is magnetically coded to store digital information. The 3 ½" disks used with a Macintosh are encased in a harder plastic to protect the fragile storage media. Though these disks appear to be "hard," they need care. Do not expose your floppy disks to excessive sun, heat, dust, or any magnets (magnets may erase some or all of the data stored on your disk).

MOUSE OPERATIONS

As mentioned before, you will use the mouse to communicate instructions to the computer. Therefore it is essential to understand how to operate the mouse. Following is a list of actions you will perform and what those actions accomplish.

Point: Hold the mouse in your hand, with the ball of the mouse firmly in contact with the mouse pad. Move the mouse to the left and watch the computer screen as you do so. You will see the mouse pointer move. Point to the various objects on the desktop — the trash can, the menus, the disk icon, etc.

Click: Click means to press the mouse button one time quickly and let go immediately.

Select: To select an object or icon, usually you will simply click on it one time with the mouse pointer.

Deselect: To deselect an object, click one time on an "empty" area of the desktop or window area.

Double-click: To double-click means to click two times very quickly. If you wait too long between clicks, the computer will interpret them as two separate clicks rather than as a double-click. Double-clicking is frequently used to start up an application, such as a word processing or paint program, or to open a document that was previous created. Double-clicking is also used to access special features of many programs.

Press: To press means to hold the mouse button down.

Drag: To drag, press the mouse button on a selected object and then move the mouse. The item will move or "drag" with the mouse.

Shift-click: A common use for shift-clicking is to select more than one icon on the desktop. To do so, click on the first icon, hold the shift key down and click on the second item. Continue until all desired items have been selected.

WORKING WITH WINDOWS

Opening Windows: A window is really a view of what is stored on a disk or a folder. To quickly open a window, double-click on a disk or folder icon. (See figure A-1.) A window will open to show you the contents of that disk or folder.

Activating Windows: Although the Macintosh allows many windows to be open at once, only one window may be active at a time. To activate a window, simply click on it one time with the mouse. Horizontal lines and the close and zoom boxes will appear on the title bar.

Moving Windows: To move a window, point to the title bar, press the mouse button, and drag to the desired location. A rectangular "ghost" shape of the window will follow the mouse pointer. When you release the mouse button, the window will relocate to the new position.

MAC Basics

Closing Windows: To close a window, click one time in the close box.

Zooming a Window: To quickly resize a window to full size click one time in the zoom box. To return the window to its previous size and location, click in the zoom box again.

Resizing a Window: To resize a window, point the mouse pointer to the resize box in the lower right-hand corner, press the mouse button and drag in any direction (either in or out). Try this several times until you are comfortable with resizing windows.

Using a Window's Scrolling Features: If your disk or folder contains more items than can be displayed in the active window, scroll arrows, bars, and boxes will appear. For example, to scroll to the left in small increments, place the mouse pointer on the left arrow at the bottom of the window and click the mouse.

To scroll in a smooth movement, hold the mouse button down on the down scroll arrow. Watch what happens. Try this action with the right scroll arrow. The up/down arrows on the vertical scroll bar (right side of the window) work in the same fashion.

To scroll in larger increments, usually window-wide, click on the grey scroll bar.

To move quickly from one side of the window to the other, or from top to bottom, drag the appropriate scroll box from its current location to one end of the scroll bar. What happens?

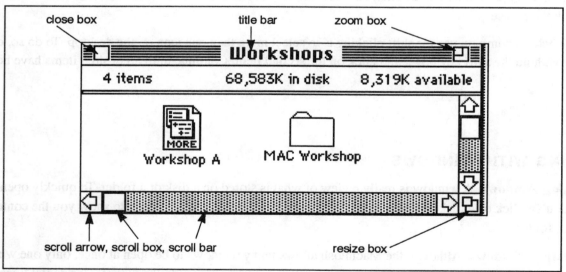

Figure A-1: The anatomy of a Macintosh window.

DESKTOP MENUS

Pulldown menus are accessed by pointing the mouse pointer at the Menu title at the top of the Macintosh window. Then, press the mouse button down and hold it down, while dragging the mouse pointer to the desired menu item. When you let go of the mouse button, the selected menu item will be performed. If a menu item is grey, that means it is currently not accessible.

The Apple Menu — desk accessories:

Desk accessories are small programs that are always accessible by pulling down the Apple menu. These menu items listed may be different on each computer system, depending upon the accessories that have been installed on that computer.

Figure A-2: The Desk Accessory Menu

The File menu:

The File menu items are designed to help you manage files and folders on your disk(s). For example, folders are created to group related documents — much as you would group documents in a file cabinet within folders. To create a new folder, pull down the File menu and select New Folder. To name the folder, immediately enter the desired name on the Macintosh keyboard. Then press Enter or click elsewhere on the Macintosh window to accept the folder name.

Figure A-3: The File Menu

The Edit menu:

The Edit menu is used to select files or folders, to Cut, Copy, and Paste filenames, to display the contents of the Clipboard, and to Undo the previous unwanted action.

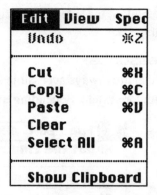

Figure A-4: The Edit Menu

The View menu:

The View menu allows you to display files and folders in a variety of ways, accommodating each Macintosh user's unique preferences and working style.

Figure A-5: The View Menu

The Special menu:

The Special menu allows you to "clean up" or rearrange your files, empty the trash (permanently throwing away any files you have placed there), erase a disk, set the Macintosh to launch an application when you turn it on, Restart, and Shutdown.

Figure A-2: The Desk Accessory Menu

THE SYSTEM FOLDER

You will notice a special folder on your hard disk window when you open it. It is called the System Folder and has an icon of a small Macintosh on the folder.

The Operating System — The system file is the single-most important file on the startup disk. Without the system file, the computer cannot run. If you have ever tried to start a Macintosh with the wrong disk (one without a system folder) it simply ejects your disk and sits there with a blinking ? in the middle of the screen.

The Finder — The Finder is the part of the operating system that locates programs and files, copies, moves, and deletes items. Without the Finder you will not be able to use the files on your disk.

The Clipboard — The Clipboard is a special place in the computer's memory that temporarily stores items that have been copied, deleted, or cut.

INITIALIZING A DISK

Initializing, or formatting, a disk prepares it for use by the computer. The initialization process divides the disk magnetically into areas called *tracks* and *segments* which are used to locate the data that you will save on the disk. Without formatting, a disk is nothing but a useless piece of plastic with a magnetic coating on it.

To initialize (format) a disk, place it in the Macintosh disk drive (the sliding metal edge goes in first, with the circular metal center down). If it has never been used before, you will see a message on screen asking if you wish to initialize the disk. Choose the Two-Sided option (one-sided is not used unless you are using a Macintosh 512K or older machine) and then click on OK when it asks you if it is ok to erase the disk. (There is nothing on it anyway, right?)

DISK AND FILE MANAGEMENT

Inserting/Ejecting Floppy Disks — To insert a disk, hold it with the metal slider away from you, and the metal circle down. Insert it straight into the disk drive. Be sure not to force the disk.

There are two ways to eject a disk:

1. Drag the disk to the trash can. (No it will not erase anything to do this — it simply removes the disk from the disk drive.) The disk icon will also be removed from the desktop.
2. Select the disk, pull down the File menu and select Eject (E). The disk will be ejected from the drive, but the disk's icon will remain on the desktop in "ghost" form.

Creating / Using Files — Files, frequently called documents are created when you use a program such as a word processor or paint program and then save it to disk. Files are represented by icons in the Macintosh window.

Launching Applications — Launching is another term meaning to start up an application. Application is another word for program. Any program designed to help you get your work done, whether it is a word processing program, an accounting program, or a page layout program (like PageMaker) is called an application. Applications are launched by double-clicking on the application's icon.

Copying Disks and/or Files

Disk-to-disk (two floppy disk drives) — to copy one floppy disk in its entirety to another floppy disk, do the following:

1. Hard lock your source disk. Insert the source disk in one drive and insert the target disk in the other. (it doesn't matter which one).

2. Drag the icon of the source disk on top of the target disk icon (you should see the target icon turn dark as if selected). Let go of the mouse button. A dialog box will appear that asks you if you want to replace the contents of the target disk with the contents of the source disk. Click OK. Then wait until finished.

Disk-to-disk (one floppy disk drive) — to copy one floppy disk in its entirety to another floppy disk, do the following:

1. Lock the source disk, then place in the floppy drive. Using the File/Eject command (E) eject the disk. The disk icon should remain on the desktop, but it will be grey, like menu items that are not accessible.

2. Insert the target disk. Drag the "ghost" icon of the source disk onto the target disk icon. A dialog box will appear that asks you if you want to replace the contents of the target disk with the contents of the source disk. Click OK. Then follow the instructions given to you by the dialog boxes: you will need to continue swapping disks until the copying process is complete.

Copying a File on its Own (Same) Disk — to make a copy of a file onto the same disk, select the file, pull down the File menu and select Duplicate.

Erasing Files — To erase a file, drag it to the trash can.

Renaming Files and/or Disks — To rename a file or a disk, simply select the file or disk and then type the new name. Press enter or return when done.

Shutting Down — To end a computer session, pull down the Special menu and select Shut Down. You should do this each time you end your Macintosh session. If you simply turn off the computer without properly shutting it down, system files on the startup disk may be damaged.

Appendix B

Keyboard Commands

Key Commands

FOR MANAGING DOCUMENTS

Menu Commands

File/New .... ⌘N
File/Open .... ⌘O
File/Save .... ⌘S
File/Page Setup .... ⌘-Option-P
File/Print .... ⌘P
File/Quit .... ⌘Q
Edit/General Preferences .... ⌘Y
Typographic Preferences ⌘-Option-Y
Page/Go to .... ⌘J
View/Fit in Window .... ⌘0
View/Actual Size .... ⌘1
Show Rulers .... ⌘R

Commands Available on the Apple Extended Keyboard

On-line Help .... Help
To beginning of document .... Home
To end of document .... End
Up one screen .... Page Up
Down one screen .... Page Down
To previous page .... Shift-Page Up
To next page .... Shift-Page Down
To first page .... Shift-Home
To last page .... Shift-End

FOR MANAGING PAGE ELEMENTS

Moving Items with Item Tool

Right (1 pt) .... Right Arrow
Right (.1-point) ..Option-Right Arrow
Left (1 pt) .... Left Arrow
Left (.1 pt) .... Option-Left Arrow
Up (1 pt) .... Up Arrow
Up (.1 pt) .... Option-Up Arrow
Down (1 pt) .... Down Arrow

Down (.1 pt) ...... Option-Down Arrow

Moving Items with Other Tools

Any direction .... ⌘-Drag
90° Constraints .... ⌘-Shift-Drag

Creating Items

Constrain to 45° .... Shift-Drag

Changing Line Widths

Increase 1 pt .... ⌘-Option-Shift->
Decrease 1 pt .... ⌘-Option-Shift-<

Menu Commands

Item/Modify .... ⌘-M
Item/Frame .... ⌘-B
Item/Runaround .... ⌘-T
Item/Duplicate .... ⌘-D
Item/Step & Repeat .... ⌘-Option-D
Item/Delete .... ⌘-K
Item/Group .... ⌘-G
Item/Ungroup .... ⌘-U
Item/Lock .... ⌘-L

FOR MANAGING TEXT

Menu Commands

File/Get Text .... ⌘-E
Edit/Undo .... ⌘-Z
Edit/Cut .... ⌘-X
Edit/Copy .... ⌘-C
Edit/Paste .... ⌘-V
Edit/Select All .... ⌘-A
Edit/Find/Change .... ⌘-F
Style/Size
    Other .... ⌘-\
Style/TypeStyle
    Plain .... ⌘-Shift-P
    Bold .... ⌘-Shift-B
    Italic .... ⌘-Shift-I
    Underline .... ⌘-Shift-U
    Word Underline .... ⌘-Shift-W
    Strike Thru .... ⌘-Shift-/

Outline .... ⌘-Shift-O
Shadow .... ⌘-Shift-S
All Caps .... ⌘-Shift-K
Small Caps .... ⌘-Shift-H
Superscript .... ⌘-Shift-+
Subscript .... ⌘-Shift-Hyphen
Superior .... ⌘-Shift-V
Style/Character .... ⌘-Shift-D
Style/Alignment
    Left .... ⌘-Shift-J
    Centered .... ⌘-Shift-C
    Right .... ⌘-Shift-R
    Justified .... ⌘-Shift-J
Style/Leading .... ⌘-Shift-E
Style/Formats .... ⌘-Shift-F
Style/Rules .... ⌘-Shift-N
Style/Tabs .... ⌘-Shift-T
View/Show/Hide Invisibles .... ⌘I
Utilities/Check Spelling
    Word .... ⌘W
    Story .... ⌘-Option-W
Utilities/Suggested Hyphenation .⌘H

Changing Font Size

Increase (preset sizes) .... ⌘-Shift->
Increase 1-pt. inc. .... ⌘-Option-Shift->
Decrease (preset sizes) .... ⌘-Shift-<
Increase 1-pt inc ..... ⌘-Option-Shift-<

Changing Horizontal Scaling

Increase in 5% inc. .... ⌘-]
Decrease in 5% inc. .... ⌘-[

Changing Kerning/Tracking Values

Increase 10/200 em .... ⌘-Shift-}
Decrease 10/200 em .... ⌘-Shift-{
Increase 1/200 em .... ⌘-Option-Shift-}
Decrease 1/200 em .... ⌘-Option-Shift-{

Changing Baseline Shift

Up 1 pt. .... ⌘-Option-Shift-+
Down 1 pt .... ⌘-Option-Shift-hyphen

Changing Leading Values

Inc. leading 1 pt...................⌘-Shift-"

Dec. leading 1 pt..................⌘-Shift-:

Inc. leading .1 pt. ......⌘-Option-Shift-"

Dec. leading .1 pt. .....⌘-Option-Shift-:

Copying Paragraph Formats

Copy format to selected
  paragraph ....Option-Shift-Click

Moving Text Cursor

Previous character...............left arrow

Next character....................right arrow

Previous word ....⌘-left arrow

Next word ....⌘-right arrow

Previous paragraph...........⌘-up arrow

Next paragraph ....⌘-down arrow

Start of line ....⌘-Option-left arrow

End of line ....⌘-Option-right arrow

Previous line..........................up arrow

Next line ....down arrow

Start of story........⌘-Option-up arrow

End of story ....⌘-Option-down arrow

Moving and Positioning the Picture within Picture Box

1 pt. increments.................arrow keys

.1 pt. increments ...Option-arrow keys

Center in box.....................⌘-Shift-M

Scaling the Picture within Picture Box

Increase sin 5% inc.⌘-Option-Shift->

Decrease in 5% inc.⌘-Option-Shift-<

Fit to box ....⌘-Shift-F

Fit proportionately to box
  ....⌘-Option-Shift-F

Simultaneously Resizing Picture Boxes while Scaling Pictures

Resize box and scale picture...⌘-drag

Resize box and scale picture,
maintaining aspect ratio
  ....⌘-Option-Shift-drag

FOR MANAGING PICTURES

(content tool selected)

Menu Commands

File/Get Pictures ....⌘-E

Edit/Cut...⌘-X

Edit/Copy ....⌘-C

Edit/Paste ....⌘-V

Style/Negative..........⌘-Shift-Hyphen

Style/Normal Contrast ....⌘-Shift-N

Style/High Contrast ....⌘-Shift-H

Style/Posterized Contrast ...⌘-Shift-P

Style/Other Contrast ....⌘-Shift-C

Style/Other Screen..............⌘-Shift-S

Appendix C

Glossary

Glossary

Ascender .... The part of a letter that rises above the body (x-height) of the letter. Examples of letters with ascenders: h, d, b, k.

Baseline .... The imaginary line upon which letters appear to rest.

Cap height .... Height of capital letters. The actual height amount will change according to typeface and size of the letters.

Crop marks .... Lines or marks that indicate the outside limits of the page.

Descender .... The part of a letter that extends below the baseline. Example of letters with descenders: j, g, p.

Em .... The size of an em (in width) is equal to the point size of the type. For example, an em for 12 point type is 12 points in width. (See Point.)

En .... An en is ½ the width of an em. (See Em.)

EPS .... Encapsulated Postscript. A format in which graphics or illustrations are saved to disk.

Footer .... Text or information that is printed at the bottom of each page of a document.

Format .... The layout of a document or area of text on a page.

Grid .... The pattern of horizontal and vertical lines on a page. As used in page layout applications, the grid lines are non-printing and can be viewed on the computer monitor.

Guideline .... A non-printing line that is used to create grids and to align page elements.

Gutter .... Space between text columns and along margins between facing pages.

Heading .... Text or information that is printed at the top of each page of a document.

Justification .... Method of spacing words in a line of text to produce either even or ragged margins.

Kern .... In QuarkXPress, kerning is defined as increasing or decreasing the space between a *pair* of characters.

Landscape page
orientation .... Orienting a page so that its long side is at the top of the page.

Layout .... Design or arrangement of page elements (text, pictures, lines, etc.) on a document.

Leading .... The vertical space between lines, measured in Quark, from one baseline to the baseline above it.

Pantone color .... Pantone® Matching System (PMS) for matching ink colors.

Pica .... A unit of measurement. There are approximately 6 picas per inch, or 0.166" per pica.

Point .... A unit of measurement. There are 72 points per inch, 12 points per pica.

Ruler origin point ... The point at which the horizontal and vertical ruler 0-points intersect.

Registration color ... A color, that when applied to an element, will cause that element to print on every plate of a color-separated document.

Registration marks... Alignment marks that are placed on each page of a document, and are used to line up overlays and color separations.

Rules .... Lines of various widths placed on a page.

Runaround .... Term used to describe how text is set around a graphic element on the page.

Typeface .... Used to describe a type "family," such as Times, Helvetica, or Palatino.

Type style .... Variations of typeface such as italic, bold, underlined, or shadowed.

Typography .... The art of type setting.

Vertical alignment ... Alignment of text between the top and bottom of a text box, or the alignment of elements between the top and bottom edges of a page.

Wraparound .... The process of automatically wrapping or shifting words from one line to the next when the first line becomes too long to fit within the width boundaries of a text box.

Appendix D

QuarkXPress
Version 3.1 Update

QuarkXPress 3.1 offers many new features that will enhance your desktop publishing productivity. These features are listed in this appendix with brief descriptions of the functions and uses for each feature.

SYSTEM 7.0 COMPATIBLE

QuarkXPress 3.1 is fully system 7.0 compatible and makes use of the new system's features.

NETWORK USER SUPPORT

QuarkXPress 3.1 allows ServicePlus™ owners who use multicopy versions of QuarkXPress to more easily update their copies on the network.

COMPLETE SAVE

The new QuarkXPress now does a complete save every time you save, including Hyphenation and Justification settings, preferences, kerning and tracking tables, previously saved only in the XPress Data Document. This means that you no longer need to keep a copy of the Data Document with your XPress document.

DON'T PRINT BLANK PAGES

You can choose not to print blank pages in a document, saving paper or film in the final output.

SHOW LAYOUT GRID

The baseline grid, previously an invisible grid, can now be viewed by selecting SHOW BASELINE GRID from the VIEW menu.

ACTIVATE HIDDEN ITEMS

Elements that are "hidden" behind other opaque elements may now be selected without having to move or resize the front elements.

STACKING

With QuarkXPress 3.0, you only had ITEM/SEND TO BACK or SEND TO FRONT options, which sometimes necessitated a tedious process of selecting each item and reorganizing the layering. With QuarkXPress 3.1, you may now accomplish selective layering — elements can be sent in front or behind other specific elements.

LIVE DRAG, RESIZE, CROP AND ROTATE

QuarkXPress 3.1 now redraws the screen while you are moving, resizing, and rotating elements or when cropping pictures. This provides more immediate feedback when you are working and a more interactive working environment.

STYLE SHEETS PALETTE

In addition to applying a style sheet from the style menu or through the use of a keyboard equivalent, QuarkXPress 3.1 now allows you to display defined style sheets on a floating palette (figure D.1). Applying a style sheet is now as simple as selecting the desired paragraphs and clicking on the style name with the mouse.

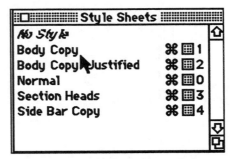

Figure D.1   The Style Sheets Palette.

COLORS PALETTE

The new Colors Palette (figure D.2) makes it easier to apply colors to text, pictures, or elements. Simply select the element to be modified, and click the mouse on the desired color.

Figure D.2   The Colors Palette.

BLEND BACKGROUND COLORS

The Colors Palette can be used to create two-color blends for box backgrounds. You can select the two colors for the fill, control the color shade value, and the angle of the blend (see figures D.3 and D.4).

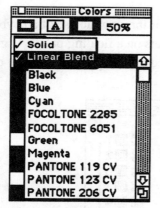

Figure D.3 *The Color Palette with Linear Blend selected.*

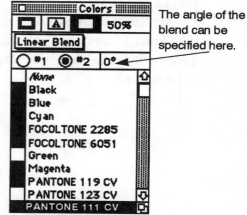

Figure D.4 *The Color Palette with the second blend color selected.*

CALIBRATED COLORS

QuarkXPress 3.1 automatically calibrates PANTONE® colors shown in a document so that the color display matches the colors displayed in the PANTONE color selector.

PROFESSIONAL COLOR-MATCHING

The new QuarkXPress, in addition to the PANTONE® color selector, now allows you to select colors from the FocalTone® and TRUMATCH® color systems.

TRAPPING INFORMATION PALETTE

You have greater control over color trapping with the Trapping Information Palette. You can control whether to overprint or knockout a color, specify custom trapping information and get information about specific elements on a page. Each element or instance of applied color can be individually specified.

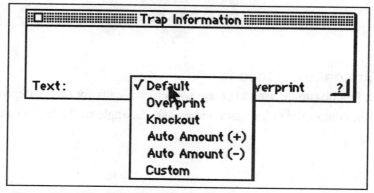

Figure D.5 *The Trapping Information Palette.*

Index

Index

A

alignment, 64, 96-98, 138, 142, 241-242,

anchored elements, 16, 205, 233

auto page insertion, 56-57, 116, 118-119, 201

automatic centering of pictures, 94

automatic page numbering, 152

B

baseline grid, 66-68, 261,

bitmapped, 124, 140, 196,

bring to front, 241

brochure, 113-117

C

changing line style, 42, 44

character specifications, 70, 98, 100

Clipboard, 30, 46, 90, 92

close box, 8,

Content Tool, 10, 26, 28, 220-223

continuation lines, 178

converting, 36

coordinate, 12, 16

coordinates, 14, 16,

copying and pasting a text box, 30

copying lines, 42

copying elements, 154

creating lines, 40

creating polygons, 32

creating text boxes, 26

crop marks, 118

D

deleting a text box, 28

deleting/cutting lines, 42

document construction, 191-217

Document Layout Palette, 17, 152-154, 156-157, 210-213, 215-216

drop caps, 124-126, 272,

duplicate, 102, 182, 237, 326

E

Edit menu

Undo, 46, 224-225, 255-256

Cut, 28, 222, 224, 255-256, 326-327

Copy, 30-31, 42, 222, 224, 255-256, 326-327

Paste, 30-31, 38, 42,

Clear, 28, 38, 222, 224-225, 256

Select All, 66, 225, 326

Clipboard, 30, 46, 92,

Find/Change, 256, 326

Preferences, 54-56, 66-67, 82-84, 225, 326

Style Sheets, 156, 160-162, 164-165, 262-265

Colors, 200, 308-313

H&Js, 156-157, 265-268, 282-283

entering text, 26, 68, 252

F

File, 6-8, 190-195, 252-255, 326-327

File menu

New, 6-8, 190-194, 326

Open, 24-25, 190-192, 326

Close, 8, 190, 192, 319-320

Save, 20-22, 192-193, 326

Save as, 20-21, 192-193, 254

Revert to saved, 194

Get picture, 86-88, 192

Get text, 104, 172-173, 326

Save text, 254

Save page as EPS, 295

Document Setup, 18-19, 194

Page Setup, 18-20, 142-143, 195-198, 326

Print, 18, 48-49, 196-200, 326

Quit, 20, 200, 326

first line indent, 156, 272-273

fold marks, 118, 120,

font size, 13, 98-99, 202, 258-260, 269-272, 326

formats, 66-67, 72-73, 124-126, 160-164, 272-275, 326-327

frame, 38-40, 235-236, 326

framing boxes, 38-39

G

General Preferences, 54-55, 83, 150-151, 201, 326

get picture, 86-88

get text, 104, 172-173, 253, 326

grid, 66-68, 82, 261, 272, 274

grouped elements, 16, 182, 237-239, 247

grouping, 44-47, 132, 182

guidelines, 58-61, 84, 209

guides display, 56

H

H&Js, 150, 156-157, 159-162, 164, 176, 182, 186, 265-268, 272, 276, 282-283

handles, 26, 28, 32, 34-36, 40, 46, 50, 69, 79, 106-108, 132, 220-221, 223, 233, 236-237, 240, 242-244, 300, 302

Hyphenation and Justification, 150, 156-158, 265-266, 268

I

imagesetter, 114, 197

import pictures, 84